GCSE
MUSIC
NEW EDITION

Richard Lambert

Longman

LONGMAN REVISE GUIDES

SERIES EDITORS:
Geoff Black and Stuart Wall

TITLES AVAILABLE:
Art and Design
Biology*
Business Studies
Chemistry*
Computer Studies
Economics
English*
English Literature*
French
Geography
German
Home Economics
Information Systems*
Mathematics*
Mathematics: Higher Level*
Music
Physics*
Religious Studies
Science*
Sociology
Spanish
Technology*
World History

* new editions for Key Stage 4

Longman Group Limited,
Longman House, Burnt Mill, Harlow,
Essex CM20 2JE, England
and Associated Companies throughout the world.

© Longman Group UK Limited 1990, 1993

First published 1990
Second Edition 1993
Third Impression 1995

British Library Cataloguing in Publication Data

Music. – (Longman GCSE revise guides).
1. Great Britain. Schools. Curriculum subjects: Music
780'.7'2941

ISBN 0 – 582 – 22845.X

Set by 17QQ in 10/12pt Century Old Style

Produced by Longman Singapore Publishers (Pte) Ltd.
Printed in Singapore

CONTENTS

EDITORS' PREFACE

Longman Revise Guides are written by experienced examiners and teachers, and aim to give you the best possible foundation for success in examinations and other modes of assessment. Examiners are well aware that the performance of many candidates falls short of their true potential, and this series of books aims to remedy this by encouraging thorough study and a full understanding of the concepts involved. The Revise Guides should be seen as course companions and study aids to be used throughout the year, not just for last-minute revision.

Examiners are in no doubt that a structured approach in preparing for examinations and in presenting coursework can, together with hard work and diligent application, substantially improve performance.

The largely self-contained nature of each chapter gives the book a useful degree of flexibility. After starting with the opening general chapters on the background to the GCSE and syllabus coverage, all other chapters can be read selectively, in any order appropriate to the stage you have reached in your course.

We believe that this book, and the series as a whole, will help you establish a solid platform of basic knowledge and examination technique on which to build.

Geoff Black and Stuart Wall

ACKNOWLEDGEMENTS

I am grateful to the following Examination Boards for permission to quote from their syllabuses and to reproduce questions which have appeared in past examination papers. Whilst the Boards have granted permission to reproduce the questions, I accept full responsibility for any solutions provided.

University of London Examinations and Assessment Council
The Midland Examining Group
The Northern Examinations and Assessment Board
The Southern Examining Group
The Welsh Joint Education Committee
The Northern Ireland Schools Examinations and Assessment Council
The International General Certificate of Secondary Education

I am grateful to Stainer and Bell Ltd for permission to reproduce 'Farewell, dear love' by Robert Jones; to the following schools for permission to include students' work:

St Christopher School, Letchworth, Herts
Coopers School, Chislehurst, Kent
Meridian School, Royston, Herts
Chislehurst and Sidcup Grammar School, Kent

I have received a great deal of support from colleagues and friends while writing this book. Particular thanks must go to Roger Pope for his erudite advice and thorough scrutiny of my text; to John Barber and David Tutt; to Noel Morgan, Adrian Pitts and Christopher Weaver for help with student compositions; to Stuart Wall and Geoff Black for their encouragement; to Tristan and Abigail for countless odd-jobs, and finally to my long-suffering wife Pam, for her infinite tolerance, understanding and invaluable secretarial skills!

The publishers are grateful to the following schools and colleges for their co-operation:
Bishop Fox's School, Taunton; Chase High School, Malvern; Derby Tertiary College, Mackworth; Impington Village College, Cambridge; Poole Grammar School; Pope Pius Comprehensive School, Rotherham; Queensbury School, Bradford; Rugby School; St Helena School, Chesterfield; St Christopher School, Letchworth; St Mary's High School, Cheshunt; Shildon Sunnydale Comprehensive School; Sir William Perkins's School, Chertsey; South Park Sixth Form College, Middlesbrough; Thrybergh Comprehensive School, Rotherham; Waddesdon Church of England Secondary School, Aylesbury; Wollaston School, Wellingborough.

AUTHOR'S NOTE

You will have purchased this Revise Guide because you enjoy music and wish to do well in the GCSE examination. No matter which syllabus you are following, the book provides useful information to maximise your success in all aspects of Listening, Performing and Composing. Although it contains many hints and ideas on final revision before you sit a written paper or submit your coursework compositions, it also contains many helpful suggestions for your various practical examinations.

The various syllabuses are clearly outlined, with their requirements explained in detail. Specimen and actual past questions from the different Exam Groups are reproduced, enabling you to familiarise yourself with different styles of question. Some have typical student answers with suggestions for improvement; others provide you with a tutor's model solution. Much emphasis is placed in this book on musical analysis – primarily to help you with the various types of questions on your set works, but also to illustrate the essential construction of many pieces, in a wide range of styles. This will also help you with your composition coursework.

Several glossaries are included at the end of the book for you to look up any information you may require on composers, instruments, people in music and theoretical terms. A list of recommended books for further reading is also included.

I hope that this book will help you to achieve your best in the examination, and further stimulate your musical appetite.

Richard Lambert
October 1989

In this new, expanded impression of the Music Revise Guide current syllabus requirements have been clearly summarised and set works from all the Exam Groups are discussed, with model questions for you to study. Only out-of-date material has been deleted on expired syllabuses; glossaries have been updated and the analyses on past Set Works have been retained so that you can prepare even more thoroughly for your own set works.

April 1993

GETTING STARTED

Music in secondary schools is now thought of as a practical subject. Over the last ten or twenty years the class music lesson has changed its emphasis from factual knowledge ('knowing that ...') to a direct practical experience of music-making ('knowing how'). Gone are the lessons with dictated notes on composers' lives; gone is the old-fashioned harmony lesson where all examination students applied countless rules which produced similar stereotyped exercises.

It is now accepted that the music teacher is no longer the single source of musical experience for pupils. With music on record, tape, television and radio so fully available to everyone, music teachers rely on this valuable resource and can expect differing interests and achievements from their pupils.

It was realised that the previous music examination at 16+ (Ordinary level) was catering for a small minority of pupils – an elite who were well experienced on an instrument or two before they even started the exam course. The exam groups could exempt candidates from one paper (usually the harmony paper) if they produced evidence of a Grade 5 pass or above on an instrument. This was a very stimulating course for pupils who loved their exclusive diet of classical music and were considering an 'A' (Advanced) level music course, and perhaps a music degree to follow. However, it excluded large numbers of pupils who enjoyed different styles of music, perhaps because they were less fortunate in their previous experience of listening or playing.

CHAPTER 1

GCSE MUSIC

GENERAL AIMS

ASSESSMENT OBJECTIVES

COURSEWORK

WRITTEN EXAMINATIONS

DIFFERENTIATION

ADDRESSES OF THE EXAM GROUPS

GRADES

SUMMARY OF TERMS USED

ESSENTIAL PRINCIPLES

The General Certificate of Secondary Education (GCSE) was first debated in 1984 and courses began in 1986. The first candidates sat their GCSE examination in 1988. Although the GCSE initially caused some controversy and worry amongst teachers, courses are now well established, and it is fully accepted that the exam allows pupils of all abilities the opportunity to show what they understand, know and can do. Also, the added benefit of assessed coursework removes some of the pressure of having an examination on a particular day.

> **Coursework removes some of the pressure of the exam.**

The GCSE sets out to reward an absolute level of achievement, without any comparison between candidates. Since it is designed for **all** pupils of 16+, it will range widely from a basic level of competence to an extremely high level of achievement in each subject. GCSE tests memory and factual knowledge as before, but with much more emphasis on understanding, practical skills and the ability to apply your knowledge. The National Criteria (standards that courses and assessment must meet) contain *grade descriptions* (as from 1994 these will be called *levels* – see page 7) which clearly inform you what you need to know, understand and be able to do in order to achieve a particular grade for any subject.

> **Listening, performing and composing are essential activities.**

It has been agreed nationally that GCSE students in music should experience three essential activities: LISTENING, PERFORMING and COMPOSING. Although we shall consider these separately for the sake of clarity, it must be emphasised immediately that a good musical education will successfully combine these three activities. Indeed, you will soon see how important this combination really is: most of the elements in GCSE music are an obvious synthesis of the three. For example, an *improvisation* is a form of instant *composition*, and a composition on paper only comes to life when it is successfully *performed* before an audience. It was necessary to separate the activities for ease of assessment.

1 ⟩ GENERAL AIMS

The National Criteria for Music sets out the educational purposes of following a GCSE music examination as follows:

a) To develop sensitivity towards music through personal experience by the exercise of imagination and the acquisition of skills and knowledge.

b) To continue and develop musical activities previously undertaken in the classroom.

> **What GCSE in Music seeks to achieve.**

c) To stimulate and develop an appreciation and enjoyment of music through an active involvement in the three musical activities: listening, performing and composing.

d) To develop performing skills to enable candidates to participate in the wide range of musical activities which can be found at present in the school and in the community.

e) To provide intellectual and aesthetic stimulation.

f) To develop a perceptive, sensitive and critical response to music of different styles in a cultural and historical context.

g) To encourage the understanding and expression of thoughts and feelings which may be more readily accessible through music than through other forms of communication.

h) To encourage the development of memory and the acquisition of skills of a more general nature such as analysis, inventiveness and co-ordination.

i) To provide an appropriate body of knowledge, promote understanding and develop skills as a basis for further study or leisure or both.

2 ⟩ ASSESSMENT OBJECTIVES

Aims are an important part of a syllabus, but not everything that we feel or think about music can be readily assessed. This is why the music exams of the past sometimes tested a candidate's *knowledge* of composers' lives, for example – facts which were either right or wrong, and so were easy to mark. This sort of testing has little to do with musicianship. After all, an intelligent but totally unmusical person can learn historical and factual information. The GCSE Exam Groups set out to encourage more satisfactory ways of providing musical experiences which pupils would find enjoyable and challenging; it therefore encompasses many more styles of music than was previously the case.

An *assessment objective* describes an ability or achievement which can be readily measured. For examination purposes everything that you write or perform has to meet these agreed objectives. Your teachers will prepare coursework tasks that will test them; the question papers will be set with the objectives in mind; and you will have to demonstrate that you can meet them! We can consider these objectives within our three activities:

1 After a satisfactory course of LISTENING, you should be able to:

- respond to the structural and expressive elements of music using technical and/or non-technical language;
- perceive the relationship between sound and symbol, using staff notation and other systems if appropriate;
- show an awareness and recognition of musical styles of the past and present.

2 With PREPARED PERFORMANCE, candidates are required to offer two of the following:

- singing or playing individually;
- singing or playing in an ensemble;
- rehearsing and directing an ensemble;

With UNPREPARED PERFORMANCE, candidates are required to offer two of the following:

- performance of previously unseen music;
- repetition of musical phrases given aurally;
- improvisation.

3 Finally, candidates are required to COMPOSE or arrange music in a traditional or in a contemporary idiom. (National Criteria)

> **Assessment objectives for the three activities.**

EXTERNAL CANDIDATES

Everything that is explained in this book applies to candidates in full-time education, where a two-year course is the normal time span for GCSE. External candidates may enter, but should write to their nearest regional exam group for further details. Addresses are given later in this chapter.

3 > COURSEWORK

The National Criteria for Music specifies that 25% – 40% of the marks have to be allocated for *coursework* (Composing). The amount actually varies from Group to Group, but Table 1.1 shows clearly the distribution of marks for coursework and the externally set parts of the examination.

EXAMINATION GROUP	COURSEWORK (Composition)	EXTERNALLY SET (Listening paper and Performance tests)
ULEAC	30%	70%
SEG	30%	70%
NEAB (syllabus 1391)	30%	70%
NEAB (syllabus 1394 see pages 14/15)		
WJEC	30%	70%
MEG (option A)	40%	60%
MEG (option B)	30%	70%
MEG (option C)	30%	70%
NISEAC	25%	75%
IGCSE (Overseas candidates)	30%	70%

Table 1.1 Distribution of available marks for the three parameters: Listening, Performing and Composing

In some subjects, the coursework has to be done by specified times during the course. With music – although you should be composing all the time – the final selection does not have to be made until shortly before the exam (probably the end of the Spring term in the examination year). Your teacher will have all these details, but do fully understand your commitment:

> **A useful check-list.**

- Make sure that you know the number of pieces required for submission.
- Make sure that you compose to the best of your ability, with all written work neatly done.
- Check up on the format for presentation. Do I need to make a tape? Do I need to write a commentary?

■ Make sure that your coursework is not lost. Most teachers keep pupil compositions at school. If your work is not with your teacher, do make certain that it is kept in a safe place.

PRESENTATION

Presentation of your coursework must follow the guidelines set down in your syllabus. Speaking generally, the exam groups give great flexibility; written scores are encouraged, but a detailed commentary and/or annotated tape is usually satisfactory. Check your own syllabus (and Chapter 3) for precise details.

Sometimes it is hard to know **how much help** you are allowed with coursework. You will probably have to sign a form declaring authenticity – that is, that the coursework is your own work. Do remember, though, that it is acceptable for your teacher to give you initial ideas, or even a theme to harmonise, and to discuss with you any problems arising with the writing of a piece. However, records of assistance must be kept and acknowledged when your work is submitted for assessment.

ORGANISATION

What is the best way to **organise** coursework? Some people make a diary of deadlines for the completion of each piece; your teacher will probably have done this anyway. It is certainly best to complete your folder or folio of compositions in good time before you start your proper revision period.

> **Performance has much in common with coursework.**

Table 1.1 shows the generous proportion of the full exam which is allotted to *Composing* coursework; but in many ways the *Performance* section can also be regarded as coursework. Although your performing has to be tested on a certain day, you will need to plan the programme and polish your performance in your own time, well in advance of the actual day. The Prepared Performance section (your solo and ensemble work) carries three or four times more marks than the Unprepared section (sight reading, memory and improvisation). (See table 3.2 in Chapter 3 for details of this.) In all these elements you will benefit from a conscientious attitude throughout the course; it is impossible to master these skills in last minute frantic practice.

With careful **planning** you should be in a confident position when the examination time arrives. Your composition folio should be finalised and out of the way. Your performance section (much of it chosen by you) should be well prepared, leaving time for you to concentrate on your revision.

4 > WRITTEN EXAMINATIONS

> **Make sure you know what is expected of you.**

The *written paper* for *Listening* will test your knowledge, understanding and response to a wide range of music. Make sure that you fully understand how many marks are available for each section of the paper. A question worth only one mark, for example, is best answered with a word or brief phrase. As with every GCSE subject the aim of assessment is that you are given marks for what you can do, rather than losing marks for what you cannot do. This is why some questions are differentiated – to allow all candidates to show what they have learned. There should be no real surprises in your written paper, because everything has been spelt out so clearly in the syllabus. If you work hard in class, taking careful note of all requirements for coursework and prepared tests, and revise properly towards the end, you will emerge with a good GCSE grade!

5 > DIFFERENTI-ATION

Setting an examination is an extremely difficult task because GCSE covers such a wide ability range. Some subjects have solved this problem by incorporating 'hurdles' – cut-off points where you can proceed no further if you do not reach a set standard. The music GCSE does not include hurdles. Instead it uses a method known as *Differentiation by Outcome*. This means that **all** candidates answer the same questions and are free to choose which ones they will answer, subject to certain requirements. This method enables all candidates to respond positively, showing what they know, understand, and can do.

Differentiation is provided automatically in the *Composing* and *Performing* sections, as candidates will compose and perform at their own ability levels. In the *Listening* section, differentiation is achieved by using *structured questions* which allow personal response at an individual level of experience and knowledge. In this way, a question may be answered 'correctly' by one candidate, while another may get more marks by offering more depth and perception in his or her answer.

6 ADDRESSES OF THE EXAM GROUPS

There are six Examining Groups which cover the whole of England, Wales and Northern Ireland. The IGCSE (International) has been formulated for Overseas Candidates. These seven groups are constantly referred to in this book.

1   University of London Examinations and Assessment Council (ULEAC)

Stewart House
32 Russell Square
London WC1B 5DN
(0171) 331 4000

2   Southern Examining Group (SEG)
Oxford School Examinations Board
The Associated Examining Board

Central Administration
  Office
Stag Hill House
Guildford
Surrey GU2 5XJ
(01483) 506506

3   Northern Examinations and Assessment Board (NEAB):

31–33 Springfield Avenue
Harrogate
N. Yorks HG1 2HW
(01423) 66991

or   12 Harter Street
Manchester M1 6HL
(0161) 953 1180

4   Welsh Joint Education Committee (WJEC)

245 Western Avenue
Cardiff CF5 2YX
(01222) 561231

5   Midland Examining Group (MEG)

Oxford & Cambridge Schools
  Examination Board
Purbeck House
Purbeck Road
Cambridge CB2 2PU
(01223) 411211

or   Elsfield Way
Oxford OX2 8EP
(01865) 54421

6   International General Certificate of Secondary Education (IGCSE)

International Examinations
  Syndicate Buildings
1 Hills Road
Cambridge CB1 2EU
(01223) 61111

7   Northern Ireland Council for Curriculum, Examinations and Assessment (NICCEA)

NISEAC
42 Beechill Road
Belfast BT8 4RS
(01232) 704666

7 GRADES

The grade descriptions are a useful guide.

Your grade is determined by your overall performance in the examination and it might conceal a weakness in one area which is balanced by a stronger performance elsewhere. The following three grade descriptions are provided to show the standards of achievement likely to have been demonstrated by candidates awarded those particular grades. Candidates attaining higher grades will also show the abilities expected for lower grades.

GRADE F

A typical Grade F candidate is likely to have shown the ability to:

- **Listen**
  - recognise changes of mood e.g. cheerful, sad, etc.
  - recognise melodic contour and relative duration e.g. leaps, repeated notes, stepwise movement.
  - identify music of different periods and cultures e.g. to recognise a genre such as jazz.

- **Perform**
  - demonstrate in a simple piece of the candidate's choice, individually and/or in the context of an ensemble, attainment either in the chosen instrument (or voice) or in the directing of others – at a level of performance where elementary skills of both technique and interpretation may be expressed. For example, control of instrument or voice would be sufficient for a performance of music well rehearsed and with good ensemble, where there is accompaniment. There would be some awareness of the relationship of phrases and section.
  - make a reasonable attempt to play short melodic phrases, e.g. a violinist would be required to use basic finger patterns in first position.

- **Compose**
  - present music in a basic form and be able to discuss it with the assessor if required. Compositions would demonstrate signs of technical knowledge and control of the medium used with design of ideas, e.g. a very simple rhythmic/harmonic accompaniment.

GRADE C

A typical Grade C candidate is likely to have shown the ability to:

- **Listen**
  - recognise changes of tonality, speed, instrumentation, etc.
  - identify harmonic progression, pitch, and rhythm.
  - identify music of different periods and cultures and the more common forms within those styles e.g. 'Blues'.

- **Perform**
  - demonstrate in a technically more demanding piece of the candidate's choice, individually and/or in the context of an ensemble, attainment either in the chosen instrument (or voice) or in the directing of others – at a level of performance where technical and interpretative skills are combined to demonstrate fluency, accuracy, sensitivity of expression with regard to style and mood, intonation, timing, tonal variety, rhythm, dynamics, and balance. There would be sufficient fluency in the control of instrument or voice at a suitable pace to achieve effective legato, staccato, and contrasts in tone. The performance would communicate an awareness of phrase relationships, climax, repose, tension, and relaxation.
  - to play musical phrases noting performance detail, e.g. a violinist would be required to observe bowing, staccato, and dynamic markings.

- **Compose**
  - present music in a finished form and be able to discuss it with the assessor if required. Compositions would demonstrate evidence of technical knowledge and control of the medium used with design and imaginative use of ideas and resources, e.g. a march for trumpet, synthesiser, piano and percussion with a contrasting middle section.

GRADE A

Not many of the syllabuses give actual criteria, but for a Grade A you will have to meet all the assessment objectives; demonstrate real expertise and show a high degree of organisation in your work. (The IGCSE syllabus includes examples of A grade descriptions.)

As a matter of interest, this is how GCSE Music students fared in the 1992 examination.

Grade A	B	C	D	E	F	G
20.9%	21.9%	21.4%	14.0%	10.2%	7.2%	3.6%

8 **SUMMARY OF TERMS USED**

You will probably hear or read most of the following words at some stage in your course. They are not musical words as such (there is a separate glossary for those at the back of the book), but words used in an educational context.

Aesthetic	A word which relates to the appreciation of beauty.
Assessment	The marking of your work; it is assessed according to criteria (assessment criteria) which have been nationally agreed and accepted by all the Boards.
Attainment Targets	The knowledge, skills and understanding which pupils of different abilities and maturities are expected to have by the end of each National Curriculum key stage.
Coursework	Work for assessment that is produced during your course, and, therefore, without the pressure of exam conditions. Composition is your main coursework.
D.E.S.	Department of Education and Science, more recently known as the Department of Education.
Differentiation by outcome	All candidates are free to answer the same set of structured questions which are then assessed according to your ability, and without comparison between candidates.
Free response	A type of question where you have the opportunity to show your knowledge through feeling and experience. The answer will not be right or wrong as such.
Grade descriptions	An account of the skills considered appropriate for a particular level of achievement. Your syllabus may have two or three grade descriptions (probably for grade F, grade C and possibly grade A). You then work out the other grades from these.
Moderation	The examiner's adjustment (up or down) of the marks awarded by your teachers so that they conform to the agreed standards.
National Criteria	Nationally agreed standards which your course and its assessment must meet. There are general criteria as well as subject-specific criteria for each of the subjects.
National Curriculum	A DES document containing provisions relating to attainment targets and programmes of study. These statutory requirements were first introduced for Music in September 1992. Music is now a foundation subject in Key Stages 1–3. Continuation of the study of music at GCSE level is not compulsory and corresponds in other subjects to Key Stage 4. The attainment targets for Key Stages 1–3 are similar to those formulated for GCSE: AT1 – Performing and Composing: AT2 – Listening and Appraising.
SCAA	The Schools Curriculum and Assessment Authority which is in control of all the GCSE examinations.
Weighting	The proportion of the total marks available that is given to one part of the examination.

COURSEWORK AND EXAMINATION TECHNIQUES

GOOD LISTENING

PERSONAL RESPONSE

NOTE TAKING

PRACTICE HABITS

COURSEWORK: COMPOSING

REVISION

TYPES OF QUESTION IN THE EXAM

GETTING STARTED

We hear music around us all the time – in the supermarket, the restaurant, while watching a film – and much of it is inevitably filtered out from our minds. Sometimes we only notice when it stops! In many ways there is too much muzak (as this perpetual background music is called); it makes concentrated listening to music of quality more difficult, as we become accustomed to being surrounded by this 'wallpaper music'.

There is a world of difference between listening with concentration to an expressive piece of music, and playing the Top Ten on your Walkman as background entertainment. Try to develop good *listening habits* from the very start of your GCSE course. Have a notebook and pen handy so that you can jot down any responses and thoughts as they occur at the time. These need not be lengthy, but making notes, which you can later refer back to, is a good way of organising your thoughts. Keep a list of all the pieces that you listen to, with brief details of who played, sang, and conducted, and also your feelings about each piece.

If you listen to too much at first, you will probably 'switch off' your attention, and what you are hearing will revert to background music. Any music that you hear in your class lessons is likely to be in short, concentrated amounts as your teacher is experienced in these matters, and realises how much is appropriate. Out of class, therefore, plan your listening in similar concentrated bouts; then think about what you have heard. Did you enjoy it? Is it a style you would like to hear more of? If you have been studying the piece at school, discuss it with your teacher and friends in class.

ESSENTIAL PRINCIPLES

<table>
<tr><td>1 > GOOD LISTENING</td></tr>
</table>

1 > GOOD LISTENING

❝ Some useful hints for listening. ❞

Try to follow your teacher's suggestions as to the choice of listening. Ask to borrow the tapes he or she has used for lesson material, or join your local record library, and reinforce a class topic by further listenings in your own time. When you have listened to a piece on tape or record, listen to it again a few days later. Are your responses the same? No doubt you will notice more details about the piece during the second hearing; you will continue to perceive new things with each hearing, as you become more familiar with it. Do not expect to 'understand' it first time; you will have a response straight away, but good music is very concentrated, and full of complex motion. 'Meaning' in music is a very difficult topic. For now, perhaps you should listen innocently, without trying to analyse the meaning of the music; one thing is certain – that you will discover new things each time you return to a work.

We mentioned near the beginning of the chapter how muzak fills up our every silence. As an experiment, try listening to film music, or TV jingles, in a new way. Concentrate on how they enhance or detract from the action. Consider whether the style is suitable for the mood of the film at any moment. Is there too much music? Would silence be effective?

There is, of course, no substitute for live music. However good your hi-fi equipment, the reproduction and atmosphere can never replace the concert hall or stage auditorium. If you have the chance to attend music in theatres, a church or concert room, notice how the musicians have been placed. Why do you think they are sitting or standing in that particular position? Is the acoustic a resonant or a 'dead' one? Did you like the way the sound carried in that particular atmosphere?

❝ Check your listening equipment. ❞

Returning to recorded music, as that is how you are likely to hear most of your music, start to be more fussy over the quality that you accept. Are the controls on your hi-fi adjusted correctly? Should there be a little less treble, and more bass for a particular piece? Many hi-fi sets now have graphic equalisers (EQ) which allow you to adjust the low, middle and high frequencies to your preferred settings. Experiment with these, and aim to be more critical with your demands for recorded music. Don't accept second best if you can help it.

2 > PERSONAL RESPONSE

❝ Personal response is important. ❞

In addition to testing your factual knowledge about a piece of music, the examiners may also be interested in your *personal response* to it. Obviously, this must come from you alone – it cannot be taught; this is why you are recommended to listen so carefully and make notes as you go along. You can be taught the things to listen for, together with numerous technical terms and signs and general musical vocabulary, but in the end a response to a piece is very much an individual thing.

Do be careful to discipline your responses. You are not asked to use music as a trigger for nostalgic experiences ('This piece is great because it reminds me of the time I went scuba diving…'); try to base any feelings you are asked to describe on the piece alone.

3 > NOTE TAKING

❝ Some good habits in note taking. ❞

In class do write down suggestions or factual statements made by your teacher. These notes will help you with any assignments that you are given throughout the course, and will be invaluable during your revision period.

The importance of recording your feelings when listening to music has already been stressed. You should develop the habit of writing down anything which could be useful at a later stage. When listening, also jot down brief details of instrumentation/voices, the words used (if applicable), the style or period, and any other relevant notes that could enhance your appreciation of it.

When working at your practical pieces, you may need to write down short notes during your lesson so that you will remember essential points for further practice later. If you have private lessons your instrumental teacher will be discussing speeds, dynamics, light and shade in expression, pauses, breathing/fingering/bowing and a wealth of other details. You may be asked to practise certain exercises, studies or scales to improve a particular technique. Write it all down!

When composing, you may need to make several sketches before you arrive at your final result. A 'theme' or idea may come to you at any time, so write it down immediately, before you forget it! Even a few squiggles on a scrap of paper will mean something later on, and can then be worked into something of musical value when you have time. You may like to keep a compositional sketch-book so that all your ideas are in one place.

4 > PRACTICE HABITS

❝Organise your time.❞

One of the new things about the GCSE music examination is that you are expected to perform on an instrument (or sing) – as a soloist and/or as a member of an ensemble. The examination is encouraging the making of music, as well as the responding to it with intelligent listening. You will need to plan out your time so that you are practising regularly and to the maximum possible effect. Your instrumental teacher will have recommended (many times, no doubt) how often you should practise, and for how long. This depends on your ability, and your particular instrument, of course, but make sure you organise your time well.

Ask yourself, am I practising correctly? Some people have the habit of playing the same thing over and over again without really trying to correct faults. Isolate a mistake, work out the best way to solve it, and when you are satisfied put it back into its context. You will 'kill' a piece if you play it too many times for the sake of it.

Do respect these recommendations. It may be that you are the sort of person who has no problems with organising time for practice; but many people 'forget' or are too 'busy' for several days at a time. As a serious music student (and it is assumed that you are, or you would not have purchased this book!) this is now an area that must not be neglected.

Depending on the options that you choose, remember that you will need to practise your solo pieces, work at sight reading, ensemble pieces, memory tests, improvisation, and rehearsing/directing an ensemble. You may even choose to use a second instrument, and it all requires regular work and self-discipline if you are to make real progress.

THE 'DOODLE BUG'

❝Do experiment!❞

This is rather a silly title for a serious habit which you should start to acquire. 'Doodling', or experimenting on your instrument, is very beneficial as well as being great fun. It can lead to proficiency in improvisation, give you ideas for composition, improve your sense of pitch and, in the case of guitar or keyboard, your sense of harmony. Composition is a long process of selecting sounds, and by experimenting fully with textures, chords and melodies before you start to write you will gradually evolve a style that you find pleasing – a style of your own. Whenever you find yourself with a few spare moments, shut yourself away quietly and improvise something. It need not be in exam format, but a fun piece where you will start to discover sounds of your own.

PERFORMING EXPERIENCE

If you are an advanced player, you will hold no fears for performing in front of your GCSE examiner. Most likely you will have played before an audience several times at school concerts or other events, and will be fairly confident that nerves will not spoil your performance.

❝Get as much perform-ing experience as you can.❞

Less experienced players should endeavour to gain some performing experience, however small. You should try, ideally, to perform often throughout the course, but if this is not possible, your chosen performance programme must be played in class or before your friends. They may be able to make constructive comments on musical details, posture, or your placing in the room, as well as inspire you with confidence!

5 > COURSEWORK: COMPOSING

Since the start of your course, you will have been composing, but not all of your work will be assessed for the exam. The good thing about GCSE is that it is all about achieving – not failing. Some of your pieces will not be your best work. You may have been under the weather when a certain piece was done, or uninspired by a certain style in which you were asked to compose. You will probably think of your first attempts as insignificant, but by the end of the course you will almost certainly have some fine pieces of work from which you can select the appropriate number for assessment.

❝Listen to your teacher's advice.❞

The various Groups have different requirements for submission of compositions, and you would be well advised to re-read the assessment objectives in your syllabus from time to time. Since your teacher will be assessing your work initially anyway, it will be a good idea to listen to your teacher's suggestions on what to include or discard. You may feel you could re-write an earlier piece rather better, if you have the time; but not if your teacher has already marked it – that is not allowed.

Have confidence in your composing. Each piece will probably be better than the last, so that nothing is ever wasted – it is all good experience. Don't make the mistake of writing only the number of pieces that are required for submission; write as many as you are able, and select from these. Plan out your time to allow yourself regular composing periods, and you will find this a satisfying and fulfilling activity.

6 > REVISION

How can you best prepare for the exam? There is no one way to revise; everyone must work out a way that best suits them. The following suggestions may help you formulate your own revision plans, but do discuss this with your teacher – he or she knows your work better than anyone, and can advise how you could work to best advantage.

> **Useful hints on preparing for the exam.**

- Check all the requirements for the examination very carefully in your syllabus: re-read the assessment objectives – the questions will be formulated around these. Check any details that you are unsure of – the numbers of pieces, length of programme, composition requirements etc.
(Details for obtaining a syllabus are given in Chapter 1)

- Be absolutely certain which options you have been entered for, and what each option aims to test.

- Find out the actual dates of your final music exams as soon as you can, then, using your classnotes, decide on your priorities for revision. You should base your weekly revision around your weakest area. Your teacher can best advise you on your strengths and weaknesses, and your mock exam will have probably shown these. Try to organise your classnotes into topics first of all, and then put these into sections. Sub-dividing your work in this way may help you focus your revision. Simply re-reading notes will not help very much at all; apply them to the musical topics so that they start to mean something.

> **Past questions are an important resource.**

- Look at as many past questions as you can. You should be able to purchase past papers from 1988 onwards. (Addresses for the various Boards are given in Chapter 1). Notice the rubric (instructions in the questions). What is each question really asking? Notice the number of marks that each question carries, for this tells you what the examiners regard as important – you can then give extra revision time to these topics and skills. It is easy to waste marks by spending too long on one question, or by not reading another carefully. Practise some of these questions against the clock so that you become used to the timing.

- If you have a computer, perhaps you can program it so that you can test yourself, on musical terms or theoretical knowledge. Spelling should not count against you if it is clear what you mean, but do try to be accurate; your computer may be able to help here.

- If your school allows you to borrow records or tapes, listen to extracts as if they were exam material – test yourself with imaginary questions on instrumentation/structure/style/period/personal response etc. You may be allowed to borrow some past examination tapes.

- Use your teacher if there are any elements of the syllabus that you are unsure about. Ask to go though a topic in class if you are unclear about it. Avoid going into an exam worried about something that you could have checked out beforehand.

- Revising with your friends and testing each other can be a useful way of revising, as long as you stick to work and don't waste time! Your family may be able to help too; you could play over your performance pieces to them, or ask them to test you on some questions.

  Most importantly – know when to **stop** your revision. If you have organised all your work, and kept to your revision timetable you will be able to enter the exam with confidence.

7 > TYPES OF QUESTION

In the written (*Listening*) paper you will come across different types of question. Examples of these are given in Chapter 4.
These may include:

> **Different types of question.**

a) multiple choice questions
b) one-line answers
c) paragraph answers
d) longer answers
e) adding detail to a score
f) response to a score (graphic or staff notation)

In Chapter 1 you will have read about Differentiation by Outcome. Some of the questions in your written paper will be structured so that credit can be awarded for depth of perception and knowledge within the answer. Obviously the number of marks allowed for a question will indicate the amount of detail that is expected for full marks. It is important to notice these when you read the question.

8 ⟩ IN THE EXAM

This is common sense but worth stating. If you have worked until the small hours, or been up since first light, you will not be in peak condition for taking an examination. Try to be relaxed, and wear comfortable clothes if you are allowed to do so. Also make sure that you have all the necessary equipment for writing or playing.

Read the examination paper very carefully. The rubric in the questions is usually very well worded to avoid any confusion; make sure that you have clearly understood what is expected of you before you begin your answer. How many marks is each question worth? You will be well prepared by having worked through past papers, but don't spend too long on each question – make sure that you have time to finish the paper. If you have studied hard, practised well and revised thoroughly you have nothing to worry about!

GETTING STARTED

The National Criteria for Music have stressed the importance of *Listening*, *Composing* and *Performing*, and emphasise the importance of combining these activities wherever possible. The GCSE examination has to consider them separately to facilitate accurate assessment, but your teacher has probably organised your lessons in such a way that you are regularly experiencing all three activities simultaneously.

Chapters 4–13 consider these GCSE elements separately with relevant details for all the Examining Groups. Although this can be a book to 'dip into', it is recommended that you work your way through the exercises and specimen questions **during the course**, as they are calculated to reinforce your musical understanding, even if a particular topic is not required by your syllabus.

This chapter will cover the elements in general, describing the requirements of the various Groups, before getting on to more detailed information later in the book. It is recommended that you obtain your own copy of the syllabus that your teacher has chosen – not to check up on him or her, but to take it upon yourself to discover exactly what GCSE Music will require of you. You will then be in a better position to plan your method of **work**, **practice** and **revision** for the duration of the course. Your teacher will have worked out an appropriate music course for you to follow that covers all aspects of the chosen syllabus, but you may not be fully aware of the weighting marks for the various elements. You will find some of this detail in the chapters that follow, but there is no substitute for looking at the current syllabus itself. You will find addresses for the Examining Groups in Chapter 1.

TOPIC AREAS FOR ALL MUSIC SYLLABUSES

LISTENING
PERFORMING
COMPOSING

EXAMINATION GROUP	LISTENING PAPER Externally set	PERFORMANCE Controlled tests	COMPOSITION Coursework
ULEAC	38%	32%	30%
SEG	40%	30%	30%
NEAB (syllabus 1391)	40%	30%	30%
NEAB (syllabus 1394)	see pages 14/15		
WJEC	40%	30%	30%
MEG option A	30%	30%	40%
MEG option B	30%	40%	30%
MEG option C	40%	30%	30%
NISEAC	40%	35%	25%
IGCSE	40%	30%	30%

Table 3.1 Distribution of available marks for Listening, Performing and Composing

For ease and clarity, Table 3.1 shows you the requirements for all Groups. For further detail, read the following paragraphs carefully, with particular reference to your particular syllabus.

E S S E N T I A L   P R I N C I P L E S

Check the requirements for Listening listed below for your exam group.

ULEAC

There will be a written paper lasting approximately 2¼ hours. This will be marked by an external examiner. You will be provided with a question and answer booklet and all musical extracts and questions will be on tape. There are three parts to this paper:

a) **Musical Perception**. You will be required to recognise, identify and show your understanding of trends and styles from Western Europe, Afro-America and other traditions. There will be questions on vocal and instrumental combinations; musical textures; and styles and structures in composition.

b) **Literacy**. You will hear a recorded extract ten times, with silences between hearings for you to answer questions based on it. The aim is to see how much detail you can perceive from these ten hearings. Your question paper will have blank staves with printed barlines – more than you will actually require. Some bars will be printed, and you may have to add to these, or answer separate questions relating to the structure of the extract.

c) **Set works**. You are required to study one work chosen from a list of works from the classical and pop traditions. You will need to be familiar with the piece and study the printed score. A recording will be played of a given printed extract, and questions set on instrumentation, structure and other relevant aspects of the work.

SEG

There is a written paper lasting approximately 1½ hours. You write your answers on the question paper. This section of the examination is in two parts:

Section A (One hour) must be answered by all candidates. Questions will be based on between six and ten excerpts of recorded music. You will be assessed on your response to music from the Renaissance to the present day, including jazz, folk, rock, blues, musicals and music from India, Africa, the Orient and the Caribbean.

Section B (½ hour) – candidates choose one of two alternatives. Either, 1. Questions on two chosen set works listed in the current syllabus or, 2. Further questions on unprepared excerpts of music.

Both papers will test your knowledge of structure, texture, instrumentation and all aspects of style. You must be prepared to answer in both staff and graphic notation. Consult the syllabus for the full list of musical concepts with which you should be familiar. The papers will be assessed externally.

NEAB (Syllabus code 1391)

The written test is in two parts lasting approximately two hours, including a fifteen minute break. You will have a question and answer booklet and the questions will be on a tape. The questions will test the breadth of your musical knowledge rather than depth. You will be given several extracts of music to answer questions on, and some of these will include a printed score, so your knowledge of staff notation should be sufficient to follow these printed extracts. You will also be tested on basic music theory, form and styles that are related to aural perception. There are no set works in this examination.

NEAB also offers a different GCSE examination which concentrates on the Listening component exclusively:

NEAB: HISTORY AND APPRECIATION OF MUSIC (Syllabus code 1394)

This syllabus comprises a) General Listening Appreciation Test (30%), b) Set Music: Listening and History (30%) and c) assessment of coursework (40%).

a) **The General Listening Appreciation** (approx two hours). This will test you on the history and appreciation of a broad musical spectrum. You will be provided with a question and answer booklet and questions will be based on taped musical extracts.

b) **The Set Music paper** (1¼ hours). This will be based on a listening study of 8 set works and an historical study of the societies from which they were generated.
Section A – A listening test. 10 compulsory questions will be set requiring identification of excerpts chosen from all eight works.
Section B – A written paper. Part one: 4 questions to be answered from a list of 8, one on each set work. Brief written answers are required. Part two: 2 questions to be answered from a list of 8, one on each set work. This time more extended answers are required.

c) **Coursework.** Two completed assignments are to be submitted, reflecting work that you have done throughout your course. The Board provides a list of topics, although you may submit a topic of your own, subject to approval. Each assignment should usually be of between 1000 and 2000 words in length. In the 1994 syllabus candidates must select two from a list of eight topics.

WJEC

The written paper will last approximately 2½ hours including a break of ½ hour in between the two parts. You will be given a question and answer booklet, and all questions are compulsory, based on music heard in the examination.

1 **Aural Perception** (60% of marks for the paper). There will be questions involving the detection of errors; comparisons of two presentations of similar material; compositional detail based on a musical extract using a skeleton score.

2 **Stylistic Perception** (40% of marks for the paper). There will be questions on the set work which was specified for detailed study, questions on the works which were set for general study, and questions on general musical knowledge based on unprepared extracts. Music from 1550 to the present day is covered, including non-Western music.

Most groups of questions will contain an incline of difficulty so that every candidate will be able to respond in a positive way, but the Listening test as a whole will not have a general incline of difficulty.

MEG

From 1994 there is a new syllabus for this Group. There are now three Options: A, B and C. By entering one of the options shown below, candidates are able to choose the assessment model which most closely matches their own skills and abilities.

OPTION	COMPONENTS	WEIGHTINGS		
A	01 03 06	Listening 30%	Performing 30%	Composing 40%
B	01 04 05	Listening 30%	Performing 40%	Composing 30%
C	02 03 05	Listening 40%	Performing 30%	Composing 30%

Components 01 and 02 are written papers. Components 03–06 are Coursework and are teacher assessed and externally moderated. The additional weighting on Listening in Option C (provided by Component 02) is a reflection of the additional time spent during the course in the study of Set Works.

Component Number	Component Title	Duration	% Weighting
01	Listening	Up to 1½ hours	30
02	Listening	Up to 2 hours	40
03	Performing	–	30
04	Performing	–	40
05	Composing	–	30
06	Composing	–	40

LISTENING

Component 01: This is taken as part of Option A or B. The 1½ hour paper will be in two sections with a 15 minute break. Questions will be set on extracts of music which will be heard on tape during the exam. There will be short answer questions, structured questions, and free-response questions which may require a longer answer.

Component 02: (2 hours with a 15 minute break) is taken as part of Option C and will be in three sections. The first two are identical to Component 1; the third section will be in two parts. Part 1 will test your outline knowledge of *two* of the Set Works. Part 2 requires you to choose *one* of the Set Works and to demonstrate both perception and knowledge in greater depth.

IGCSE

Most of the content of this examination relates to Western European music, but this syllabus encourages an open-minded interest in world music. Any common non-British terminology will be included in the questions where possible. IGCSE has two schemes of assessment. Grades C–G are available to candidates who take the Core curriculum papers, and Grades A–G can be awarded to those who take the papers for the Extended curriculum.

Core curriculum – Paper 1 (one hour without a break). All of the questions are compulsory, and will be set on musical extracts with a wide range of styles. A cassette tape will be used and you will be provided with a question and answer booklet. The questions will require short answers or will be of the multiple-choice type. There will be three sections to the paper:

Section A – questions based on Folk music from around the world: European, Latin American, African, Indian and Far Eastern traditions.
Section B – questions on two instrumental or vocal works from the Baroque, Classical and Romantic periods.
Section C – questions based on twentieth century extracts, including non-European. A question may be set to test response to 'programme' music.

Extended curriculum – Paper 2 (two hours with a ten minute break). The format is as for the Core curriculum Page 1 (above) but candidates will also sit Sections D and E (approx 1 hour).

Section D – questions on one or more further extracts of music. Candidates will be required to identify chords I, IV, V and VI, and cadences aurally; to insert rhythm or melody into gaps in a score.
Section E – Questions on two set works.

NISEAC

This two-part paper will last two hours with a fifteen minute break, and will be presented on tape. Paper 1 will last ¾ hour and will count for 15% of the total marks; Paper 2 will last 1¼ hours and will count for 25% of the total marks. The two papers will cover: response to mood and character of music; identification of musical detail in given extracts; questions on staff notation when following a simple score; identification of different styles – past and present; aural questions are given on eight set works. Inclines of difficulty are included within the questions to achieve differentiation.

---

2 > PERFORMING

“ Know the difference between prepared and unprepared performance. ”

The Groups offer options for Performing in GCSE. These fall into two categories:

Prepared Performance – singing or playing individually (see Chapter 6 'Solo Performance') – singing or playing individually as a second instrument [IGCSE only] (see Chapter 6) – singing or playing in an ensemble (see Chapter 7 'Ensemble Work') – rehearsing and directing an ensemble [not IGCSE] (see Chapter 8).
Unprepared Performance – the performance of previously unseen music (see Chapter 9: 'Sight Reading') – singing at sight [WJEC only] (see Chapter 9) – the repetition of musical phrases given aurally (all Boards, but compulsory for MEG) (see Chapter 10: 'Memory Tests') – instrumental or vocal improvisation (see Chapter 11 'Improvisation').

Table 3.2 shows that the Prepared Performance elements carry more marks than the unprepared elements. Table 3.2 also shows how the options are to be chosen and their respective weighting. Further details for each of the options in Performance are given in separate chapters as indicated above. You should consult your current syllabus carefully for precise information – it is not possible to include everything here.

3 > COMPOSING

Check the requirements for composing listed below for your exam group.

EXAM GROUP	TOTAL % FOR PERF. SECTION	PREPARED			UNPREPARED		
		Solo	Ensemble	Rehearse – direct an ensemble	Memory	Sight reading	Improv- isation
ULEAC	32%	12%	12%	12%	4%	4%	4%
SEG	30%	10%	10% 40 mks each	10%	5%	5% 20 mks each	5%
NEAB (1391)	30%	12%	12%	12%	3%	3%	3%
WJEC	30%	12%	12% 36 mks each	12%	Choose two out of three (18mks each) + compulsory singing at sight (6mks) Section totals 6%		
MEG Options A and C	30%	60 mks total			compul- sory 6mks	either 8mks	or 8mks
MEG B	40%	90 mks total*			6mks	either 4mks + or 12mks	8 mks + not rqd
NISEAC	35%	13½%	13½%	13½%	4%	4%	4%
IGCSE	30%	Compul- sory 12% + either 2nd inst't 9%	or ensemble 9%	not rqd	compul- sory 3%	either 6%	or 6%

i) Shaded areas indicate that the candidate should choose two options out of three within a section.

ii) Marks have been given where percentages were not available. They show relative weightings and are not necessarily out of 100.

* Option B MEG: candidates should choose 2 or 3 elements. If only 2 they should offer 2 contrasting pieces in one element.

Table 3.2 Prepared and unprepared performance: mark distribution

ULEAC

You are required to submit between 2 and 4 contrasting pieces, lasting up to ten minutes. You are free to compose or arrange existing music in any style you wish, but ULEAC envisages that you will use the simpler traditional forms – binary, ternary, variation, rondo etc. A score and/or a commentary should accompany a recording of each piece. Your teacher will mark your work according to established criteria, and external assessors will then moderate this initial assessment. Your pieces must be sufficiently long to demonstrate your ability, and you should indicate where you have received any extra help. A declaration must be signed and sent to authenticate your work. Full details of teacher assessment are in the syllabus if you wish to read these. One group composition may be submitted, provided that the individual contribution by each candidate is clearly identifiable and authenticated on the score and tape.

SEG

Your teacher will assess your work throughout the course, noting how you draft out and improve each composition. A minimum of five minutes selected work must be submitted for moderation, each piece being accompanied by a detailed commentary (written or recorded), a recording of the piece if possible, and a signed statement of authenticity. You may write in any style, including arrangements – there are no restrictions. If you present a score in graphic notation you should provide a clear key to the symbols you use.

NEAB

You are asked to submit a folio and/or tape of compositions or arrangements. You may use any form of notation, or submit an annotated tape if that is more suitable. Free choice of style of composition is given. It is suggested that you select from works composed during the course, up to a maximum playing time of five minutes, and that your pieces should display an understanding of variety, balance, form and unity, etc.

WJEC

You are required to submit a selection of compositions or arrangements not exceeding five minutes playing time. You may use any form of notation, or recording if more suitable, but these must be accompanied by an explanatory commentary or notes. The commentaries may be written or put onto tape. You should indicate clearly where any part of a composition is not original – a given opening, or a theme for variations, for example. You are asked to sign a declaration that your folio is authentic work.

MEG

Options A, B and C (see page 15 for details)
Component 05 – you are asked to submit three compositions or arrangements. A completely free style is permitted, and notation can be staff or graphic. Annotated tapes may be submitted instead of scores.
Component 06 – Four pieces must be selected from your coursework, for initial assessment by your teacher. Your compositions or arrangements may include annotated tapes or freely notated music.

IGCSE

Three pieces are to be selected from your coursework for initial assessment by your teacher, and then submitted for moderation to Cambridge. The compositions may be written in any style, and free notation may be used if appropriate, but the pieces should be contrasted in character. The syllabus gives a list of fourteen possibilities which are offered as suggestions only, but candidates aiming for Grades A and B should work one or two of their pieces (not all three), according to a second list in the syllabus which encourages a traditional European harmonic style. It is recommended that you consult the syllabus for more details.

NISEAC

You are required to submit a selection of compositions or arrangements which you have composed during the course, lasting about five minutes in all. Initial assessment will be made by your teacher and moderated by inspection by the Council. Your compositions must be presented in the form of a written score or annotated tape, or both. Any form of notation is valid.

A FINAL STATEMENT

Having now studied your relevant syllabus thoroughly, you should have a clearer idea of what is expected of you in GCSE Music. The following chapters will break down the three main components of Listening, Performing and Composing, so that you can more easily meet the objectives for all elements of the examination. By all means 'dip' into the book for advice or suggestions, but do try to work at the questions and exercises that have been included. There are model questions and actual examination questions; pupil answers and compositions, and tutor's comments and compositions. There is plenty here for everyone.
    Good luck!

LISTENING: MUSICAL PERCEPTION AND LITERACY

INDIAN MUSIC

CHINESE MUSIC

JAPANESE MUSIC

AFRICAN MUSIC

INDONESIAN MUSIC

AFRO-CARIBBEAN MUSIC

GETTING STARTED

You will have read in Chapter 3 of the different requirements specified by the Groups for the Listening component. The old-style GCE and CSE (Certificate of Secondary Education) exams encouraged an interest in, and an awareness of, music of different periods, by giving set works and selecting a particular period of musical history to be studied. While this may have been successful with those students who enjoyed and appreciated the serious music of the Western European tradition, it excluded large numbers of pupils who showed a preference for pop, jazz, rock, or the wealth of other musical styles from around the world. These were not included in the syllabuses at that time.

GCSE makes up for this 'oversight' by encouraging 'a perceptive response to music, including the aural recognition and identification of musical features and the critical appraisal of the expressive and structural characteristics of music' (National Criteria 1.3.1). The Groups continue to draw on the styles and trends from Western Europe, but now include Afro-American styles and other traditions, such as Chinese, Japanese, Indian, Balinese, and South American, as well as the aforementioned popular styles.

In Chapter 15, sections 1–5 cover the main developments in Western music, its styles and composers from 1550 to the present day. Read these carefully and follow the suggestions for listening and follow-up work. You can read about jazz, its development and important musicians in section 6, and about pop music from 1950 onwards in section 7.

ESSENTIAL PRINCIPLES

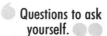
Questions to ask yourself.

Part of this chapter aims to cover music from around the world. As you listen to some recordings of music from other traditions, try to consider the following points. What instruments are being used? Are they similar to instruments that you know? Are there whole families of these instruments, or are they played singly? How do you respond to the music? What sort of mood does it convey?

Although the list is by no means complete, you should be aware of the main characteristics and instruments used in the music from the following areas:

1 India
2 China
3 Japan
4 Africa
5 Indonesia
6 Afro-Caribbean

Try to listen to examples of music from other countries.

The following information about music from these parts of the world, although deliberately concise, is quite sufficient for the sort of questions that you are likely to encounter in GCSE. It is essential that you should hear some examples of music from these countries, for words are never adequate for describing music. Try, too, to find some illustrations of the instruments mentioned in a good book on musical instruments; it will help you to see the similarities between instruments from different countries.

1 INDIAN MUSIC

You will possibly have heard the sitar and tabla in a pop recording at some time: The Beatles, Pink Floyd, Rolling Stones and several other groups have used these Indian instruments, with their evocative timbres. For this study you should obviously become familiar with an authentic Indian raga.

Melody is the fundamental component in Indian music. Each raga portrays a different mood or emotion which is developed through the musical skills of a particular artist, and it has its own scale pattern which can be different in its ascending and descending forms. Ragas can be associated with a certain time of day, a colour or a season, and every performance (which is totally improvised after the chosen raga is played) will try to convey the feelings of that particular raga.

The most commonly used melodic instrument is the sitar with its seven melody strings and approximately twenty 'sympathetic' strings (so-called because they vibrate in sympathy when the main strings are plucked). The neck has adjustable frets which are moved to accommodate the chosen raga scale. You may also notice a perpetual drone when listening to Indian music. This will be played on the tambura, which resembles the sitar but has only four strings. This somewhat hypnotic drone is provided by a continuous strumming of the strings.

Having listened to some Indian music, what will you remember most about it? Did you enjoy it? Write down your thoughts and feelings on listening to it, and it will help you with further recognition.

Here is a specimen question on an extract of Indian music.

Practice question

This 'extract' will be played TWICE with a silence of half a minute between each playing. After the second playing you will have ONE minute to complete your answers.

i) Name the percussion instrument heard in this extract.
Instrument _____ (1)

ii) a) From which part of the world does the music come? Choose your answer from the following list and underline the correct area. (1)

    Bali (S.E. Asia)   America   Caribbean
    Russia   Japan   India

  b) What do you hear that suggests your answer?
    Reason _____ (1)

Note: make sure that your answers are pertinent to the examination extract. Avoid such answers as 'India, because it sounds just like something I heard in an Indian restaurant'. This may seem flippant, but has been seen several times on examination scripts. You need to explain that you have recognised the sitar or tabla, or whatever, **in the extract** itself. Remember that you are being tested on what you know, what you understand and what you can do – your answers must be completely relevant to the music.

2 CHINESE MUSIC

Oriental music may sound strange to our ears at first, but here is a fascinating range of new tone colours for us to appreciate. Early Chinese music was used for court or ritualistic purposes, and it was believed that music should imitate the mystic harmony between Heaven and Earth. References to this date back at least 2500 years.

There are several types of scale in common use, but the pentatonic (five-note scale – see Chapter 14) is the best known. In fact five is a sacred number to the Chinese. They also discovered the so-called circle of fifths, C – G – D – A and so on, on which our Western scale system is based.

> **Some traditional instruments.**

Chinese music does have notational systems. The oldest that can be understood today dates from about 500 AD, and was used for qin (zither) music. The qin (pronounce it 'chin') has seven silk strings stretched over a wooden soundboard. The erhu is the principal bowed instrument in China. Probably a thousand years old, this folk instrument has the horsehair of the bow located between the two strings; it is moved by the right hand fingers to sound either of the two strings. The erhu is now becoming increasingly popular in the concert hall. The pipa is another very old stringed instrument, this time about 1500 years old! It has a pear-shaped body rather like a lute, with four strings, and is used for accompanying songs. You may also come across the sheng mouth organ, and the beautiful sounds of the 'moon' guitar.

3 JAPANESE MUSIC

The Japanese musical tradition owes much to the Chinese influence, and to some extent, to that of India. The koto derives from the Chinese qin. Over six feet long, it has thirteen silken strings that pass over movable bridges. The biwa (lute) derives from the Chinese pipa (see above), and the Sho mouth organ from the Chinese sheng. The samisen first appeared in China too. This is a three-stringed fretless instrument with a very long neck, and is plucked percussively with an axe-shaped plectrum that is very large in comparison with Western plectra.

Note: write down anything that will help you to remember the style of music that you listened to. Was it very different from the Chinese music? If so, why?

4 AFRICAN MUSIC

To an ethno-musicologist (an expert in the musical culture of a particular group of people) there would be many different styles within the music of such a large continent. For our purposes, we can only generalise.

> **Percussive instruments are important.**

In many African tribes, percussive instruments are surrounded by taboo, and they are used in all the important rituals. Although harmonic structure is often not important, most African music is certainly very complex rhythmically. There is an infinite variety of drums, played singly, in pairs or in large groups. Besides their use in tribal ritual, drums are an important method of communication – a sort of bush telephone service! Try to hear a recording of the so-called 'talking drums', or the Nigerian hour-glass drum, where tension in the drum heads is rapidly changed to vary the pitch of the drum.

Note: how different is African music from everything else that you have heard? What will you remember about it that will help you recognise further examples of it? How does African singing differ from Western-style singing?

5 INDONESIAN MUSIC

The characteristic sounds of the gamelan orchestras of Bali and Java are unforgettable, and once heard you should have no difficulty in identifying them. A typical gamelan will consist of several different sized gongs (the bonang), metallophones with bronze keys (the saron), many different types of wooden xylophones, and metal and leather drums (including the kendang drum). The characteristic bell-like sound quality is created by the method of tuning; the instruments have the same note tuned slightly differently to set up a 'beat' between them. There may be any number from twelve to about thirty players in a gamelan and each village has its own version. Depending on locality there may be simple flutes or stringed instruments added. For example, the island of Bali has a musical sound that is distinct from that of Java, but for GCSE purposes you will simply need to recognise the overall South East Asian percussive sound.

6 ▷   AFRO-CARIBBEAN MUSIC

You will read a little about reggae, ska and rock steady in Chapter 15 section 7. These popular dances and instrumental styles originated in Jamaica. But from Trinidad, just off the coast of South America, comes another type of folk music – the steelband. Apparently the Trinidad authorities had banned the use of bamboo instruments on the grounds of noise! It is said that someone thought up the idea of making steel drums in the process of mending his dustbin.... What happens now is that oil drums are converted into steelpans. The top is sunk with a hammer and the positions of the notes worked out. The initial tuning is a careful process after the pan has been burnt to improve its tone. Steel drums are made in different sizes and played with rubber-ended sticks to produce the distinctive steelband sound.

Note: how can you tell the difference between gamelan music and steelpans? Write it down!

HOW YOU ARE TESTED

The Groups all have different ways of testing your knowledge of and response to music. There may be multiple-choice questions, short one-word or -line answers, or questions requiring longer and more detailed answers. Be sure to understand what each question is trying to test. Read each question, and listen to the cassette recording carefully to avoid misunderstanding.

Here is a check-list of topics or concepts that you should be familiar with to feel confident in this part of the examination. You can use the index and glossaries at the back to find further information as required, as most of these words are discussed in detail somewhere in this book. They are words that can be applied to many styles and trends of music:

> 66 Concepts to know. Check with the index and glossaries at the back of the book. 99

sequence	ostinato/riff	simple/compound time
phrasing	development	tempo
form or structure	variation	dissonance/consonance
ornamentation	instrumentation	unison/polyphony/antiphony
dynamics	tonality	harmonic figuration
counterpoint	modality	harmonic movement
imitation	atonality	chromatic
modulation	texture	rubato
timbre	syncopation	Alberti bass

PRACTICE QUESTIONS

Finally, here are some specimen questions to show the wide variety that may be asked. You cannot fill in the answers in this book, but you should read the questions several times, and ask yourself how you would go about answering them. Notice the number of marks that are available and gauge your response accordingly:

Question 1

You will hear an extract of rock music in three main sections. Write briefly on each section, mentioning the speed, mood and instrumentation.

Section 1 _____

_____

Section 2 _____

_____

Section 3 _____

_____ *(6)*

(**Note:** the question is very clear. It states that your answer must be brief, and tells you exactly what to write about.)

Question 2

What are the two solo instruments in this extract?

i) _____

ii) _____ *(2)*

Is the extract taken from a symphony, an oratorio, an opera or a string quartet?

_____ *(2)*

What period does the extract come from: Renaissance, Baroque, Classical, Romantic or Modern?

_____ *(2)*

(**Note:** here you could possibly work out your answer by a process of elimination (knowing what it cannot be) or alternatively by being familiar with all the stated types of music or period styles.)

Question 3

For WJEC you may be played a short melody with differences in pitch to your printed version. You may be asked to indicate where the mistakes occur, and state whether they were too high or too low.

Question 4

For ULEAC, in Section B (Literacy), you will be given a partial score of some music, and asked to answer ten or more questions with ten hearings on tape. You will be given time to digest all the questions thoroughly before the first hearing. Some of the questions may require straightforward factual answers that could be done without the tape. Organise your time carefully here, and don't mis-read the questions!

Here are some specimen questions on an imaginary extract of thirty-five bars:
  i) The key of this piece is Bb major. Insert the key signature where necessary. *(2)*
  ii) Name the instrument which first plays in bar 13. *(3)*
  iii) Insert the following signs (Fig 4.1) at appropriate places within bars 1–12.

Fig. 4.1

(3 × 2)

  iv) Insert the missing accidental in bar 4. *(2)*

(**Note:** i) and iii) are simple tests of music theory – you will need to learn this. In ii) remember to count the bars throughout each hearing of the extract, for you cannot guess this sort of answer.)

Question 5

Listen to these three versions of The Floral Dance and then write briefly about each one under the following headings:

  a) Treatment of melody.
  b) Instrumentation.
  c) Any other points of interest.

You will hear each version once in order, and then each version twice.

Version A _____

_____

_____

_____ *(6)*

Version B _____

_____

_____

_____ *(6)*

Version C _____

_____

_____

_____ *(6)*

(NEAB Music 1988)

(**Note:** this question is clearly worded. Answer the three points equally if you can, and the amount of space allowed for your answer gives you some idea of the detail required for maximum marks.)

Question 6

The next extract is from a symphony. Name the instrument playing which is not usually heard in a work of this kind and indicate the word which best describes the closing section of the extract. The extract will be played twice.   (2)

Instrument _____

CANON / FUGUE / OSTINATO / OBBLIGATO / RONDO
(Underline your answer)

(WJEC 1991 Paper 2 Stylistic Perception : General Musical Knowledge)

Question 7

The verse of the song has four phrases. Which of the following best represents its structure?

AABB   ABAB   ABBA   ABBC

(IGCSE 1991 Paper 1 Unprepared Listening)

Question 8

You are going to hear two examples of folk music from different parts of the world. Each extract will be played *four* times with a pause between each playing.

Music A1
The diagram below represents Music A1.
Look at the diagram and read through questions 1 to 6.
Now listen to Music A1 and answer the questions.

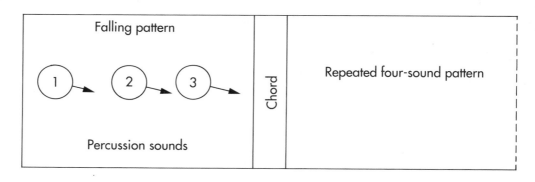

1   Which pair of instruments is heard in this extract?
  ☐ banjos
  ☐ guitars
  ☐ harps
  ☐ violins   *(1)*

2   The second of this pair of instruments does not play at first. When does it enter?
  ☐ at the beginning of falling pattern 2
  ☐ during falling pattern 2
  ☐ at the beginning of falling pattern 3
  ☐ during falling pattern 3   *(1)*

3 Briefly comment on the rhythm of the percussion sounds.

_____ *(1)*

4 Complete the following sentence, including *some* of the bracketed words in your answer:

(notes, chords, discords, octaves, broken, rising, falling, by step, by leap, repeated)

Each repeated four-sound pattern consists of _____

_____

_____ *(2)*

5 Which statement describes the complete repeated four-sound pattern section?
   ☐ It is all in the same key
   ☐ It has one change of key
   ☐ It is in several keys
   ☐ It is not in any key   *(1)*

6 Of which country or part of the world is this style of music typical?

_____ *(1)*

(IGCSE 1992 Paper 2 – Listening)

Question 9

This extract will be played THREE times.

'Prithee pretty maiden, will you marry me?
Hey but I'm hopeful – willow willow waly,
I may say at once I'm a man of propertee–
Hey willow waly O!
Money, I despise it, many people prize it,
Hey willow waly O!

Gentle Sir although to marry I design,
Hey but he's hopeful, willow willow waly –
As yet I do not know you and so I must decline,
Hey willow waly O!
To other maidens go you, as yet I do not know you–
Hey willow waly O!'

  i) In the first verse – which line repeats the music of line 1?

_____ *(1)*

 ii) There is an example of *sequence* in verse 1. Write out the words of the line where it appears.

_____

_____ *(1)*

iii) Name the two types of voice in this duet.

_____ *(2)*

 iv) Give the number of a line where the two voices sing together

_____ *(1)*

  v) Which of the voices sings this phrase in the second verse?

_____ *(1)*

 vi) Name the cadence at the end of each verse.

_____ *(1)*

(NISEAC 1991 Paper 1 – Listening)

Question 10

You will hear three examples taken from the same choral work. The examples will be played one after the other as a set, and you will hear the set twice. After a short pause the set will be played again and after another pause you will hear it for the fourth and final time.

a) List *three* features which the examples have in common.

_____

_____

_____   *(3)*

b) Is this music from an opera, a mass, a madrigal or a musical?

_____   *(1)*

c) Ring *one* of the names given below as the composer of this music.

Gershwin   Haydn   Purcell   Rachmaninoff   Shostakovich   *(1)*

d) Are the examples mainly in the major key, the minor key or a mixture of both?

_____   *(1)*

e) Write a brief paragraph on *each* of the *three* examples.

Base your answer on the following:

forces used, both vocal and instrumental;

how many parts;

types of voices;

harmony, modulation;

musical devices such as ornamentation or sequence;

text;

comment on the way each example ends, e.g. in terms of a recognised cadence.

_____

_____

_____

_____

_____

_____   *(18)* another whole page in addition to these lines was given.

(SEG 1991 Paper 1 Listening)

These few questions are intended to give some idea of what to expect in the Listening examination. All the Groups will test both general and particular listening skills (and set works, which are discussed in the next chapter). Your teacher will not be able to cover the whole range of world music – it is a vast subject – but will select appropriate examples for you to listen to throughout the course, bearing in mind the details of your syllabus. Remember with GCSE that the background factual content of music is less important than the discipline of listening.

REVIEW SHEET

✎ What is a Raga?

_____

_____

✎ Tabla are the hand drums used in Indian music. What other instruments would you expect to hear?

_____

✎ What type of scale is commonly used in Chinese and Japanese music, and often other folk cultures?

_____

✎ How is the scale constructed?

_____

_____

✎ Comment on the use of drums in African music.

_____

_____

✎ What do we call the 'orchestras' from Bali and Java?

_____

_____

✎ Name some of the instruments that you might hear in these 'orchestras'.

_____

✎ How are steelpans made?

_____

_____

✎ Explain the following musical terms:

(a) Alberti bass

_____

(b) ostinato

_____

(c) dynamics

_____

(d) a sequence

_____

(e) syncopation

_____

(f) development

_____

(g) counterpoint

_____

(h) atonality

_____

(i) compound time

_____

(j) polyphony

_____

(k) rubato

_____

(l) imitation

_____

(m) chromatic

_____

SET WORKS

GETTING STARTED

To its devotees, music is the most fascinating and purposeful activity known to man. Many people are quite content to listen 'innocently' without bothering to think of the historical importance of a work, its structure or its instrumentation. Indeed, a great deal of pleasure is to be gained in this way, and people must be free to listen to music in any way they wish. But there are several different responses when listening to music – physical, emotional, imaginative, intellectual; of these, the intellectual response is the most sophisticated, and occurs when music is enjoyed and appreciated for its sheer beauty and the way the composer has manipulated musical form. Therefore the greater the knowledge of the way the music is constructed, the greater the response intellectually.

Naturally, it is possible to have several of these responses at the same time. With simple pop music even an untrained ear can respond immediately in a physical and emotional way. With GCSE we are aiming a little higher – the course aims to develop your capacity to respond to, and appreciate, all that is to be found in the music you play and hear.

Elsewhere in this book you will find explanations and examples of musical structure, technical terms and details of instruments which are mentioned in this chapter. Here some specimen analyses are given which should help you prepare and revise for your set work, even if yours is not included here. Remember that composers did not write their music so that exam candidates could analyse them – they are works of art that sometimes defy being put into categories. There is often more than one way to analyse a piece; you may even disagree with your teacher! Thinking out the different ways of explaining its construction will help you clarify your own thoughts on the work.

ESSENTIAL PRINCIPLES

❝ You can learn the principles involved in any analysis. ❞

Use the given analyses as 'models' for your own set work. The principles used in the analyses will help you approach any particular set work.

1 ➤ ANALYSIS 1: VIVALDI

VIVALDI: "WINTER" FROM 'THE FOUR SEASONS' Op. 8 no. 4

(Set by ULEAC and SEG in 1990)

❝ Some hints for your analysis. ❞

1   First of all make sure that you are using the correct edition of the work. The Examining Group will obviously base its questions on the stipulated publication; early works tend to differ substantially. (For this study we are using Edition Eulenberg No. 1223.)

2   Listen to and follow through the set work as many times as you can, improving your score-reading as you do so. With an orchestral score you may need to follow the melody lines first of all. You won't have time (in faster music) to read every note. Learn to scan – and if you count carefully, at least you should be in the right bar! Follow the shape of the melodies at first; it will certainly become easier with practice.

   "Winter" has many interpretations on record – you may like to listen to more than one. Some use original instruments and small orchestras; others modern instruments and perhaps a larger group.

3   Pencil Vivaldi's Sonnet into the relevant areas of the score (see the translation on p. VII of the score). It is assumed that the composer wrote these words himself, to explain the winter programme of his concerto. When you follow through now you will be able to see and hear more easily what Vivaldi is describing in sound.

4   Read about Vivaldi. When did he live and where did he work? How many Concertos in the style of "Winter" did he produce? Listen to more concertos by him, especially the three other 'Seasons'.

5   Be sure of the difference between a Baroque concerto such as this, and the eighteenth- and nineteenth-century Concerto with its elements of display.

6   Read up about Basso Continuo and the whole Baroque convention of figured bass.

❝ Don't forget the background notes. ❞

You will often find helpful background notes in the score itself, as we do here in the Preface to "Winter". "Winter" is the final concerto in the well-known set of four entitled 'The Four Seasons' – for solo violin, strings and basso continuo. We are not sure when they were actually written, but we know that they were published in 1725, by which time Antonio Vivaldi (c. 1675–1741) was a mature composer. While he was music director at a girls' orphanage school in Venice, Vivaldi was composing prolifically for the orchestra there. In his lifetime he composed over 400 concertos, nearly forty operas and much church music (including the popular 'Gloria'). Although he was ordained in 1703, a chronic chest complaint prevented him from entering the priesthood, but his nickname 'il prete rosso' (the red-haired priest) apparently stuck!

The Concerto is in F minor and cleverly depicts various winter activities and characteristics, such as 'chattering teeth' (see Fig. D in the score) which inspires an effective use of tremolando from the upper strings and soloist (Fig. 5.1).

Fig. 5.1

solo violin

'Stamping of feet to keep warm' (see Fig. C) employs a favourite Vivaldi device, the sequence shown in Fig. 5.2.

Fig. 5.2

solo violin bars 23-24

The opening 'shivering' orchestral build-up is produced by the simplest of means – trills in the solo part (Fig. 5.3).

Fig. 5.3

Notice the figures below the bass notes in this opening section. For example, bar 7 is labelled $\frac{6}{4}$ (below the bass F) and the harpsichord player is required to add the chord (Fig. 5.4).

Fig. 5.4

This chord (B flat minor), can be played in an appropriate way at the discretion of the keyboard player – if it was not marked at all he would simply play an ordinary chord of F (minor) (Fig. 5.5). This is a straightforward and effective musical shorthand, and at the time saved composers a good deal of writing, especially with their lengthy operas!

Fig. 5.5

Notice in bar 3 the indication 'stacc. sim.' (staccato simile). This saves the repeated printing of the staccato notes as in bar 1, and it is easier on the eye not to see so many score markings.

The soloist makes a dramatic entry at Fig. B (bar 12) with a rapid demisemiquaver figure depicting the icy wind. The orchestral strings continue to punctuate this solo with references to their opening 'shivering' figure. This section has been in C minor. (Notice the necessary B naturals which confirm this key. Always look for these accidentals; they are usually new leading notes which affect the modulation into a new key for variety.)

At bar 19, the E natural brings us back to the tonic key of F minor for the strongly rhythmic 'foot-stamping' theme at Fig. C, already mentioned above. The solo violin embarks on more demisemiquavers and extends this figure with only basso continuo as accompaniment (bars 26–33). It remains in F minor throughout. The ripieno (backing strings) re-enter at bar 33 with a 'wind' figure of their own (= another shorthand way of writing repeated demisemiquavers). Bars 34–5 are written in B flat major (A natural is the new leading note), and using a rising harmonic sequence to change key, Vivaldi goes to C minor at bars 35–6 (B natural is the leading note), then E flat major by means of the returned B flats in bars 36–7. So we finish this section and start the new one in E flat major (bar 38).

This next section is based on the opening material and feels slightly different, being in the major key this time. Notice the sequences again with full strings (41–44), and once more with the soloist (44–46). Fig. D, we have already discussed with its effective 'chattering' tremolando – an easy effect to produce for string players. This starts in C minor. Notice how Vivaldi gives tonal variety in this section by omitting the bass instruments altogether – the viola is the lowest instrument here. The movement is completed by a rousing return to F minor with the stamping figure first heard at Fig. C. Only 63 bars long altogether, the movement is a highly effective piece of descriptive string writing.

Think of the variety Vivaldi has achieved within his first movement – moments of drama (Fig. C) with a chance to shine for the harpsichordist; thinner textures where the soloist is accompanied only by continuo; and memorable harmonic figures throughout.

The delightful slow middle movement is only eighteen bars long! It is in the major key and calmly depicts someone resting peacefully by the fireside while outside it is pouring with rain. The composer establishes this restful contentment with an eight-bar solo violin melody which modulates to the dominant key of B flat major. The second half reiterates the melody and works back to the tonic, then adds two bars as a miniature coda. The rain is portrayed by simple means – pizzicato semiquavers in the 1st and 2nd violins (this also serves as a momentum to the music). The bass part throughout consists of repeated quavers ( ) and the viola is printed with a static line (marked 'con l'arco' – an instruction to use the bow, that is, not play pizzicato like the others). In some recordings this viola line is decorated and given more movement, and most effectively too.

The final movement, in 3/8 time, returns to F minor, and the programme is concerned with walking and slipping on ice which finally cracks and breaks. The winds blow furiously and bring the concerto to a furious dramatic conclusion.

The opening is for solo violin, with a tonic pedal sustained on continuo cello. (The words 'tasto solo' inform the harpsichord player not to fill in with chords; and 'arcate lunghe' simply means 'long bows' for the cellist.) This first melody is sometimes performed in a flexible rhythm to suggest the trepidation of someone walking on thin ice (Fig. 5.6).

Allegro

Fig. 5.6

Notice how the pedal note changes to a dominant pedal (on C) at bar 21. The rhythm turns to quavers (♩ ♩ ♩) in the upper strings from Fig. G, then the downward scales at various speeds from Fig. H suggest a fall on the ice. The word 'tutti' at bar 48 implies that the harpsichord should play again from here. A staccato semiquaver figure commences at Fig. I in the solo violin, depicting another attempt at walking on the ice – this time with more confidence (Fig. 5.7).

Fig. 5.7

Observe the tonic pedal notes this time are held in the 1st and 2nd violins (bars 51–60); the violas act as the bass part, while the basso continuo is silent. 'Tasto solo' is again indicated from bar 61–123 where the solo violin has most of the musical interest. Notice the soloist's strongly rhythmic figure at bar 73–9, its commencement is shown in Fig. 5.8.

Fig. 5.8

This section is built over the pedal note of G which is the dominant of C minor. Fig. L is where the ice cracks and breaks (Fig. 5.9).

Fig. 5.9

The Sirocco wind is depicted from Fig. M in C minor – a theme not dissimilar to Fig. G (although describing different things; Vivaldi is conscious of the need for a sense of musical repetition). Fig. M–N is hesitant at first, but the soloist interrupts at 120 with a rapidly scurrying scalic passage in E flat major. This is completely unaccompanied to begin with, then punctuated with tremolando demisemiquavers (♪♪♪ | ↾ ⁷) by the full orchestra every so often until 137 where the texture becomes thicker to the end. Bar 125 is back in F minor, and it remains in this key except for a brief transitory modulation at 131–134. This is a most exciting climax to the concerto.

Obviously, teachers will pick out different points when working through a score with pupils – some may emphasise the programmatic content (i.e. Vivaldi's sonnet), others may place more importance on chords, keys, themes and rhythms. The overall intention is for you to get to know the work very well and see how the composer has constructed it.

Here are some specimen questions on "Winter". When answering try to show your knowledge as clearly as possible – remember some of the questions are differentiated. In other words, you may be 'correct' with a minimum answer but try to give more detailed information if this is relevant. You can only expect good marks for a question if it is answered both fully and clearly.

A favourite, and obvious, question is to present the candidate with a page of the score and ask for it to be put into context: e.g. 'Where exactly in the work does this extract occur?'

Be precise! Supposing bars 9–13 of the slow movement (i.e. p.16) were to be identified. A good answer would be: 'This extract comes from the slow middle movement (largo); it is from the second half where the solo violin presents the main theme in the dominant key of B flat major. The other strings continue as before and their individual pizzicato rhythms effectively depict the rainfall.' (A weak answer would simply state 'this comes from the slow movement'.) Obviously the detail required for a particular answer depends on the number of marks it carries. **Use your common sense!**

> **Make use of the practice questions below.**

PRACTICE QUESTIONS
Question 1

ULEAC (1989) gave bars 1–12 of the first movement of "Winter" as a full printed extract. The following questions were asked. (Answers are not provided here; refer to the text above or glossaries at the back). Notice the amount of marks available for each question.

a) Where exactly in the work does this extract occur?   (2)
b) Name the key at the end of the extract.   (2)
c) The bottom stave in each system is marked B.C. What does this mean, and which instruments would you expect to play in this part?   (2)
d) Comment on the harmony of this extract.   (2)

Question 2

The second movement has one texture throughout. Describe this.   (8)

Question 3

Write a description of the third movement. You should refer to keys, texture, structure and any other matters which you consider would help a listener to understand this movement. You may if you wish give musical illustrations.   (14)

Things to do: VIVALDI: 'GLORIA' (Nos 1 – 5) is set by MEG for 1994 and 1995 (using the Oxford University Press vocal score, ed. Graulich ISBNO19 3384450).

Having carefully studied the notes on 'Winter' and using the glossaries at the back of this book, try to answer the following questions on the Vivaldi 'Gloria'.

1) In the first movement, is the choral writing mainly homophonic or contrapuntal?
2) How important is this musical figure in the opening 'Gloria' movement?:

3) Why has Vivaldi used the key of D major to open the work? (see Glossary 3 [trumpet] and page 165 question 3).
4) In the second movement, 'Et in terra pax hominibus', find examples of (a) counterpoint (b) homophonic writing (c) sequence.
5) [In SEG style]: You will hear six different examples taken from throughout the Prepared Work. In each case give the name of the movement from which the excerpt is taken.

Movement 1, 2, 3, 4 or 5

a. _____
b. _____
c. _____
d. _____
e. _____
f. _____

6) In what key is the 3rd movement, 'Laudamus te'?
7) In what key does No. 4 'Gratias agimus tibi' begin and in what key does it end? Why are they different?
8) Comment on the vocal imitation in No. 5 'Propter magnam gloriam'. Is the gap between the entries of the voice parts always the same?

2 >   ANALYSIS 2: HANDEL

HANDEL: 'MESSIAH' (Nos. 2–4 and 44 only)

(ULEAC 1994 and 1995, Nos 1–8 only, IGCSE 1994 Nos 27–8 and 40–44)

Handel's oratorio 'Messiah' is a lengthy work containing fifty-three separate numbers divided into three Parts. The three extracts come from Part I which prophesies the coming of Jesus Christ (the Messiah); it tells of His birth, and sings of the joy which His nativity inspires.

The work is performed very regularly, although some numbers are sometimes cut because of its great length. Handel worked with amazing speed when composing this oratorio; it took him only twenty-four days in August 1741, and this was in the days before electricity – no light and no photocopiers! He used previously composed material for just four of the numbers, but everything else was new. 'Messiah' was first performed the following year in Dublin.

The first three numbers considered here appear immediately after the Overture:

No.2: Tenor recitative: 'Comfort ye my people'
No.3: Tenor aria: 'Ev'ry valley shall be exalted'
No.4: Chorus: 'And the glory of the Lord'

QUESTIONS AND ANSWERS

The following questions and answers are designed to inform you on many aspects of the set extracts. You will not have so many questions on one work in the examination.

Question 1

What is an oratorio?

Answer 1

An oratorio is a musical setting of a Biblical story, for solo voices, chorus and orchestra.

Unlike an opera, there is no acting or costume, and performances today are usually in a church or concert hall rather than a theatre. Oratorios are constructed with separate numbers, with a mixture of recitatives, arias, duets (and other solo combinations) and choruses. The orchestra accompanies the voices primarily, but there would usually be an Overture and some interludes for orchestra alone.

Question 2

Where do the words for 'Messiah' come from?

Answer 2

They come from different parts of the Bible and were compiled by Handel's friend, Charles Jennings.

Question 3

Give a general description of No.2: 'Comfort ye my people'. (12)

Answer 3

This number employs two styles of recitative. The first, from the opening as far as figure C, is very lyrical with a gentle orchestral accompaniment. It is unusually tuneful for a recitative. The second style is in the last eight bars and is rather like 'recitativo secco' – dry, punctuated chords (although the strings are used here, not just harpsichord and cello as for true 'secco' style) with a dramatic vocal line in keeping with the words: 'Prepare ye the way of the Lord, make straight in the desert a highway for our God'. This piece ends with the customary perfect cadence, which, although written directly beneath the last words, is always delayed until the singer has finished. Another convention at this point is the singer's added passing-note, see Fig. 5.10.

Fig. 5.10

for   our   God __   (V-1)

This is a very popular piece, and is frequently used by singers as a separate solo item, together with the aria that follows.

It starts in E major, and the calm three-bar introduction not only sets the mood, but is used as a link throughout the piece (bars 14–15, 21–22, 27–29). This is common practice with Handel and other Baroque composers. Handel has two unaccompanied bars (8 and 20) where full attention is focused on the soloist. He starts to make the change to the more dramatic vocal style in bar 23: 'that her iniquity is pardon'd', where the solo line becomes more angular. There is a final statement of the introductory figure, this time in the dominant key of B major, before the final dramatic eight bars (ending in A major) which lead on to the companion aria.

Question 4

No.3: 'Ev'ry valley shall be exalted' follows on from No.2 with the same soloist. Comment on any similarities or differences between the two pieces. (5)

Answer 4

Recitatives generally give information and set the scene with little or no repetition of words. They are often sung by a tenor voice as it carries well when there are so many words to hear and comprehend. Arias, on the other hand, are more reflective and the repetition of lines allows the listener to dwell on the meaning of the words. Arias are commonly preceded by recitatives, sung by the same singer.

The recitative in No. 2 has more repetition than normal and is unusually tuneful to begin with. The aria, also starting in E major, is very melodic and makes extensive use of melisma (many notes to one syllable) and word-painting, (see Answer 5 for more details on this.) Both pieces use the occasional unaccompanied bar which draws full attention to the solo line. There are similarities too in the use of the orchestra, as Handel gives it both a melodic and harmonic accompaniment role in the two pieces. The chords in bars 56–58 of No. 3 simply punctuate the singer's melodic line, which is similar to, but less dramatic than the final few bars of No. 2.

Question 5

Comment on Handel's use of word-painting in No. 3.   (5)

Answer 5

It is quite usual for composers in all periods to illustrate musically (or word-paint) the text that they are setting. Handel was no exception. Here he depicts a feeling of exaltation very effectively by using many notes (forty-eight to be exact!) in a rising sequence in E major (bars 15–19). Similar treatments of the same word are used in bars 21–24 and 47–51. A simple portrayal of height and depth is given in bars 24–26 (Fig. 5.11).

Fig. 5.11
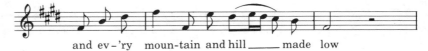
and ev-'ry moun-tain and hill _____ made low

Crookedness is given an angular melodic line in bars 33–34 (Fig. 5.12).

Fig. 5.12

the crook – ed straight

While in bars 29–32, and 36–41 he suggests a feeling of plainness by using a smoother melody (Fig. 5.13).

Fig. 5.13

and the rough pla-ces plain _____

Question 6

Write a general description of the Chorus: 'And the glory of the Lord'. You should comment on keys, structure, texture and anything else which you feel would help a listener to understand this extract. Use relevant musical illustrations if you wish.   (15)

Answer 6

The choruses in 'Messiah' are one of the chief glories in the work, and are justly popular. Handel's long experience as an opera composer accounts for the dramatic verve and confidence to be found in his later sacred music. After the composer's death, choral societies up and down the land performed 'Messiah' and some of his other oratorios with massed choirs and huge orchestras. Sheer size inevitably sacrificed much of the clarity and wit that has been re-discovered more recently, with the use of smaller forces in keeping with Handel's original conception.

'And the glory of the Lord' has a rich variety of choral styles: single line writing (as in the first alto statement); homophonic full choir (all parts moving rhythmically together); simple imitation ('shall be revealed'); dramatic doubling of parts ('for the mouth of the Lord hath spoken it' where tenors and basses sing powerfully together); two musical ideas sung simultaneously (bars 110–113 where the sopranos add the 'shall be revealed' figure to the lower parts 'and the glory' figure (Fig. 5.14). There is a dramatic silence near the end, followed by a grandiose adagio plagal cadence. Handel uses this type of ending frequently in his choral music.

Fig. 5.14

The chorus commences in A major, and passes through the dominant (E major) at bars 21–43; A major returns at 43 until bar 64 where the D#s bring back the dominant until that changes to its own dominant key, B major, with its A#s at bar 72 until bar 87. E major from bar 88 for the last time leads to a return of the tonic key at 102.

There are four melodic figures deployed throughout the chorus (Fig. 5.15). All four ideas are initially stated as a single line, then developed in various ways. There are passages in two-, three- or four-part harmony as well as single lines. Two ideas are used as orchestral interludes – bars 38–42 using b), and bars 73–76 using a); and there is invertible counterpoint (bars 129–134 invert bars 51–55), where the two lower parts singing figure d) swap their lines with the two upper parts singing figure c).

These comments are but a sample of the wealth of Handel's ingenuity in this exciting first chorus from 'Messiah'.

Fig. 5.15

Question 7

Give an account of the 'Hallelujah' Chorus (No. 44), commenting especially on the differing styles of vocal writing.

(8)

Answer 7

This rousing Chorus so moved King George II on first hearing it, that he rose to his feet and audiences have traditionally followed ever since! It is probably its simplicity that makes it so popular. Set in the triumphant key of D major it makes good use of trumpets and kettledrums. After the short orchestral introduction the homophonic choral "Hallelujahs" are sung in straightforward harmony based on primary triads. "For the Lord God Omnipotent reigneth" is in unison with powerful octave leaps – a strong contrast before more chordal "Hallelujahs". At bar 22 the two ideas are combined – the "Hallelujahs" becoming a highly rhythmic accompaniment to whichever voice part is taking the "Lord God Omnipotent" theme. The intricate counterpoint continues until an effective drop in volume at the words "The kingdom of this world is become (suddenly loud) . . . the kingdom of our Lord". Bars 41–51 are a complete fugal exposition (see page 147) to the words "And He shall reign for ever and ever". This breaks off with a most effective "King of Kings and Lord of Lords" gradually rising in the sopranos, while the lower voices interject "for ever" and "Hallelujah". The basses return to the fugal theme at bar 69 before the movement ends with a coda based on previous material culminating in a grand plagal cadence (see page 127).

ANALYSIS 3: HAYDN

HAYDN: TRUMPET CONCERTO (MOVEMENTS 2 AND 3)

(Set by WJEC in 1990 and IGCSE in 1991)
Boosey and Hawkes edition no. 275

This is a different type of concerto from Vivaldi's "Winter". Classical Concertos used a solo instrument which was contrasted with a larger backing symphony orchestra. Concertos were usually written in three movements – fast, slow, fast – and generally kept to the structural principles which had been evolved by the chief exponent, Mozart. Piano and violin tended to be the favourite solo instruments used by classical composers for their concertos – there are few existing trumpet concertos.

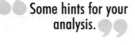
Some hints for your analysis.

1   Check that you are using the correct edition of the score.
2   Follow the score through several times. Listen to the whole work, not just the stipulated movements, so that you get the full perspective. You may find the score reading a little harder than for Vivaldi's, but do persevere. The trumpet part should be easy to hear, although there are two other trumpets playing in the main orchestra. Be aware that the page divides into two! Look out for the ∥ on the left hand side of the page which denotes this split. Remember to count and you shouldn't get lost too often when following through. Score reading is something that improves with practice; remember to scan and not attempt to read all the notes.
3   Mark into your score any important points that you have been taught, or any that you find in the following analysis. This will help you to remember things as you become familiar with the score.

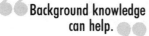
Background knowledge can help.

4   Read up on the life and works of Haydn. You should have a working knowledge of his background: humble beginnings – choir school in Vienna – the Esterhazy years – retirement and success with two London visits. There are many good books available on Haydn. Ask your teacher to advise you on this. Be certain which instruments are required for the concerto, and find out all you can about the differences between the trumpet for which it was originally composed and its modern counterpart.
5   If you are unsure of any key signatures and scales when working out modulations, refer to the first section of Chapter 14.

Space permits only a concise analysis here, but it should be detailed enough for you to understand how Haydn constructed the two movements in question. You should work through these notes alongside the score several times to gain full benefit. It doesn't really matter if this is not your set work. It will be useful extra practice in helping you to think analytically.

Joseph Haydn composed his only trumpet concerto in 1796 for the Viennese court trumpeter Anton Weidinger. Weidinger performed on the newly invented keyed trumpet, and so for the first time could play all the notes of the chromatic scale. Before this time trumpeters had used the natural trumpet which could play only natural harmonics, rather like the bugle. This new instrument (although soon superseded by our modern valved instrument) allowed the composer the opportunity to write free chromatic movement for the first time (Fig. 5.16).

(2nd movt: bars 18-24)

Fig. 5.16

The overall key for the concerto is E flat major, but the middle, slow movement (Andante) is in the subdominant key of A flat major. It is constructed in ternary form, that is A + B + A. To begin with, theme A is played by the first violins, and then repeated at bar 9 by the solo trumpet (Fig. 5.17).

Fig. 5.17

This short opening section ends with a simple perfect cadence (chords V–I) at bar 16.

The B tune, initially played by first violins and flute, is handed over to the trumpet at bar 18. (See the first quotation above.) By bar 24 Haydn has modulated to the distant key of C flat major, and by bar 27 he is in D flat minor. A dominant of the original tonic is reached at bar 30, pulling the tonality back to A flat major for the second A section at bar 33. This time the trumpet plays first. The short coda, starting at bar 41, is based on the material from Section B.

The finale (third movement) is back in E flat major, and is built in Sonata-rondo form. This is a mixture of sonata form and rondo form (A–B–A–C–A), where the first episode (B) is initially in a key other than the tonic, but appears later in the tonic key (as the second subject would in true sonata form).

The first subject is presented by the upper strings only (bars 1–12) and then repeated tutti (by the full orchestra) at bar 13 (Fig. 5.18).

Fig. 5.18

(vln.)

The second subject is 'hinted at' in bar 27, but here it is still in the tonic, of course The soloist enters at bar 45 after a stirring build-up. The exposition is re-stated and extended, this time with the trumpet accompanied by strings playing piano (p). A transition, or bridge passage, follows at 68–80. Notice the semiquaver imitation (♪♪♪♪) between the two violin parts at bars 71–75; as expected, these few bars are used to change the key towards B flat major, the dominant, for the second subject at bar 80 (Fig. 5.19).

Fig. 5.19

This starts with trumpet and violin imitating each other. Notice the tricky new trumpet motive at bar 86 (Fig. 5.20).

Fig. 5.20

A second theme appears at bar 98 which is still part of the second subject (Fig. 5.21).

Fig. 5.21

And a third idea at bar 116 (Fig. 5.22).

Fig. 5.22

which provides a link back to the main theme in E flat major at bar 125. This time there is a canonic imitation from the flute at bar 127. This section 'A' starts as before, but changes at bar 141 by modulating into A flat major, the subdominant key. A freely-modulating section follows, which develops material from the first subject only, and passes through the following keys: F minor (bars 148–154); A flat major (155–156); F minor again (157–158); B flat minor (159–160); A flat major (161–162); F minor (163–167); C minor over a dominant pedal (168) and finally a reiterated dominant 7th chord (B♭ D F A♭) at 177–180 leads back to E flat major at bar 181.

The recapitulation (bar 181) is considerably shorter this time – 11 bars instead of the 68 in the exposition! In fact bars 181–191 could be compared with bars 57–67. The transition (at bar 192) is also shortened, changing at 196 by avoiding the previous imitation, and arriving at the second subject (in the tonic of course, this time) at bar 200. The new figure for the trumpet at bar 204 (Fig. 5.23) bears some resemblance to that in bar 86, but the second theme of the second subject is this time omitted. The third theme does appear however, at bar 220 in the first violins, repeated rather more fully in the woodwind at bar 224, then handed back to the strings at bar 232. This leads to a re-statement of the main 'A' theme by the trumpet at bar 238, but it disintegrates by merging into the coda. Notice the trumpet trills (see Chapter 14) at bars 249–253.

Fig. 5.23

A fortissimo tutti at bar 256, with tremolando (𝄐) in the lower strings to increase

ff

the tension, leads to an unexpected pianissimo B natural in all the strings, but Eb major is very soon reconfirmed (272). The pause mark ⌢ at 279 is an indication that a cadenza (solo 'display' passage) may be played, if required. This is left to the discretion of the soloist and conductor. At 280 there is a pp reference to the main theme, but the music quickly whips up to form a brilliant ending with typical Classical semiquaver configuration.

PRACTICE QUESTIONS

Now test yourself with the following questions. The answers are all in the text above, or in the glossaries:

Question 1

How many trumpet concertos did Haydn compose?

Question 2

Haydn used ternary form for the slow movement. What form did he use for the last movement?

The remaining questions are in IGCSE format. Refer to bars 13–25 of the second movement in the score (think of it as the printed extract – but you will not be told bar numbers). You would hear it in the exam TWICE. Questions 3–7 relate to the extract, and question 8 relates to the last movement which is not included in the recording. Tick the box that has the correct answer:

Question 3

Which part of the extract is this taken from?

☐ The opening
☐ Very near the beginning
☐ The middle
☐ Near the end

Question 4

What key is used at the start of the extract?

☐ Bb major
☐ Ab major
☐ F minor
☐ Eb major

Question 5

At what interval apart do the oboes play in bars 22–23?

☐ in thirds
☐ in fourths
☐ in unison

Question 6

In bars 19–21, what effect do the violas, cellos and basses produce?

- ☐ a glissando
- ☐ a ground bass
- ☐ a pedal
- ☐ a cadenza

Question 7

Which statement is true concerning the trumpet theme in bars 18–24?

- ☐ It comes from the opening of the second movement
- ☐ It first occurs just before the given extract
- ☐ This is the first occurrence

Question 8

(Last movement) When does the trumpet first play?

- ☐ Right at the beginning
- ☐ A few bars into the movement
- ☐ A long way into the movement

MOZART: CLARINET CONCERTO, 2ND MOVEMENT

(Set by NISEAC in 1990/1991)

This delightful concerto was one of Mozart's very last works, written in 1791, the year of his death. It is catalogued as K.622 out of a total of 626 works, an incredible amount of music for a composer who died at the age of thirty-six.

Mozart was fond of the sound of the clarinet; there is also a Clarinet Quintet, K.581, composed two years earlier for the same player, Anton Stadler. Stadler was a fine player who contributed to the technical development of the clarinet; he also played the basset horn, and his mastery of both instruments was well recognised and appreciated at the time. Stadler's experimentation led to the clarinet's range being extended downwards, thus improving the richness of the instrument. It was for this extended clarinet, now known as the basset-clarinet, that Mozart wrote his concerto, but it soon became obsolete as it was difficult to play. The work is generally performed today on an A clarinet with some of the impossible lower passages revised upwards; however, modern basset-clarinets have been made and a fine recording by Thea King (Hyperion KA 66199) uses one – try to hear how the Concerto may have sounded in Mozart's time.

The second movement, a beautiful Adagio in 3/4 time, is composed in D major, the subdominant key. It is quite usual to have a different key from the original for a middle movement to provide tonal variety. Simple ternary form (A–B–A) is used, the restrained outer sections contrasting with the middle section with its more intricate solo part. If you have access to a score of the music, you will notice the clarinet part is written a minor 3rd higher (in F major) than the orchestral parts; remember that the clarinet in A is a transposing instrument where its written notes sound a third lower (see the section on Transposing instruments in Chapter 14). The horn players in Mozart's orchestra would have had to insert a D crook (extra tubing) into their instrument to produce the correct key for this movement, for they had no valves and relied on the 'natural' notes.

QUESTIONS AND ANSWERS

The following questions would be answered without reference to a score:

Question 1

What wind instruments, excluding the clarinet, are used in the concerto? (2)

Answer 1

Two flutes, two bassoons and two horns in D.

Question 2

How are the French horns used in this movement? (4)

Answer 2

They are used primarily as an accompaniment with long-held notes mostly in octaves, although the first horn also doubles the melody in the first orchestral tutti.

Question 3

How does Mozart provide musical contrast in the middle section of the movement?   (8)

Answer 3

The middle section is twenty-seven bars long. While the strings and wind continue to provide a supporting role, the clarinet line has many more notes – rapid demisemiquaver runs, sextuplets ( ), arpeggios and a trill. This intricate solo part is more intent on display than the outer sections, and the line is less smooth. Towards the end of the middle section there is tremolando ( ) and syncopation ( ) in the string writing which increases the momentum. The use of dynamics also provides a contrast – the p f p f markings are quicker-changing.

Question 4

Mozart puts a pause in the score over the last clarinet note before the 'A' theme returns. What does this mean?   (2)

Answer 4

It is an indication that the soloist is free to play a cadenza, an appropriate solo passage of his own making. It is not thought of as a pause in this context.

Question 5

Explain how the second 'A' section is different from the first.   (12)

Answer 5

Mozart varies the second section, firstly, by omitting the orchestral (tutti) repetition of the main theme. He substitutes this with the descending second theme instead. This figure does receive its tutti restatement but Mozart re-scores it by giving the bassoons a more melodic part this time. After twenty-four bars (the length of the first section) Mozart adds a fifteen bar coda which echoes the style of the middle section and explores a wide range of notes on the clarinet. It is quite usual for a composer to vary a section in this way; the overall effect is the same and the symmetry is unaffected.

As a follow-up to this work, listen to the Clarinet Quintet and the Clarinet Trio K.498. You will be able to compare Mozart's treatment of the solo instrument and observe the difference in sound between a Trio and a Quintet. Which do you prefer, and why?
The Piano Concerto No. 23 in A major, K.488 is set by NEAB (History and Appreciation of Music syllabus) for 1994 and 1995. The Piano Concerto No.21 in C major, K.467 (2nd movt only) is set by NISEAC in 1994. Listen to both of these works if you can, and use the following suggestions for effective study (making sure that you have first read the notes on Haydn's Trumpet Concerto and Mozart's Clarinet Concerto, as this will give you a good background to Classical concertos):

1   Note the instrumentation used in the Concertos. Are they both using exactly the same instruments? Is this different to the Haydn Trumpet Concerto and the Mozart Clarinet Concertos? Are the instruments used in similar ways in all the Concertos?
2   How is the backing orchestra used in these concertos? Is it playing all the time, or does the piano have substantial stretches where it is allowed to play unaccompanied? How is the melodic content of each concerto shared between soloist and orchestra?
3   How does Mozart give variety in the sound he creates? Is it accomplished through varying the orchestral texture, through volume changes, speed changes, thematic variety or mood changes?
4   Here is a specimen NISEAC question (as applied to another set work in 1991).
    You will hear TWO performances of part of this (concerto). Performance A followed by performance B will be played TWICE. There will be a pause of 30 seconds between the first two performances of the music; the final playings will follow after a pause of 1 minute.

i)   Write briefly about the differences between the two performances.   *(8)*
ii) Which performance do you prefer and why?   *(2)*

[With a question such as this, do not be frightened of stating the obvious. If you have noticed something relevant that is worth stating, then do so! Part (i) is worth more marks so make sure that you get down several different points – such as differences in speed, volume, size of the orchestra, pitch (one version might be slightly higher than the other), clarity of recording etc. In part (ii) the reason you give is probably the most important part of your answer. Justify your answer clearly]

5 ⟩ ANALYSIS 5: BRAHMS

BRAHMS: ACADEMIC FESTIVAL OVERTURE, Op. 80

(Set by NISEAC in 1990/91 as a Special study)

For effective preparation of this set work you will need an orchestral score. Instead of studying this work in analytical detail, here it will be presented, again, as a series of questions and answers. The questions will be formatted along GCSE lines – ranging from straightforward one- or two-line answers to full paragraphs. There are far more questions than in the actual exam so that we can cover the work in suitable detail. Remember that you are rewarded for what you know; to merit top marks you must display a thorough acquaintance with the score.

QUESTIONS AND ANSWERS

Question 1

How old was Brahms when he composed this work?   *(2)*

Answer 1

He was about forty-seven years old. Brahms (1833–1897) wrote this overture in 1880.

Question 2

For what occasion was it composed?   *(2–8)*

Answer 2

The Chair of Philosophy at the University in Breslau (now called Wroclaw in present-day Poland) had conferred an honorary Doctor's degree upon Brahms in 1879, describing him as 'the most famous living German composer of serious music'. He was asked (and expected) to write an orchestral piece in return. By summer 1880 Brahms had composed two Overtures – the 'Tragic', and the so-called 'Academic Festival Overture'. Both were performed at the degree ceremony in Breslau in January 1881.
(Notice that you are usually told how many marks are available for each answer. Use your judgement to decide how much detail is required. 'A university degree ceremony in 1881' would gain two marks, whereas a higher mark allocation would require more of the above information.)

Question 3

What instrumentation does the work have?   *(5)*

Answer 3

The overture is scored for a larger than normal nineteenth-century symphony orchestra (and the largest Brahms ever used): piccolo, two flutes, two oboes, two clarinets, two bassoons, double bassoon, four horns, three trumpets, tuba, three timpani, cymbals, triangle and strings (1st and 2nd violins, violas, cellos and double basses). The piccolo, the extra trumpet and larger percussion section add to the festive atmosphere.

Question 4

Give a brief account of Brahms' orchestral music.   *(8)*

Answer 4

Brahms composed four symphonies, between 1876 and 1885; a Violin Concerto, a Double Concerto for violin and cello, two Orchestral Serenades, two Piano Concertos, The Tragic and the Academic Festival Overtures, and the Variations on a Theme by Haydn (St Anthony Variations).

Question 5

Write about the structure of this Overture. (12)

Answer 5

The Academic Festival Overture, like many other Concert Overtures, is composed in Sonata Form – albeit modified. The first subject group has several themes: a) bar 1 in the strings, C minor, pp; b) bar 25, strings and horn, F major moving to D♭ major, pp; c) bar 46, tutti, E minor, forte; d) bar 64 in the higher brass over a pp drum roll, C major. These are the main themes, but it must be stated that this part of the exposition is itself rather like a Rondo as the composer re-states the main theme every now and again: bars 41–5 in C minor, bar 88 in the tonic major and tutti.

The second subject commences at bar 127 in E major (not the expected 'Classical' key-change which would go to the dominant here), although its second theme, bar 139 is in G major, the expected dominant of C minor. The third theme also starts in G major with the bassoons at bar 157 and is used to finish the exposition at bar 240.

The development (bars 241–269) is extremely brief. It contains a variation of the opening theme, and the third theme in F minor at bar 255.

The recapitulation (from bar 269) varies the first theme of the first subject, and this time Brahms makes it considerably longer, as if to compensate for a short development section.

The second subject arrives at bar 314 in C major. The darkness of C minor has now disappeared. Bar 324, the second theme now in E♭ major, corresponds to bar 139 in the exposition. The long section (bars 157–229) of the third theme is omitted this time (although the section beginning at bar 346 is related to the earlier one in the third theme at bar 211). The tutti version of this theme (from bar 231 in the exposition) is played ff at bar 367 where the brass again plays the major role.

The coda played maestoso (majestically) in a readjustment of the tempo is the first statement of the popular German student song 'Gaudeamus Igitur' ('Let us rejoice therefore'). Here it is a brass theme with rushing string scales to round off the work in noble fashion.

(N.B. This is a very detailed answer. An acceptable C grade answer would cover the basic sonata form structure; the A grade student would be more specific by highlighting the modifications to the regular sonata form).

Instead of writing generally about the whole work, you may be asked to write in detail about a specified section:

Question 6

Using the given extract of bars 64–87, comment on Brahms' use of the orchestra. (10)

Answer 6

Brahms had used here a student song called 'Wir haben gebaut ein stattliches Haus'. He chose this carefully for the occasion of the work's first performance, for it expresses the students' pride in the university. The opening, in C major, is for higher brass initially, marked softly and sweetly, over a dominant timpani roll which overlapped from the previous section. The roll is doubled by basses and shortly afterwards by the cellos to add to the increasing crescendo. This section is a dramatic build-up to the climax at bar 88.

Other instruments are gradually added to the three trumpets; by bar 80 all except piccolo, clarinets, the other percussion and upper strings are playing. The cellos commence a tremolando (♪) to help increase the tension at bar 78. The upper strings, doubled by bassoons, and piccolo at 87, enter with rapid rising scalic passages, which increase in length and volume until the fortissimo statement, tutti, at bar 88.

6 ▷ ANALYSIS 6: DEBUSSY

DEBUSSY: CHILDREN'S CORNER SUITE FOR PIANO

(Set by SEG in 1990)

1   Doctor Gradus ad Parnassum
2   Jimbo's Lullaby
3   Serenade for the Doll
4   The Snow is Dancing (not no.5)
6   Golliwog's Cake-walk

Debussy (1862–1918) possessed an incredible 'ear' for musical sound. If you examine his printed music you will find the utmost precision with notational detail. He won, as a student at the Paris Conservatoire, the coveted Prix de Rome (a chance to compose in Italy for three years), but he did not become well-known until after the first performance of his orchestral 'Prélude à l'après-midi d'un faune' in 1894. He was a remarkable pianist, and composed much fine piano music in an individual style, using, for example, blocks of chords, the whole tone scale, the pentatonic scale, pedal and harmonic effects – in all a very original harmonic style.

This suite of six pieces, composed between 1906 and 1908, was dedicated to his daughter, 'To my dear little Chouchou, with her father's fond apologies for what follows'.

No.1 – 'Doctor Gradus ad Parnassum' is a humorous homage to the set of piano studies written in 1817 by Clementi. The Latin words mean 'Steps to Parnassus', and refer to the sacred mountain of the Muses who are supposed to inspire creative artists. It is a gentle parody of a child practising a piano study in C major. The child starts off confidently enough, but distraction soon sets in and as practice time approaches an end, the last few bars are hurried through and the piano-lid is slammed somewhat angrily!

Points to notice:
a) The French words to indicate speed and expression.
b) How this short piece has some substance, unlike many of the studies it satirises.
c) The frequent key signature changes.
d) The clefs are continually changing too, as the range of a piano is so wide.

QUESTIONS AND ANSWERS

Question 1

Give the meaning of the following French terms encountered in this piece:
a) modérément animé (bar 1)
b) égal et sans sécheresse (bar 1)
c) un peu retenu (bar 21)
d) Animez un peu (bar 37)
e) Très animé (bar 67).

Answer 1

a) moderately lively
b) evenly and not harshly
c) held back a little
d) a little more lively
e) very lively.

Question 2

How does Debussy give a feeling of unity at the start of each section?

Answer 2

He uses the same musical material so that bar 33 (in B flat major) is the same figure as at the opening, but now in quavers (augmentation), and similarly in bar 37 (in D♭ major).

No.2 – 'Jimbo's Lullaby' is full of imagery for young children. We would call it 'Jumbo', of course – it is an elephant piece! Debussy uses the pentatonic scale some of the time to bring out the simplicity of mood. Notice the low, lumbering melody of the opening which depicts the slow, heavy creature. You can imagine that a stuffed elephant is being told a fairy tale by the child.

Question 3

Name the key of the piece, and comment on the style of piano writing.

Answer 3

It is written in B flat major. Although the treble clef is used Debussy concentrates on the middle and lower registers of the piano to illustrate the physical character of 'Jimbo'. As before, he is meticulous with compositional detail and the general dynamic level is extremely soft, there being one bar marked mf, but nothing louder. There is a prominent use throughout of chords using the interval of a major 2nd.

There are numerous French terms in this piece:

doux et un peu gauche (bar 1): gently and a little awkwardly; un peu en dehors (bar 21):

as if outside (distantly); marqué (bar 34): marked, pronounced; un peu plus mouvementé (bar 39): a little more movement; sans retarder (bar 74): no slowing up.

No.3 – 'Serenade for the Doll'. Debussy requests that the performer uses the soft pedal throughout the piece, even in the passages marked f. Some writers have commented on Debussy's psychological undertones in this seemingly innocent piece – how the child has authority over her doll with its fixed smile – but this is something we cannot explain for certain and must be left for the listener to decide. Again note the precision with detail, and how the melody is sometimes below the accompaniment. The overall key is E major.

Question 4

Comment on the varying textures in the piano writing in this Serenade.

Answer 4

Debussy was a master of pianistic expression. Besides requiring the soft pedal throughout the piece, there is a wealth of varied detail. The texture ranges from the effective silent bar (bar 65) to the single line writing, pp and staccato, (bars 61–2); two note chords (bars 66–68); ostinati figures (bars 1–2, 43–4 etc); chordal writing in the treble clef only (bars 30–34); an Alberti bass effect (bars 106–114); common arpeggios (121–2); and arpeggiated chords (bars 90–96). These are only some of the piano textures in this delightful and artistic miniature.

No.4 – 'The Snow is Dancing' seems to suggest a feeling of sadness in a child as he or she observes snow falling, perhaps for the first time.

Let us suppose for this piece that you are presented with the first page (say fifteen bars as in the *Peters Edition* No. 7252) and asked the following questions:

Question 5

The key at the opening of this extract is ambiguous. Name the two possibilities.　　　(2)

Answer 5

It is a mixture of F major and D minor.

Question 6

Is there a melody in this extract?　　　(2)

Answer 6

Not in the conventional sense of having a melody with separate accompaniment. The repeated semiquavers are drawn from the rising figure of bar 1, and there is a line of semibreves (bars 3–10) which may be treated as a melodic line. Much of the musical effect here is one of perpetual movement rather than a melody as such.

Question 7

How does Debussy continue the piece after this effect?　　　(8)

Answer 7

There are sixteen more bars of perpetual semiquavers in similar style before it dissolves at bar 34 into a soft quaver-triplet counter-subject above the original rising four-note figure. Snowflakes dancing? The climax to this section is at bar 49 with heavy accents and repeated notes. There is a recapitulation of the first idea starting at bar 57 but Debussy omits the first six bars, (so it corresponds to bar 7). The final few bars mix the two ideas gently together (e.g. bar 68 treble clef = 40 bass clef) and it ends softly with a bare D minor chord with no third (F).

No.6 – The final piece in 'Children's Corner' is the well-known 'Golliwog's Cake-walk'. Debussy, although trained extensively in the Central European classical tradition, was to develop a highly original composing style, comprising such wide-ranging interests as Balinese gamelan music, medieval plainchant and the then-contemporary ragtime from America, as in the 'Golliwog's Cake-walk'. We see the familiar ragtime syncopation (♫ ♩ ♫) and the unexpected ff chords. (bars 4, 12, 20, 24, 40, etc.). What is less well-known or understood is the rather impertinent satire towards Wagner, the nineteenth century musical giant whose harmony was much revered and emulated (but despised by others, of course). Here Debussy parodies the opening of Wagner's 'Tristan' opera of 1865 in the middle section, commencing at bar 61 until about bar 80 (Fig. 5.24).

Fig. 5.24

avec une grande émotion (with much feeling)

This serious original melody is now given the undignified but harmless treatment of added staccato quavers with teasing acciaccaturas (♪), but Debussy would have to admit that

Wagner at one time had been a temporary influence on him!

Question 8

Comment on Debussy's use of rhythm in this piece.   *(2)*

Answer 8

As is common with ragtime, the use of syncopation is paramount. There are also numerous accents on weak beats. The off-beat rhythms in the G flat major section (bar 47) are lightened further by acciaccaturas. The more legato movement in this section (when it mocks Wagner) is satirical partly by means of the added staccato and ornaments.

7 ▶ ANALYSIS 7: BARTOK

BARTÓK: CONCERTO FOR ORCHESTRA (MOVEMENTS 2 and 4 ONLY)

(Set by MEG in 1990)

Béla Bartók (1881–1945) was commissioned by Serge Koussevitzky, the Conductor of the Boston Symphony Orchestra, to write a work for the orchestra in memory of his wife. Although Bartók was a sick man, dying, in fact, of leukaemia, he managed to complete this dazzling five-movement work – which shows off every instrument as a soloist in its own right, hence its unusual title – and it received its first performance at Carnegie Hall, New York in December, 1944.

Bartók had decided to emigrate to America when things had proved unacceptable to him in war-torn Hungary. He was an international pianist and authority on Hungarian folk-music; unfortunately these meant very little to America at the time and he had the unenviable prospect of building his reputation again from the beginning. But ill health dogged his work; recognition was slow, and he was forced to lighten his personal and intense style of composing to suit American tastes. He died in 1945.

No. 2 Gioco delle coppie ('Play of the Pairs')

This is a cleverly constructed movement in ternary form, where pairs of similar instruments are presented one after the other, each pair being harmonised in parallel fashion, a different interval apart.

After a side drum introduction, played mf and without the snares, the order is as follows:

a) bassoons in 6ths
b) oboes in 3rds
c) clarinets in 7ths
d) flutes in 5ths
e) trumpets (muted) in 2nds

As a middle section and as a contrast, the brass instruments play a restrained chorale-like melody, followed by the four horns in similar mood. The side-drum is used intermittently as a quiet link at the ends of phrases. The upper woodwind imitate each other using the first three notes of the bassoon duet (from bar 8) as a way of returning to a recap of the first section.

The recap (bar 165) starts with exactly the same order of instruments, set at the same intervals apart as before. The main differences are as follows:

a) now has an extra bassoon added to the original pair
b) a pair of clarinets join the oboes
c) the two flutes join the clarinets
d) all the woodwind add to the original flute duet
e) the string writing which accompanies the pair of muted trumpets is more sophisticated; the tremolando is higher this time, and two harps playing glissando vary the texture still further.

The movement finishes the way it started with a quiet side-drum rhythm, which this time fades away to nothing.

QUESTIONS AND ANSWERS

Question 1

Which instruments that Bartók used for the first movement are not required for the second movement?   (3)

Answer 1

The 3rd flute (which doubles piccolo); the 3rd oboe (which doubles cor anglais); the 3rd clarinet (which doubles bass clarinet); the 3rd trumpet and bass trombone; bass drum, tam-tam, cymbals and triangle.

Question 2

Describe some of the technical effects that Bartók demands of the string players in this movement.   (5)

Answer 2

Throughout the 'Play of the Pairs' the string section is playing a subservient role to the duettists, but it is a most important background part. They set off the various duet themes with their pizzicato chords; muted (con sord.) trills; tremolando ( ) and glissando ( ); harmonics (where a string is touched lightly to produce a higher, weaker note); normal bowing and some playing at the point of the bow (punta d'arco); spiccato (bouncing the bow to produce short, crisp notes); and sul ponticello (bowing near the bridge), which produces an eerie sound.

Question 3

How does Bartók create a contrasting middle section in this ternary movement?   (5)

Answer 3

Having used five different pairs of instruments one after the other, Bartók provides a more restrained middle section before the pairs return. This middle part is given to the brass without horns, who play a smooth mf chorale-like melody. The side-drum reminds us of its presence with quiet references to its opening rhythm at the end of each brass phrase. The four horns, aided by the tuba, enter with an imitative figure which remains undeveloped. The upper wind hint at the bassoons' theme with imitative 3-note figures ( ). This quieter section of music, with less emphasis on display, seems the perfect contrast before the return of the 'Play of the Pairs', which is even more intensified this time.

No. 4 Intermezzo Interrotto ('Interrupted Intermezzo')

It is said that Bartók heard a performance of Shostakovich's 'Leningrad' Symphony (No. 7) and, thinking little of its somewhat banal march tune, proceeded to denigrate it by subjecting it to musical ridicule in this movement. To be fair to Shostakovich, his war-time seventh symphony, written to help uplift the citizens of a besieged Leningrad, was itself parodying the goose-steeping Nazi enemy in the march tune. Bartók uses it as a somewhat forced interruption to his own inimitable music.

Question 4

Comment on the time signatures used in this movement.   (2)

Answer 4

Bartók commences with a 2/4 time signature, but intersperses the opening theme with occasional 5/8 bars, which provide an infectious unpredictable rhythm. When the viola introduces the second idea (bar 42), there are bars of 6/8 3/4 5/8 7/8 and 2/4. The 'Shostakovich' interlude commences at bar 75 in 8/8, then changes to ¢ for the duration of the march. The viola theme (now rescored more fully) and the return of the opening theme (bar 135) retain their constantly changing time signatures as before.

Question 5

Disregarding the changes of time signatures, how does Bartók compose his opening statement in this movement?   (3)

Answer 5

He writes a four-bar string introduction: B A# E F#, then the oboe melody uses these notes as its sole material, and the accompaniment, too, consists predominantly of these same four notes.

Question 6

How does Bartók satirise Shostakovich in the 'Interrupted' section of this Intermezzo? (*10*)

Answer 6

He takes a fragment of Shostakovich's march tune from the 'Leningrad' Symphony, and proceeds to make it sound as 'corny' as possible. Bartók uses vamping (oompah) in the accompaniment, shrill mocking laughter in the woodwind, trombones blowing a 'raspberry' by means of loud glissandi; and an exaggerated (and later upside-down) version of the march theme itself. All these contribute to a satirical knock at Shostakovich.

Question 7

How does Bartók produce a laughing effect in the 'Interrupted' section of this movement? (*2*)

Answer 7

This occurs three times. An initial discordant high woodwind trill gradually falls away, with different rhythms implying dying laughter. For example, ♩♩ ♩ in the flutes fit against

♪♩♩ ♩ in the oboe and clarinets, producing an effective cross-rhythm. It is the mixture of these three elements: dischord, cross-rhythm and the callous trilling which produces music full of mockery.

8 ▷ SUMMARY

❝ Two suggestions for your own study. ❞

If you have read and carefully studied all the pieces discussed so far in this chapter, you should now be well acquainted with the thought processes that are required for this type of work. You probably now feel confident to undertake some study on your own. You know now what things to find out about, and most importantly, you have learnt what to listen for.

To conclude this chapter and by way of a summary, we shall now encourage you to study some more set works on your own:

The ever-popular Musical 'Cats' by Andrew Lloyd Webber has extracts set by two Boards:

a) 'Skimbleshanks', 'The Old Grumbie Cat', 'Mungojerrie and Rumpleteazer' and 'Mr. Mistoffelees' are set by MEG for 1994 (using 'Ten Songs from Cats' published by Faber Music)

b) 'Magical Mr. Mistoffelees' and 'Memory' are set by NISEAC for 1994

Working independently now, use the following points to make your own study of these extracts:

❝ Some hints for your analysis. ❞

a) Listen to the songs that are relevant to your syllabus (or preferably all of them for further experience), thinking firstly of the emotional impact that each song makes on you. Did you like it? And if so what appealed to you in particular? Write down your initial reactions and feelings – you are studying a great deal of music and it is important to keep careful records of your work.

b) Make notes as you research into the construction of the songs:
   1) How important do you think the words are?
   2) How does the melody relate to the words used?
   3) What instruments are of importance in the song? What solos are played?
   4) Does the mood stay the same throughout the song? If not, how does it change?
   5) Can you work out the structure of the song? Think in terms of verse/chorus/solo etc. Sometimes it is helpful to use the labels A + B + A and so on.
   6) How important is the record production to the song itself? Would it exist satisfactorily in a less polished version?
   7) Find out some background information on Andrew Lloyd Webber. Listen to other pieces by him to add to your familiarity with their style. You would enjoy 'Variations' (set by SEG for 1994).

8) You should know something about T.S. Eliot, the distinguished poet; read through his cat poems in 'Old Possum's Book of Practical Cats'. Did Lloyd Webber use them in the original version, or were they re-worded in places? Who did he collaborate with?

Here are some model questions which could be asked on any of the above songs. They are based on actual questions used by several Boards.

a) Give the name of the song from which (this extract) is taken.
Name of song _____ (½)

b) Name two instruments being played in the instrumental 'break' in (this extract)
Name of instruments _____ and _____ (1)

c) Describe briefly the overall structure of the song from which (this extract) is taken.
_____
_____ (2)

d) Describe the song .... Pay particular attention to the structure, and melodic, rhythmic and harmonic patterns. If you wish you may give musical illustrations.
_____
_____ (14)

EXAMINATION QUESTIONS

Here are some actual past questions for you to try after a thorough study of the 'Cats' songs.

LLOYD WEBBER Cats: (Overture), Skimbleshanks, Memory, Mr. Mistoffelees

(The excerpt for each question is played twice)

1 a) i) Give the name of the piece from Cats that this music comes from
_____ (1)
   ii) Whereabouts in the piece does the excerpt come? _____ (1)

b) Name two instruments which play the melody line at the start of the excerpt
   i) _____ ii) _____ (2)

c) After the singer finishes, the tune is heard again but it is different in several ways. Write down two of these differences
   i) _____ ii) _____ (2)

(SEG, 1989)

2 a) The rhythm at the start of this excerpt differs from that at the start of the number.
How? _____ (2)

b) This excerpt portrays the Railway Cat. What is there in the music that paints a sound-picture of this title, and how?
   i) (What) _____ (1)
   ii) (How) _____ (1)

c) The words that follow the end of this excerpt are – 'Do you like your morning tea weak or strong?'.
   i) How does the composer set these words? _____ (1)
   ii) What voices are used? _____ (1)

(SEG, 1989)

3 Give three examples of word-painting from this excerpt, i.e. where a word or words are expressed by the music, either by the shape of the tune or in the accompaniment. In each example, quote the word(s) and say how the music paints them.

a) Example 1
   Word(s) _____ (1)
   How _____ (1)

b) Example 2
   Word(s) _____ *(1)*
   How _____ *(1)*

c) Example 3
   Word(s) _____ *(1)*
   How _____ *(1)*

(SEG, 1991)

4   Describe 'Skimbleshanks', concentrating particularly on points of musical interest.
(20)

(IGCSE, 1991)

5   Describe all the features of the music and accompaniment in 'Skimbleshanks' that help create the effect of a railway train.   *(20)*

(IGCSE, 1992)

STUDENT ANSWER WITH EXAMINER COMMENTS

Here is a pupil's answer to question d) on page 47, with the examiner's comments:

Describe the song 'Memory'. Pay particular attention to structure, and melodic, rhythmic and harmonic patterns. If you wish you may give musical illustrations.

In this song Andrew Lloyd Webber does not use T.S. Eliot's words exactly. He asked Trevor Nunn to arrange them to make them more suitable for use as a song. It is a good song, well constructed, with a wide range of emotional power. Not surprisingly, it became the hit song from the Musical.

The character Grizabella sings the first two stanzas to the same tune. It is basically in 12/8 time with occasional bars of 10/8 and 6/8 to allow the words to fit satisfactorily. These changes of time signature are effective, breaking up a predictable four in a bar pattern.

The next part of the tune ('Every street lamp...') has less movement. Lloyd Webber makes good use of sequence here, especially effective on the rhyme: 'mutters' and 'gutters'. The brightening effect of the keychange at this point is dispelled by a return to the original key and the first theme.

There is a complete change of key to the flattened sixth which lifts the mood of the song. This was a modulatory trait from the Romantic period. Here Lloyd Webber employs it well. He uses the orchestra alone for the first eight bars of the main theme, before the vocalist re-enters with the second idea, lower in the voice this time and more restrained, which underlines the sad and nostalgic quality of the song.

The climax occurs after an orchestral build-up to the main tune on the words 'touch me'. The song ends quietly with four bars for orchestra, using music from the introduction. The overall structure could be described as A A B A A B A.

Good. An informative and interesting opening to an answer.

Good. Clear details of rhythmic structure.

Rather vague on melody – more detail required.

Good. An awareness of other influences here.

Some understanding of the structure, but no mention of the important modulation here.

We are not told very much about the melody itself. Answer each part of the question.

Most of these questions are concerned with facts about the music, but any factual information about a work is only relevant if you can apply it intelligently to your emotional understanding. Any personal response to music must come from you. This book is designed to show you how to study effectively, and to give you a selection of examination questions for each area of the syllabus – it does not set out to cover everything in detail for all six examining Groups.

No one can make you enjoy a piece of music, but familiarity with it from the inside, through constructive analysis and repeated listening, will increase your appreciation of it. Overall, the prime reasons for musical analysis are these:

- to further your understanding of how music works, and to increase your enjoyment of it.
- to realise that no two works are alike.
- to develop further understanding of how composers adopt standard forms to suit their artistic purpose.
- to appreciate how a work belongs to its time and how contemporaries and forerunners influence the content of a composer's work.
- to encourage an intellectual and aesthetic advancement; to develop your experience of thoughts and feelings through sound.

You should be listening regularly to all styles of music – from all corners of the world – and you will gradually gain a rewarding insight into the rich and diverse world of musical sound.

REVIEW SHEET

✎ What period of music predominantly used the Basso Continuo and figured bass?

_____

✎ What is the difference between a Baroque Concerto and a Classical Concerto?

_____

_____

✎ What favourite Vivaldi device is used here?

solo violin bars 23-24

_____

✎ What are the differences between an opera and an oratorio?

_____

_____

✎ What is 'mood-painting' in music?

_____

_____

✎ What is meant by:

(a) 'tremolando'

_____

(b) a crescendo

_____

(c) 'pizzicato'

_____

(d) a 'pedal' note?

_____

✎ Describe some of the ways in which variety is given in a typical chorus by Handel.

_____

_____

✎ How did the the trumpet develop into the instrument we have today?

_____

_____

✎ What key did Baroque composers tend to use when making predominant use of trumpets and drums?

_____

✎ What type of melody is Haydn using in these bars?

(2nd movt: bars 18-24)

_____

✎ What are the following:

(a) Ternary form?

_____

(b) Rondo form?

_____

(c) Sonata-Rondo form?

_____

✎ What is a transposing instrument?

_____

✎ Describe some of the different piano textures that a piano composer (such as Debussy) might employ in one of his pieces.

_____

_____

_____

✎ For what reason does Debussy use this phrase in the "Golliwog's Cake Walk"?

avec une grande émotion (with much feeling)

_____

_____

✎ Bartok uses several different string effects in his Concerto for Orchestra – some are quite common, others more unusual. Name some of these, explain what they mean and show how they are written down.

_____

_____

_____

_____

_____

_____

✎ In Bartok's Concerto For Orchestra, Movement 4, comment on his use of time signatures.

_____

_____

_____

_____

_____

_____

CHAPTER 3

SOLO PERFORMANCE

EXAM GROUP REQUIREMENTS

WHAT THE EXAMINER LOOKS FOR

HINTS TO PERFORMERS

CHECKLIST FOR INSTRUMENTS

GETTING STARTED

Music is essentially a performing art, and the GCSE music exam aims to encourage people to become involved in as much music making as possible, either individually or in groups. The *solo performance* section encourages you to work hard at your instrument or voice throughout the course, perfecting technique, developing interpretative skills and allowing opportunity for performing in front of others. This area of the coursework will probably be left to you and your *instrumental teacher*. Your *class teacher*, once satisfied that you are aware of the requirements for solo performance, is likely to leave you to practise until just before the exam, as there are so many other things in the syllabus to be covered.

ESSENTIAL PRINCIPLES

The Exam Groups vary in their requirements for this component. These can be summarised as follows:

ULEAC

This is an option within the Prepared Performance Element. You are required to sing or play one or two pieces of your own choice, and the examiner will listen to you for about five minutes. An accompaniment should be provided if your music requires it. You should have a copy of the score (or failing that a commentary) available for the examiner. 'It is expected that the music prepared for performance will give the candidate an opportunity to reveal the highest standards in his or her study.'

SEG

This is an option within the Prepared Performance section. You are required to sing or play at least one piece individually. You should choose music which is long enough to demonstrate your ability, and the examiner may stop you when he has heard sufficient to judge that. Ideally, you should produce a score for the examiner, but failing that, introduce the piece in such a way that you clearly present its nature.

NEAB

This is an option within the Prepared Performance section. You are required to sing or play at least one piece of your own choice. If you wish, you may offer a second instrument.

WJEC

This is an option within the Prepared Performance section. You are asked to sing or play a selection of music of your own choice which adequately displays the following skills:

a) clarity and accuracy of rhythm and pitch;
b) the use of appropriate tempo;
c) effective use of dynamics;
d) fluency of performance;
e) sensitive balance of phrasing;
f) stylistic awareness;
g) technical control of the instrument.

You may use one or two instruments for your performance, but you should not exceed five minutes in all.

MEG

(For full details see Chapter 3)
Component 03 is taken as part of Option A or C, and prepared performing is an element within this (the others being Ensemble Playing and Rehearsing and Directing an ensemble). Candidates are required to offer *two* of these elements, and there must be one performance in each of the chosen elements. Total playing time should not exceed 10 minutes. Candidates should record their performances on tape throughout the course.

Component 04 is taken as part of Option B, and prepared performing is an element within this (the others being Ensemble Playing and Rehearsing and Directing an Ensemble). Candidates are required to offer *two* or *three* of these; those offering two elements must offer a performance of one piece in one element, and two contrasting pieces in the other. Candidates offering three elements must offer one performance in each element. Total playing time should not exceed 15 minutes. Candidates should record their performances on tape throughout the course.

IGCSE

To sing or play individually is a compulsory part of this Prepared Performance section. You also need to offer either an additional solo instrument (or voice), or singing or playing in an ensemble. Pieces are of your own choice, and can be accompanied as necessary. The full section should last up to ten minutes.

NISEAC

This is an option within the Prepared Performance section. You are asked to play one or two pieces, and you may offer an instrument, voice, instrument and voice or two instruments. You have free choice of music in any style, and your programme should last between three and five minutes. Solo performance can be accompanied as appropriate.

Do practise performing

You are certain to practise your chosen pieces many times, but you possibly haven't thought of practising *performing*. Playing in front of an examiner (or an audience of course) is not the same as playing at home; and taking a practical examination is very different from having a lesson with your own instrumental teacher.

2 > WHAT THE EXAMINER LOOKS FOR

Be aware of what the examiner is looking for.

You have seen how the Groups vary slightly in their requirements for this examination. Assume that whatever syllabus you take the examiners' approach will be much the same. Most examiners will have spent time themselves preparing students for examinations and know all the pitfalls. They will all be looking for the same thing: evidence of musicianship. A lower grade performance will gain credit for playing the correct notes in an acceptable tempo; a higher grade candidate will be rewarded for expressive fluency and a sensitive musical interpretation.

Examiners are sometimes faced with the difficult task of assessing a performance by a student who has chosen a far too ambitious programme. The examiner has to mark what he actually hears; he cannot give credit for the potential ability of a candidate. It is disappointing for a talented performer to be given low marks because the chosen programme was unsuitable for him at that time.

'Musicianship' is most important.

Before we go any further, it will be worthwhile to try to define the word *musicianship*, as it is much used in this book, and is that vital ingredient which examiners seek in any performance situation. In a nutshell, musicianship is that element of feeling in a performance which is intelligently added to the showing of technical skills. As stated elsewhere, it is more or less taken for granted that you will have mastered the correct notes and rhythms for your chosen programme.

Indeed, having said that, most examiners would prefer an expressive and sensitive performance of a piece that contained a few wrong notes to one that was clinically perfect in the technical sense, yet lifeless and unfeeling. **Feeling** must be added to a piece sensitively, however. There is much more to expression than 'loud' and 'soft'. **Light** and **shade** are continually varied in most pieces of music, and each phrase needs to be considered both individually and in the context of the whole before the piece is ready for public hearing. It is worth remembering that most pieces have a fair balance between a state of tension and relaxation. You should plan, in a longer piece, where the climaxes come; it is just as unsatisfactory for a performance to be perpetually 'laid back' as tense all the time. Think in terms of **climax** and **repose** and how you can shape these convincingly.

While emphasising the importance of the expressive content, it must also be stressed that a good technical facility is no less important; it is the successful combining of the two that leads to a satisfying, and moving performance. Singers and wind players will need to solve and master any breathing problems before they can hope to give a sensitive performance; similarly, string players will spend time considering their bowing, and the brass or wind player will need to concentrate on maintaining a good embouchure (mouth position on an instrument). The pianist will produce a satisfying tone only when a good sense of touch has been mastered.

3 > HINTS TO PERFORMERS

Useful hints for performers.

Before we go further into detail for the different instruments, here are some general points of advice to performers.

- Choose your programme with great care. You need a piece or pieces that allow you to show what you can do, but don't try to impress the examiner by playing something that is beyond your technical and interpretative ability.

- If your syllabus allows you time to play more than one piece, aim to create a well-balanced programme. Try to choose pieces of contrasting style, character or period so that you will be able to show different aspects of your performing personality.

- Certainly try to gain some experience of playing for other people, at a school concert perhaps, or by playing your pieces over to your family or friends. Listen carefully to any constructive comments they may have. You will probably find that nervousness affects you physically, so trial runs will help you learn how to overcome this. Remember a little nervousness can be a good thing – most people are at their best when 'psyched up'.

Don't neglect rehearsal time.

- Once you have mastered all the notes and basic details in your piece, give careful attention to the expressive qualities. If you require an accompanist make sure that you have adequate rehearsal time together. You need to get used to hearing the piano part, and then decide how best to interpret the piece as a whole. Think of the balance between the two of you. Sometimes the accompanist will have a share of the theme and you will need to play down. Always listen to the music so that you can form a constructive opinion on how each section should be played. The natural acoustics of the exam room are rather important, so certainly rehearse in there several times if you can. If it is a resonant room you may have to play slightly slower than you originally planned. Conversely, a 'dry' or more dead acoustic may persuade you to increase the tempo to keep the piece alive. This all takes careful listening and planning – don't leave it until the actual day!

Know the various Italian terms.

- You will learn a lot about interpretation by discussing a piece with your instrumental teacher. Should it be cheerful or morose? Jumpy or smooth? You will find the understanding of Italian terms helpful here. Although they are daunting to learn, all experienced musicians instinctively know how to achieve a required mood when they see, for example, the word 'pomposo' in a Baroque piece, or 'nobilmente' in an Elgar composition. (It must be admitted that Elgar cheekily made up this word to sound Italian, but musicians understand the mood he means to set.)

- This may sound contradictory, but be careful not to over-interpret. The performance of a study which is essentially a technical exercise should not be 'expressive' for the sake of it. Similarly, ensure that your expression is suitable for the period of the composition. It would be considered bad taste, for example, to use excessive rubato (free tempo) in a Bach Prelude.

- The use of dynamics requires more thought than may at first seem likely. After all, if the music is written 'p' then surely it is simply played softly. But how soft is soft? Dynamic markings such as this are bound to be relative – a pianissimo for a tuba will not be quite the same as one for a violin! Of course this goes without saying, but it is a necessary consideration when you start to think historically. Romantic composers had a different way of using dynamic markings to Classical composers, whereas Baroque composers tended not to use them very much at all. In early and Baroque music you have the added problem of deciding whether to follow the suggested editorial dynamics, which are often printed in parentheses, or to work out your own. Would it be suitable to add ornaments? Can you miss out some of the difficult trills which have been suggested? Should you vary the volume when you go back for a repeat? Would it be correct to slow down at the end?

Use your own musical judgement, taking advice where appropriate.

We have come back to the main point: you simply must use your ever-developing musical judgement, with the advice, of course, of your teachers. Try to listen to a recording of your piece if at all possible. It may not be played in the way that you want to perform it, but it should give you some useful ideas for your own interpretation.

- The use of a metronome is a good way to set the composer's recommended tempo when you first come to study a piece, but it is not advisable to play along to the machine in a mechanical way. In fact composers often seem to contradict their own metronome markings when you listen to them conducting their own recordings. Again, trust your own musical judgement. The speed of a piece is right for you when you can play it convincingly in the chosen acoustic. The metronome marking should only be regarded as a guide.

4 > CHECKLIST FOR INSTRUMENTS

The following criteria are intended as a summary of things to work at for a successful Solo Performance. They are not arranged in order of importance and they are by no means exhaustive – you will probably think of other important things to consider. Most of the

Useful hints for solo performance on various instruments.

points have already been mentioned above, but you should find this a helpful checklist for your particular instrument.

WOODWIND

Accuracy of intonation
Good breath control
Good tone control
Good embouchure
Good technical control

Good fingering technique
Good articulation – legato and tonguing
Good interpretation
Good posture

BRASS

Accuracy of intonation
Good breath control
Good tone control
Good embouchure
Appropriate use of mutes
Good slide or finger technique

Good hand and bell technique for horn players
Good articulation – legato and tonguing
Application of a wide dynamic range
Good interpretation
Good posture

STRINGS (bowed)

Accuracy of intonation
Good control of tone, with correct vibrato
Good posture: correct holding of instrument and bow
Correct type of bowing (spiccato, staccato)

Appropriate fingering
Good use of pizzicato, mutes etc
Application of a varied dynamic range
Good interpretation

PERCUSSION (untuned)

Good co-ordination of hand, fingers and feet
Correct use of various sticks and beaters
Good control of rhythm and tempi

Good response to dynamic changes
Production of effective tone and timbre
Correct setting up (e.g. snare drum tension)

PERCUSSION (tuned)

(first read the list for untuned percussion)
Good knowledge of keyboard
Quick and accurate tuning of timpani
  (and re-tuning against other musical sounds)

Use of single and double sticks
Variation of touch
Good balance of melodic line against accompaniment
Accurate use of pedals

VOICE

Accuracy of intonation
Good breath control
Good, clear diction
A tonal balance throughout your range
Equally clear vowels throughout your range

Pleasing presentation
Clear projection of your voice
Good interpretation
Good posture

STRINGS (plucked e.g. guitar)

Good intonation – careful tuning
Good hand positions
Good balance of melodic line against accompaniment
Good plucking technique
Good left-hand technique
Pleasing tone

Correct posture and footstool placing
Wide dynamic range
Control of special effects (tremolando, harmonics)
For electric guitars – appropriate volume settings
Good interpretation

KEYBOARDS

Good variety of touch (legato, staccato, accented)

Good co-ordination of hands

Good balance of melodic line against accompaniment

A musical sense of phrasing

Appropriate and systematic fingering

Good use of pedals

Good interpretation

Good posture

(For electronic organ – musical use of effects and pre-set buttons)

(harpsichord – control/choice of registration)

PIPE ORGAN

In addition to keyboard list, as relevant:

Appropriate choice/good control of registration

Accurate use of the pedal board

Good co-ordination of hands and feet

Suitable phrasing as appropriate to the instrument

Good interpretation

ELECTRONIC KEYBOARDS AND SYNTHESIZERS

Good knowledge of the keyboard and effects

Good control of rhythmic effects

Understanding of synthesizers generally

Good imaginative/creative use of the instrument

Good interpretation

A FINAL STATEMENT

Subject reports give useful clues.

The Subject Reports published by the Groups after each examination session make interesting reading. In the Solo Performance section it is evident that a significant number of gifted candidates gave performances at a standard higher than 100% level. Likewise, a good number gave musical performances of simple music. It can be deduced from the wording in these reports that it is more sensible to offer pieces that you can perform to a good technical and musical standard, rather than risk a mediocre play-through of a piece that is technically too demanding. Also it is clear that offering a less good second piece may bring down your overall mark when the mark is an average of two. Potential candidates are reminded that their chosen pieces should not be too short, and that an accompaniment should be included where it is an integral part of the composition.

ENSEMBLE WORK

EXAM GROUP REQUIREMENTS

HINTS FOR ENSEMBLE PLAYING

INTERACTING WITH OTHERS

CHECKLIST BEFORE REHEARSING

GETTING STARTED

Music is a social activity. Making music with others can be highly rewarding – and not just financially! Singing or playing as part of a group brings that sense of teamwork as in any sport. Playing as a member of an *ensemble* should be one of the most enjoyable parts of GCSE music and, assuming it all goes well, you will feel a real sense of achievement.

This section of the examination does not carry an enormous number of marks, but it is aiming to encourage that feeling of team spirit – a corporate activity to stimulate an interest that you may want to pursue for the rest of your life. For those of you not well-versed in French, the word *ensemble* literally means *together*, so that musically it implies a small group of players who are aiming to create an intimate and close musical performance. Smaller professional ensembles (such as string quartets) do not usually have a conductor; with all parts being treated as equal, they learn to work and play together without a director. It is very important to realise that each member of your ensemble must listen to the others carefully and respond accordingly.

In terms of the examination, an ensemble may be regarded as two or more members, but it is recommended that you try to choose music that will involve three or four or more. (Remember that your Solo Performance, of course, can include an accompanist and there is then no real difference between performing as a soloist and playing in an Ensemble of two). Many of you will play regularly in a rock band, wind band, orchestra, or sing in the school choir. As long as the part you take is readily identifiable (and for some Groups, not doubled by other people) and is a valuable contribution to a piece, then any combination of two or more performers is perfectly acceptable.

ESSENTIAL PRINCIPLES

The Groups vary in their requirements for this item. They are summarised as follows:

ULEAC

This is an option within the Prepared Performance element. You may sing or play in the ensemble and there is no limit on the number of people taking part. Make sure that your part is easily identifiable and not hidden amongst all the others. You may submit one or two pieces of your choice, and the examiner will hear about five minutes.

SEG

This is an option within the Prepared Performance section. You are required to sing or play in at least one ensemble piece of your own choice, where your part must not be doubled by other members of the group. There is no specified length for your piece or pieces, but choose something which shows your contribution adequately and to best advantage. You should try to produce a score for the examiner's use, but failing that, be prepared to explain the nature of your chosen piece.

NEAB

This is an option within the Prepared Performance section. You may sing or play in the ensemble, and you are permitted to offer a different instrument from the individual performance. The ensemble should number from two to five players, and your own part should not be doubled. You are required to prepare at least one piece.

WJEC

This is an option within the Prepared Performance section. You are required to perform music of your own choice in an ensemble of at least two players (the other players need not be exam candidates). An accompanied performance would qualify for this section if the music were appropriate. Your part must not be doubled elsewhere in the ensemble.

MEG

(For full details see Chapter 3)
Component 03 is taken as part of Option A or C, and Ensemble Playing is an element within this (the others being Solo Performance and Rehearsing and Directing an ensemble.) Candidates are required to offer *two* of these elements, and there must be one performance in each of the chosen elements. Total playing time should not exceed 10 minutes. Candidates should record their performances on tape throughout the course.

Component 04 is taken as part of Option B, and Ensemble Playing is an element within this (the others being Solo Performance and Rehearsing and Directing an ensemble. Candidates are required to offer *two* or *three* of these; those offering two elements must offer a performance of one piece in one element, and two contrasting pieces in the other. Candidates offering three elements must offer one performance in each element. Total playing time should not exceed 15 minutes. Candidates should record their performances on tape throughout the course.

For both components 03 and 04, an ensemble may consist of two or more performers, but the candidate's part may not be doubled consistently by any other performer and must be aurally identifiable.

IGCSE

This is an option within the Prepared Performance section. (Ensemble Performance is offered against Solo Performance on a second instrument – there is no Rehearsing/ Directing of an ensemble for IGCSE). There could be two or more players in the ensemble, but note here that if you used an accompaniment for your Solo Performance (the compulsory item in this section), then your Ensemble must consist of three or more players. You may sing or use the same voice or instrument as in your Solo Performance, but your part must not be doubled by anyone else. You have free choice of pieces and your full performance section should last up to ten minutes.

NISEAC

This is an option within the Prepared Performance section. You are required to offer one or two pieces where your part is not doubled elsewhere in the ensemble. Members of the ensemble need not be examination candidates and the performance should last from three to five minutes. You may offer an accompanied performance (as in Solo Performance) but different pieces must be performed. You are permitted, in total, to offer a) one instrument or b) one instrument and voice or c) voice or d) two instruments.

---

2 > HINTS FOR ENSEMBLE PLAYING

" Some useful hints for ensemble playing. "

" Don't leave things to chance. "

" Learn your individual part thoroughly. "

The suggestions to be made in this chapter are doubtless duplicated elsewhere in this book, for performance standards for Ensemble playing are not so very different from those for a soloist. (For more complete notes on performance technique, see Chapter 6). The following ideas are common sense really, but must be stated.

■ If you are requested to submit a copy of the score of your piece for the examiner to see during your performance, then every effort must be made to do so. A commentary is usually acceptable if you cannot provide a score, for example with a Rock song where the group has not worked from printed music. Make sure that you explain fully to the examiner how the musical strands are employed throughout the piece. After all, you are probably performing a short two or three minute piece, and the examiner will need to see at a glance exactly what you are supposed to be playing.

■ Be completely set up for the performance before the examiner arrives. Your teacher will have worked out a detailed schedule for the day so that time is not wasted. Have all your music ready, stands set up, amplifiers and speakers in place (with volume checked in advance!), and be fully warmed up and in tune with each other. Not only does this create a good impression and save time for all concerned, but it is, indeed, good performance practice.

■ Thinking musically now, the question of balance is most important when playing with others. Once again, common sense should prevail here, but if you have a melodic instrument playing a tune, then your part should be more prominent than if you are supporting with an accompaniment figure. Taste and sensitivity – in other words, *musical judgement* – must be used at all times. There is far more to group playing than merely getting the correct notes. You must also be able to blend well with the others. Having said this, however, your chosen piece of ensemble music will probably be written in such a way that your part is a combination of melody and accompaniment, where each player takes a turn at the tune. For most people this is probably very obvious and would happen automatically, but it must be stated again: think carefully all the time about your part in relation to the other players. Should this section be more prominent? Is this an important theme or counter-melody, or is it merely a harmonic background? Music is often written as a sort of dialogue, where themes are handed from player to player in a conversational way. This sensitivity becomes second nature to experienced musicians eventually; the process may happen sub-consciously, but it certainly still goes on. No doubt your teacher will be available to advise you, or even direct rehearsals, but it will also require an intelligent contribution from you. Think musically, and listen critically to all the parts whenever you rehearse and perform.

■ Once the ensemble music has been chosen, it is your responsibility to learn your individual part thoroughly. You will be sure to know when you are likely to rehearse the piece all together, so organise yourself so that you have sorted out any technical problems with notes in good time. When an ensemble is ready to start working at a finer interpretation of a piece there is nothing more infuriating, and time-wasting, than to find that one player is still struggling with his sharps and flats, bowing, phrasing or whatever. Most GCSE candidates will be having instrumental lessons out of class, so it may be a good idea to take the music to that teacher for specialist help – he or she may well have helped to choose the piece in the first place and will therefore be more than willing to oblige. The more time that the ensemble can spend on achieving a balance of sound, sensitive phrasing and agreed general interpretation, so much the better.

■ Regarding the choice of ensemble pieces, it is impossible here to give actual titles of pieces that you might play, for every combination of instruments and abilities is quite different. It can only be suggested that you **spend time** carefully choosing a piece where each player is adequately involved, without his or her part being too difficult. It is better, surely, to perform a slightly easier part well than to take on a more showy part, only to spoil it in the examination where you have only one chance.

> **Watch the conductor.**

- If the ensemble has decided to use a conductor (your teacher, perhaps, or a musical classmate), make sure that you keep an eye on him or her. Remember that a conductor is there to express the music as well as to keep a steady beat. The alternative is for one of the ensemble players to be appointed as leader or director. Rehearse thoroughly so that he or she is well prepared for the difficult task of starting and finishing the piece with just an up-bow, a breath or a nod. A polished opening and ending, with chords sounded perfectly together, is vital to the success of your performance.

3 > INTERACTING WITH OTHERS

> **Be ready to listen to other viewpoints.**

It was stated above how important it is musically to blend well with others. Similarly, you should endeavour to blend well socially when working with other musicians. In a small group such as this, everyone has the right to offer their views and opinions to help improve the standard of the piece. However, there may come a time when a particular member has to eat humble pie and accept the judgement of the majority, or your rehearsing will never achieve a satisfactory performance. It is surely an important part of the experience to learn to interact with others. You may be the only player of your instrument and therefore know its technical limitations or characteristics best, but the final interpretation in an ensemble should be the result of a mixture of opinions.

Your teacher, of course, may decide to direct the piece in all rehearsals and the final performance. In this case you will need to behave as if you are in a professional orchestra – the conductor is the maestro, and is entirely responsible for interpretation. Your responsibility is to play your instrument in a way which responds accurately to the conductor's directives.

These are two very different ways of contributing musically and you must accept your teacher's method of working. Both methods have their place and can be very satisfying. Nothing will be achieved satisfactorily in a group unless you all show some initiative and cooperation. Having suggested that no one member should dominate an ensemble, the other danger is that no-one will take any responsibility! Try to be helpful in an unselfish, yet contributory way.

4 > CHECKLIST BEFORE REHEARSING

> **Some useful points for rehearsing.**

Before rehearsing with your ensemble you will find it helpful to check the following points:

i) Am I totally accurate – in pitch, rhythm, and intonation?
ii) Are details such as breathing/tonguing/bowing/fingering/pedalling all sorted out?
iii) Have I mastered the expressive aspects of the music – phrasing, dynamics, expression marks?
iv) Am I able to play my part fluently in the correct tempo?
v) Am I playing it the 'correct' way stylistically?

A FINAL STATEMENT

The reassuring thing to remember about GCSE is that any candidate may be part of an ensemble, even with the most modest performing skills. Do not assume that you have to be a brilliant performer. The Groups take into account the difficulty of your individual part by using a difficulty multiplier in the marking scheme. Your chosen pieces are divided into categories – very easy, intermediate difficulty and reasonable difficulty – and you are assessed accordingly. Examiners are also well aware that some instruments are more demanding technically than others, and this, too, is taken into account.

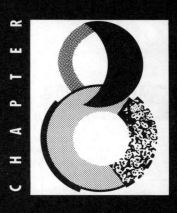

GETTING STARTED

Rehearsing and directing an ensemble is less likely to be chosen as a Prepared Option by many candidates. It is good that most GCSE Groups offer this option, but it will probably be chosen only by those candidates with an interest and an ability to conduct, who have good aural skills and the confidence to go with it.

Before you finally decide on your options for Prepared Performance, read this short chapter through carefully and consider what is involved – there is more to it than standing up in front and beating time!

REHEARSING AND DIRECTING AN ENSEMBLE

EXAM GROUP REQUIREMENTS

USEFUL HINTS AND TECHNIQUES

CONDUCTING TECHNIQUE

LAYOUT OF ENSEMBLE

RECORDING PROGRESS

ESSENTIAL PRINCIPLES

1 ▶ EXAM GROUP REQUIREMENTS

The Groups have slightly different requirements for this item, which can be summarised as follows:

ULEAC

This is an option within the Prepared Performance section. You are required to rehearse and direct an ensemble of singers and/or players in the performance of one or more pieces of your own choice. There should be at least six performers in the ensemble. About five minutes will be heard by the visiting examiner, and a score (or commentary, where no score is available) must be supplied for him to see.

SEG

This is an option within the Prepared Performance section. You are required to rehearse and direct an ensemble of more than two performers. Members of the chosen group should be given copies of the music (of your choice) one week before the examination to enable them to prepare their parts, and they should never have rehearsed the piece together previously. You will be assessed on your direction of this first rehearsal. While it is understood that you may not achieve performance standard during this one session you will be expected to work with the group as if towards an eventual performance. The rehearsal should last for ten to twenty minutes. Marks are awarded for your effectiveness as a musical leader rather than for the perfection you manage to achieve.

NEAB

This is an option within the Prepared Performance section. The examiner will hear a performance of at least one piece of music which you have previously rehearsed with your ensemble. A written and/or taped record should be submitted, in which you explain your choice of music, your preparation, the schedule of rehearsals over an extended period and comment on progress made. The line-up need not be the same for each piece, but there must be no fewer than three performers. Equal marks are available for each of the following:
a) the selection of suitable music; b) the realisation of the music; c) the understanding of the instruments and voices at your disposal; d) the direction of the actual performance of what has been rehearsed.

WJEC

This is an option within the Prepared Performance section. It is expected that candidates will direct several rehearsals of their chosen music during the course, and the examiner will need to observe a further rehearsal of one or more of these pieces, lasting up to ten minutes. Marks are awarded for your organisation, and qualities of musical direction. You should also be prepared to discuss any aspect of the rehearsal with the examiner afterwards. Before the examination rehearsal you should give a score (or outline) of the music to him. If a score is not available you should give an oral description of the piece. The members of your rehearsal group need not be exam candidates.

MEG

(For full details see Chapter 3)
Component 03 is taken as part of Option A or C, and Rehearsing and Directing an ensemble is an element within this (the others being Solo Performance and Ensemble Playing.) Candidates are required to offer *two* of these elements, and there must be one performance in each of the chosen elements.

Component 04 is taken as part of Option B, and Rehearsing and Directing an ensemble is an element within this (the others being Solo Performance and Ensemble Playing.) Candidates are required to offer *two* or *three* of these; those offering two elements must offer a performance of one piece in one element, and two contrasting pieces in the other. Candidates offering three elements must offer one performance in each element.

For both components 03 and 04, candidates will be assessed on rehearsal and performance, for which marks available will be in the ratio of 2:1. Any help given during the rehearsal must be acknowledged. The work chosen to be directed need not be a published piece – it could be a composition or arrangement by the pupil, teacher or anyone.

IGCSE

This is not an option; instead you have the opportunity to offer a second instrument for another Solo Performance.

NISEAC

This is an option within the Prepared Performance section. Candidates are expected to direct rehearsals of various pieces over the two year course. The visiting examiner will then need to observe you working on another piece, previously unrehearsed, but which the performers will have an opportunity to prepare in advance. You will have ten to fifteen minutes for the rehearsal, and you should provide either orally or in writing an overall plan and a plan for the assessment rehearsal.

2 ❯ USEFUL HINTS AND TECHNIQUES

If you do choose this option, remember that the examination 'rehearsal' is fifteen to twenty minutes long for some Groups. You will need to choose your music with care, plan the rehearsal thoughtfully and decide on the standard of performance that you are aiming for.

Here are some thoughts for guidance which are relevant for all the syllabuses that include this option.

- First of all, prepare an **overall plan**.
  Choose music within your own ability, so that it is not too difficult for you to detect any mistakes and inaccuracies. Also take into account the ability of the group you are to direct. If you choose a piece that is too demanding you will probably not have time to move beyond correcting basic technical errors; conversely, if it is too easy for them there will be little opportunity for you to display your skills of direction.

   **Choose your music carefully.**

  Bear in mind the instrumentation and balance of your ensemble, and if you are preparing more than one piece aim for some variety or contrast.

  Give careful consideration to your score and decide what your priorities will be. Prepare it very thoroughly yourself so that you form a clear idea of the composer's intentions, and can more quickly recognise problems as they arise. Try to anticipate sections in the music where things are most likely to go wrong, or which you feel will need particular attention in the rehearsal.

- Make a **rehearsal plan**.
  What are you aiming to achieve in your rehearsal? A perfect performance is unlikely, of course, given such a limited time – so what emphasis will you place on correct notes and reasonable tuning, as against the more expressive considerations? Remember, this all depends on the abilities of your players and the relative difficulty of your chosen music, but you must consider what standards you intend to achieve.

- Think of the **content** of your rehearsal.
  You will need to be able to recognise basic errors such as wrong notes and poor tuning, for example, and simultaneously give attention to aspects of rhythm, phrasing, dynamics, blending and ensemble. (By ensemble, we mean synchronised chording, especially at stops and starts, and a sense of 'togetherness' generally.)

  Have definite targets.

  Aim to develop an ability to work on particular weak spots rather than try to cover too much. In a timed exercise such as this it is better to 'perfect' a shorter section than just play through a larger section. Should the melody be more expressive here? Was someone not watching you hold that pause? Was the accompaniment figure too prominent? Your performers are probably reading from a single line and will look to you for clear direction, both spoken and through meaningful conducting.

- As the person in charge of the ensemble you will need to develop and demonstrate a sense of **musical leadership**.
  You must convince the examiner (and the players, ultimately) of your competence in musical interpretation. Perhaps the most important skill for this option is the ability to communicate exactly what you want to your players.

You must establish a good relationship with the group. Control of people does not mean you must be unfriendly! Think of yourself as first among equals.

Aim to make decisions quickly, and try not to change your mind, which may confuse the players – they must always know where they are.

- The **presentation** of your rehearsal is important.

  Were the methods you employed the correct ones? Were they suitable to achieve your required aim?

  Alter the pace when rehearsing to give variety. Although people won't get bored in your short rehearsal, sustain their interest by varying your voice occasionally to avoid monotony and keep things moving along.

  Could people understand what you were saying? Were you loud and clear? Be articulate without talking too much. Good conductors communicate with musical actions more than their voices.

  Did you involve everyone satisfactorily in the rehearsal? Or were you so intent on one particular section that the poor trumpeter was almost forgotten and only played three notes?

- What **overall impression** do you think you gave?

  Did you sense the group enjoyed it all and felt a sense of shared achievement?

  Did you manage to interpret the music according to the composer's intentions? You may have achieved the right notes but were the tempo, dynamics and phrasing appropriate?

> Presentation is important.

3 > CONDUCTING TECHNIQUE

Beating time is just one aspect of being a conductor, but a vital one. You can practise giving a good, clear beat on your own in front of a mirror at home – you could even conduct your own records! Assuming that you are likely to work with a fairly small group, it is not necessary to use a baton. Bare hands can be perfectly clear and sometimes more expressive than using a stick. Try both ways during practice and use whichever is the most comfortable for you.

Your down beat is the most important, and must be very clear; see Fig. 8.1

Fig. 8.1

two in a bar

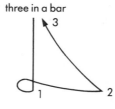
three in a bar

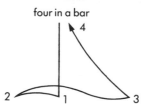
four in a bar

The diagrams in Fig. 8.1 are for right-handed people; reverse the direction of beats 2, 3 and 4 if you are left-handed. Notice the curved beats; this is rather more graceful than robotic straight lines. After all, you are trying to express the feeling of the music as well as keep a clear and steady beat. Your other hand will not move around so much, but is used for further expression: softness, loudness, tenderness, anger.

Don't overdo the hand movements – aim for clarity; you are not giving a gymnastic display! Use your face, and especially your eyes to maintain a rapport with your players. Whereas words can help you explain your musical intentions in a rehearsal, in a performance you are totally dependent on gesture – body language, in fact. To an experienced player, even a slightly raised eyebrow can be a clear signal as to how the music is to be played. A smile or frown from you will be obvious enough. Of course, the sort of gesture you give will depend on the music and your personality. There are many ways to interpret music physically, and in the end you will have to work out your own salvation. Whatever you do, be clear – don't try to be a showman on this particular occasion!

> Useful hints for conducting.

4 > LAYOUT OF ENSEMBLE

Finally, one or two suggestions concerning the layout for your ensemble. Again, this is common sense really, but worth stating. Plan out how you want your players to sit. If there are only a few, then a semi-circle is the obvious setting. With more players, you may have to use ranks making sure that all the players can see you and that you have eye-contact with them. Problems of balancing a group of players musically, can be partly solved by careful placing. You would not have a percussionist too close to the front, for example.

> Think about layout.

Also check that the music stands are placed at a sensible height: too low and the players play down to the floor; too high and they can't see you over the top! If you are directing a group of singers, arrange it so that they are grouped fairly close together in a way that they can hear each other, but also ensure that they can all see you for clear direction. You may well have to experiment (well in advance of the examination) with placing of voices or instruments. Some rooms have 'dead' spots where the sound is particularly poor. Remember that carpets and curtains absorb sound; it may be a good idea to open curtains to increase the resonance and 'flatter' the sound.

5 ▷ RECORDING PROGRESS

Points for self-evaluation.

NEAB requires a written and/or taped record of your progress in rehearsals. Use the following points to help you consider what you say in this commentary:

a) Why did you choose your particular pieces?
b) How often did you rehearse and how long for?
c) How did you organise your rehearsals?
d) What musical difficulties did you encounter?
e) Did you feel a sense of progress during the rehearsals?

The Boards vary in their requirements for the preparation of the examination rehearsal. With SEG and NISEAC you are not permitted to rehearse the actual examination piece in advance. This is perfectly reasonable, for it can so easily become staged – a rehearsed rehearsal. Whatever syllabus you work from, make sure that you get plenty of experience by working with several different pieces so that you feel fully confident on the day.

A FINAL STATEMENT

Good luck with your directing! Remember that for top marks the examiner is looking for confident and clear direction leading to a well thought out and well controlled performance.

9

SIGHT-READING

EXAM GROUP
REQUIREMENTS

THE KEY SIGNATURE

THE TIME SIGNATURE

SCANNING

COUNTING

SPEED

LOOKING AHEAD

EXPRESSION

SIGHT READING TESTS

GETTING STARTED

'Previously unseen music must be presented to the candidates in notation appropriate to the voice or instrument concerned. Where a choice is possible this shall be made by the candidate.' (National Criteria 4.2.6)

This is not a favourite activity for most music students, but it is a necessary exercise if you are to become fluent in reading music. Most Groups include sight-reading as an option within the Unprepared Performance element, so that you may not be obliged to tackle this section. A specified preparation time is allowed for each test, under supervision. If you wish to sing the tests, don't worry too much about the quality of your voice as long as you can sing in tune. In fact, tests using voice may be sung, whistled or hummed at the candidate's choice, and will be transposed where necessary.

ESSENTIAL PRINCIPLES

1 ▷ EXAM GROUP REQUIREMENTS

The criteria vary for each Group. These can be summarised briefly as follows:

ULEAC

To sing or play four pieces, which will be graded in difficulty and unaccompanied. You are allowed half a minute to prepare each passage before the first of your two attempts at it. You need to show confidence in vocal or instrumental sight-reading at an elementary level. The tests are presented to you one at a time by the examiner, who will then decide whether or not you should progress to the next test.

SEG

To sing, whistle or play up to four graded tests, the first of which will be a rhythm written on a single-line stave, and the second a pitch test with no reference to rhythm. The third and fourth tests will be printed in staff notation and of graded difficulty. Separate tests are provided for different instruments and for voice. You are allowed up to one minute of silent preparation for each test.

NEAB

To sing or play 2 tests, of which the second is the more difficult. You are allowed up to one minute of silent preparation for each test, and will be awarded marks on the best of two attempts. Where appropriate, signs for breathing, bowing and fingering will be added to the music.

WJEC

With this Group, Singing at Sight is compulsory. You are required to sing (or whistle!) a simple melody in a major key not exceeding an octave in range. This single test will be given in staff notation and you may sing it using tonic sol-fa. The examiner will support the vocal line with a simple piano accompaniment and you will be given a copy of this. Two attempts are allowed, but if the second attempt is made one mark will be deducted from the total mark awarded for the test. One minute is allowed for preparation.

If you choose the *Previously Unseen Music* option for WJEC (the other options are memory tests and improvisation – choose any two of the three) there are three graded tests to sing or play, all using staff notation. Two attempts are allowed for each test, but one mark will be deducted from the total mark if a second attempt is made. One minute is allowed to prepare for each test, and you may use your instrument for this.

MEG

(For full details see Chapter 3)
In component 03 candidates are required to offer Memory Tests and *either* Sight Reading *or* Improvisation. In component 04 candidates must offer *either* Memory Tests, Sight Reading and Improvisation *or* Memory Tests and Sight Reading only. The Sight Reading pieces may be either vocal or for one instrument only, at the candidates' choice. Three minutes preparation time is permitted before each test. During this time the piece may be played.

IGCSE

To sing or play 2 graded tests from a choice that is selected by your teacher – and unseen by you! You are allowed ten minutes preparation time with your instrument, but vocalists are not allowed any instrumental help. Each of the tests will have expression marks which you should observe. Both of the chosen pieces will be assessed and the better mark of the two awarded.

NISEAC

You are asked to sing or play up to three tests, depending on your ability. The pieces will be of a similar standard to Grade 2, Grade 4 and Grade 5 sight-reading tests respectively, and full marks are available only to candidates who attempt all three. Each piece will be eight to twelve bars long and five minutes preparation time is allowed with your instrument.

Before you set to work on your sight-reading, read through the following points and you may learn a new approach; with regular practice you will start to achieve better results.

2 > THE KEY SIGNATURE

Always keep the key in mind.

The key signature is the first thing to check carefully when you play a new piece. You should know, by glancing at the number of sharps or flats at the beginning of the line, exactly what key you are in (see Chapter 14 if you need to refresh your memory). You must keep this in your mind throughout the exercise. Remember that an accidental lasts a whole bar, so that:

for example, contains two B naturals because they are both within the same bar. These are more likely to appear in the more advanced tests.

3 > THE TIME SIGNATURE

The next thing to look at is the number of beats in a bar. Candidates usually take more note of this than the key signature, but be careful in particular with your counting in 6/8 time which can be rather tricky. Remember that you can either count the six quavers individually; or count in two main beats, where the quavers are grouped into threes. For example:

count 1 2 3 4 5 6 for a slower speed, or 1——— 2——— for a quicker tempo.

In Chapter 14 the section Rests and Note Values, explains this in more detail. The easier tests are likely to be in 3/4 or 4/4 where the counting is more straightforward.

4 > SCANNING

Scanning can help.

The preparation time may not be long enough to 'play' the tune through mentally at the intended speed. Try to **scan** through the line of music, noticing key signature and time signature as already suggested, and then observing any difficult areas – an accidental to remember, perhaps, or a tricky rhythm that requires careful counting. Make a mental note of what it is and where it occurs.

5 > COUNTING

Count each beat quietly to yourself.

This should go without saying really, but some candidates do seem to forget all about counting. Correct rhythm is fundamental in all music, and accuracy can only be guaranteed by counting each beat quietly to yourself. Besides helping the rhythm it will keep you in a strict time.

Here are some of the problem areas in sight-reading rhythm:

i) The difference between  and

If you rely on 'feel' and don't know the piece (as in any sight-reading) you can so easily mix up these two rhythms; but when you count, there is no excuse for error:

example a) $\frac{3}{4}$ 1 2 3   **example b)** $\frac{3}{4}$ 1 2 and 3

In example a) the dotted quaver + semiquaver both fit into the first beat, and in example b) you must count 'one – two' before you play the quaver. Mentally say the word 'and' (as shown above) to be sure of getting it right. If you are still unsure on this ask your teacher to help you further, and give examples for you to practise. This is a very common error in all music examinations.

ii) The triplet sometimes catches people out. In a beat it fits into one beat: $\frac{4}{4}$ 3 1 2 3 4 it must be played as three equal notes. Very often it is inaccurately performed as because, generally speaking, people rush the triplet. **Remember** a triplet is three notes played equally in the time of two of the same kind.

iii) Be sure to take rests into account. Do count them carefully! It is easy to mix up minim and semibreve rests: = a semibreve (4 crotchet beats) and

= a minim rest (2 crotchet beats).

Also take care when you see this sort of rhythm: $\frac{4}{4}$ 1 and 2 and 3—4

Here you should count the quaver rest as 'one' then play immediately, fitting the single quaver in before the second beat.

iv) Simple syncopation may be included in an advanced test: $\frac{4}{4}$ ♪ ♩ ♪ ♩ – the notes

1   2   3 – 4

do not fit on the beats as you can see by the numbers underneath, producing a characteristic jazzy rhythm. Practise this one carefully. (You may find this easier if you count it as: $\frac{4}{4}$ ♫ ♫ ♩)

1 and 2 and 3 – 4

6 ▷ SPEED

❝ Don't rush; err on the side of safety. ❞

Err on the side of safety. An examiner will forgive a rather slow speed if the performance is fluent and accurate within that speed. It is harder to give credit for a rushed, yet hesitant and unmusical rendition. Choose your overall speed by looking at the most difficult fragment. It is no good slowing down when it gets difficult and then changing gear for the easier bits!

7 ▷ LOOKING AHEAD

You must be mentally ahead of the notes that you are playing, to give yourself time to perceive the information, process it and then perform it correctly. Don't stare at a long note while you are playing it; by all means count its value, but at the same time be solving the next immediate problem or your music will sound hesitant and disjointed.

8 ▷ EXPRESSION

Some Boards give tests which contain phrasing and expression marks. You should make every effort to apply these. Obviously you are going to concentrate mainly on notes and rhythm, but all music has a wealth of added detail to indicate how it should be played. In a normal practice session you would probably work at these fine points after mastering all the notes, but here (in a simple test) you should aim to incorporate as much as you can straight away. All music – even simple exercises – consists of more than the printed notes. Try to be expressive, even if there are no markings indicated.

9 ▷ SIGHT-READING TESTS

Figs. 9.1 and 9.2 are some sight-reading tests for you to look at. They are to help you gauge the standard required as well as provide extra material for practice. These exercises are graded from A to D in order of difficulty. Figs. 9.3 and 9.4 are actual examination questions. Have a go!

Fig. 9.1

PIANO AND ELECTRONIC ORGAN

Fig. 9.2

(ULEAC 1992)

(ULEAC 1992)

Fig 9.3

Here are some 1991 SEG Sight Reading tests for you to practice:

Performing at sight – All candidates must attempt Test (a). You may have up to one minute to prepare before you begin.

Test (a) Tap or clap the following rhythm *(3)*

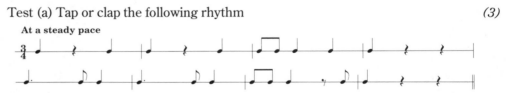

All candidates must attempt Test (b). Candidates should choose a pitch and clef suitable for their instrument or voice. Candidates choosing voice must be given the first note. You may have one minute to prepare before you begin.

Test (b) *(3)*

Test (c) CLASSICAL GUITAR
Play the following passage. *(5)*

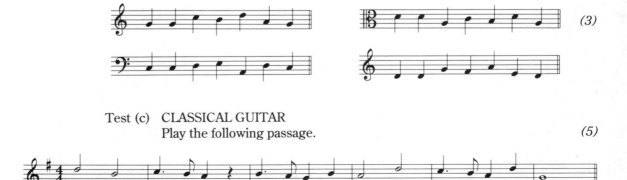

Test (d) TRUMPET/CORNET (suitable for B flat, C, D or E flat)

BRASS BAND INSTRUMENTS (suitable for B flat cornet, B flat flugelhorn, E flat soprano cornet)

(9)

Fig 9.4

A FINAL STATEMENT

You are advised not to leave this element of the syllabus until the last moment. For those of you who receive instrumental tuition outside of class, you can always ask your teacher to give a short test as part of your lesson. Courses for Grade exams should have included this anyway, although sight-reading practice is often sadly neglected. If you don't have private lessons then your class teacher will be pleased to find you some tests of a suitable standard. Do discipline yourself to practise sight-reading 'little and often' throughout the course; it cannot be crammed – it demands regular practice. Sight-reading may not be the most exciting part of music-making, but it does pay dividends. Before long you will be reading much faster and more accurately.

R E V I E W   S H E E T

✎ What two main things should you observe immediately when sight-reading a piece?

The _____

and the _____

✎ What should you remember about accidentals?

_____

✎ What is the difference between 6/8 time and 3/4?

_____

✎ Is this tune in 3/4 or 6/8 time?

CLARINET

_____

✎ Is this tune in 3/4 or 6/8 time?

VIOLIN

_____

✎ What is the key signature of this bar?

_____

✎ What major key signature has six flats?

_____

✎ What key signature is this tune in?

PITCHED
PERCUSSION

_____

✎ What is syncopation?

_____

What should you do to make sure that you have played a syncopated passage correctly?

_____

✎ How many beats are indicated by each of these rests?

_____

_____

✎ Comment on the phrasing in this piece.

OBOE
or
SAXOPHONE

_____

✎ What is the key signature of this piece?

Can you now add some expression marks to convey the mood in which this piece might be played?

✎ Add some phrase marks to this simple melody.

VOICE
(transpose
as necessary)

MEMORY TESTS

EXAM GROUP REQUIREMENTS

USEFUL TECHNIQUES

MEMORY TEST EXERCISES

GETTING STARTED

A good musical memory is a considerable asset to a musician. If you are a singer, you will obviously learn your songs or choral parts much quicker; if you work in the pop field, and don't normally use written music, you will progress much faster with a good memory. Some people will find this part of the course quite easy – singing a short tune back will be quite natural to them, especially if they had plenty of singing experience in their Infant and Junior schools. Others, perhaps with little or no use of singing voice behind them, will feel embarrassed at having to sing. Boys especially seem to feel vulnerable, with their recently lowered voices, when it comes to having to pitch a note. With practice, and increasing confidence, most people manage these tests rather well in the end. Also, many candidates will have had experience of memory tests in their Grade exams. Either way, don't worry – it is relatively painless!

ESSENTIAL PRINCIPLES

The criteria differ for the various Groups. An outline is given below:

ULEAC

This is an option within the Unprepared Performance Element. Four graded tests are given, suited to your voice or instrument. You are required to sing or play back the passages which will be played twice before your first attempt and once again before your second attempt. The key chord will be played and named first, and the starting note will always be given.

SEG

This is an option within the Unprepared Performance section. Three graded tests are given, played on the piano. You may use an instrument if you wish, the tests being transposed where appropriate, or you may sing, hum or whistle them back.

NEAB

This is an option within the Unprepared Performance section. Two tests are given, the second being more difficult than the first. You may sing, whistle or play them back on an instrument. Each test will be played twice, then you are allowed only one attempt. Where an instrument is used, the first note and the key will be named by the examiner.

WJEC

This is an option within the Unprepared Performance section. You will be asked to repeat three phrases, graded in difficulty. Each test will be played twice on the piano, then you will be allowed only one attempt. The Board expects that most candidates will sing the phrases, but instrumentalists may prefer to play them back, in which case they will be told the key and given the first note.

MEG

(For full details see Chapter 3)
Component 03 is taken as part of Option A or C. Candidates will be required to offer Memory Tests and *either* Sight Reading *or* Improvisation.

   Component 04 is taken as part of Option B. Candidates will be required to offer *either* Memory Tests, Sight Reading and Improvisation; *or* Memory Tests and Sight Reading. For both Components candidates are first required (a) to clap/tap a rhythm played twice; and (b) to sing or play the same phrase after it has been played two further times. The phrase will be 4–8 bars in length.

IGCSE

This is a compulsory test in the Unprepared Performance section. All candidates are required to clap or tap a rhythm after hearing it played twice on the piano. After a further hearing candidates must then sing or play the same phrase.

NISEAC

This is an option within the Unprepared Performance section. Four phrases will be given for you to sing, whistle, hum or play back on an instrument, each being played twice on the piano. The tests are graded, ranging from two to four bars; and from a simple crotchet beat to compound duple time.

This is obviously not an area of work that you can revise for at the last minute. Memory work needs continual practice, especially for the longer exercises. Although most Boards give you the option to use your instrument it is usually recommended that you sing these tests, unless you have an exceptionally fine ear and memory.

   Regular practice with any form of aural tests is far better for you than last minute cramming. You will find after a while that your memory will gradually improve, as you start to feel the patterns within a given melody. Most short tunes are based on scalic figures or arpeggios, and sequences (repeated patterns at a higher or lower pitch) are not uncommon. Try to hear groups of notes, or a whole phrase, rather than single ones. After all, when we listen to someone speaking we don't hear single words at a time – we take in a whole sentence.

Don't try to tackle the advanced tests until you are capable of regular success with the easier ones. In fact, any practice that you can do with singing will add to your increasing confidence; even singing well known melodies quietly to yourself will improve your memory skills.

However, for boys whose voices have recently changed, the problem is not so much remembering the tune, but in finding the pitch of the first note within the new voice range. You can often overcome what amounts to a loss of vocal confidence by testing yourself at a keyboard with single notes. Usually boys who have not used their singing voice for a few years will automatically attempt to sing at their lowest pitch, which is frequently an octave too low. This does not really matter at first, for the important thing is to make that low note in tune. Try doing this several times – you should easily manage on your own, even if you are not a keyboard player – or you can ask a friend to work with you. Soon you should graduate to two- or three-note tests, but make sure that you keep it at a comfortable pitch. When you are achieving success with this every time, extend it to a two-bar phrase and so on. You will obviously need someone else at this point to play the tunes for you, and do insist on a pitch range that suits your voice! Until you are well used to singing again, you will probably sing too low and out of tune so that if the test is set too high for you, you are back where you started.

> **Make that low note in tune.**

You may be able to persuade your class teacher to give you some singing-back practice on your own. Experience has shown that boys who normally sing very little lose all confidence when confronted with the prospect of singing in front of their class-mates. To cover their embarrassment, notes are often grunted back with little or no sensitivity or attention to rhythmic detail. You will almost certainly be more confident on your own at first, and when you feel more able to do it well you will probably not worry so much about the audience. You will have to sort this out for yourself.

3 ▷ MEMORY TEST EXERCISES

> **Work with a friend.**

Space permits the printing of only a few exercises; ask a friend (who is musically reliable!) to play these over to you, then sing them back according to the requirements of your Examining Group. Once you have become used to the style and length of these exercises, you will be able to find others for someone to help you with. (Aural books for the Associated Board or Trinity College of Music exams can be useful here).

The exercises are drawn from the different Groups, and are included for you to see the standard that is required. But for extra practice you should tackle, throughout the course, some that are outside your actual syllabus. Move on to the more difficult ones when you feel ready. It all helps.

Each time you are given a memory test, either in practice or in the examination, concentrate intently and sing it back immediately before you lose it. You will see from the criteria for these tests at the beginning of the chapter how the Groups vary in their requirements. Most Groups allow just one attempt at singing back. Don't forget that there is more to music than mere notes – for full marks you will need to be perfectly in tune, and also completely accurate in relation to rhythm and tempo.

Practice exercises

The tests in Fig. 10.1 may be transposed for the appropriate voice.

The practice exercises are graded from A to C in order of difficulty.

Hum, sing or whistle the following:

A.

A.

Fig. 10.1

Fig. 10.2 gives two actual tests for you to use.

Test A (ULEAC 1991) is suitable for Soprano voice, Tenor voice, Descant recorder, Tenor recorder, tuned Classroom Instruments and Guitar.

Test B (ULEAC 1992) is suitable for Bass voice, Cello and Bassoon.

Fig. 10.2

A FINAL STATEMENT

If you stop to think, we all have incredible powers of memory. Thinking musically, everyone can remember hundreds of songs, both melodies and words. We learn these without trying; when we enjoy hearing a song many times, somehow it all stays in the memory, often for years after having last heard it. This is all the more amazing when you consider how similar tunes can be. Bearing this in mind, it should not be too daunting a task for you to sing back a short phrase with no words. Do practise regularly, however, and don't leave it until it is too late!

IMPROVISATION

GETTING STARTED

Improvisation is **instant composition** – an impromptu expression of musical thought. Students tend to be wary of demonstrating this 'subconscious music' at first, feeling that it is insufficiently prepared. A written composition demands considerable effort, whereas an improvisation is spontaneous music; hence the initial attempts tend to be extremely short. As confidence is gained, so the length increases – sometimes too much so, making pruning necessary!

As with any other music, a framework is necessary upon which to build your improvisation. Using a particular chord scheme as a structure will help to give this 'instant music' some suitable repetition and a sense of shape. The examiner will be looking for three main things:

a) a fluency within the given style or theme, or an adherence to the chosen topic.
b) evidence of development in melody, rhythm or harmony.
c) an overall structure or form.

ESSENTIAL PRINCIPLES

Once again, the Groups vary in their requirements.

ULEAC

This is an option within the Unprepared Performance Element. The candidate is required to improvise one piece, either instrumentally or vocally, lasting up to three minutes. The improvisation is to be created *either* around a specified idea with a musical element (e.g. 'sad piece using chords'); *or* modelled on a short motif of about two bars, notated and played by the examiner. After being given the necessary instructions you will have up to 10 minutes to prepare before the actual test. A choice of ideas/motifs will be offered.

SEG

This is an option within the Unprepared Performance section. You are required to improvise one short piece on any instrument or vocally. There will be a range of ideas for you to choose from as a starting point for your music. These could include a title or written extract, a short musical opening to be continued, a chord sequence, or a melody to be worked over a given accompaniment. Once you have chosen, you will be allowed ten minutes in which to prepare with your instrument, and you may hear the given theme or topic as many times as you wish. For this test, you may use a different instrument to that used for your Prepared Performance tests.

NEAB

This is an option within the Unprepared Performance section. You are required to improvise one piece, either instrumentally or vocally. The choice of ideas is as follows: a short rhythmic pattern; a short sequence of notes; a complete melody; a short sequence of chords; or a short verse (e.g. a four-line stanza). You will be allowed five minutes preparation time with your instrument.

WJEC

This is an option within the Unprepared Performance section. You are required to improvise one piece, either instrumentally or vocally. Three ideas are offered for you to choose from: a short rhythmic pattern; a short melodic phrase; or a short sequence of chords. The examiner will play the three ideas over to you, and you will be given a notated copy – the test for the chordal sequence will be written as guitar chords and Roman numerals, as well as in staff notation. You are allowed ten minutes preparation time with your instrument.

MEG

(For full details see Chapter 3)
Component 03 is taken as part of Option A or C. Candidates will be required to offer Memory Tests and *either* Sight Reading *or* Improvisation.

Component 04 is taken as part of Option B. Candidates will be required to offer *either* Memory Tests, Sight Reading and Improvisation *or* Memory Tests and Sight Reading.

Candidates for both components are required to improvise in free style on one of the following tests:
a) rhythm – a short rhythmic pattern in conventional notation.
b) note pattern – a short sequence of notes in staff notation with letter names
c) a short melody in staff notation
d) a short sequence of chords with or without bass part, using staff notation, with the chords indicated by numbers, letters and tablature notation.
e) a set of words – e.g. folk song, hymn, classical or pop.
f) a graphic score – with given symbols.
Candidates have 15 minutes to prepare for this test.

IGCSE

This is an option within the Unprepared Performance section. You are asked to choose one idea from a list of three given to you ten minutes before the examination, and then improvise on that idea for no more than three minutes. There will be a rhythm, a note pattern and a sequence of chords. They will be written out in staff notation and played twice to you if required. Vocal candidates have ten minutes in which to prepare a melody in any suitable style to a chosen set of words: folk song, hymn, classical, modern, pop etc.

NISEAC

This is an option within the Unprepared Performance section. The test has two parts of which only the first is compulsory. This involves improvising answering phrases to three given phrases of not more than four bars each, maintaining a suitable style. The second part is to improvise for about one minute by continuing a melody, or responding to a progression of chords or a given rhythm. The extracts will be provided on tape and in notation.

Before we consider actual examination questions, or suitable topics for you to practise full-length improvisations, there is a more fundamental question to answer. Which instrument will you use? Bear in mind that it is extremely difficult to improvise on given topics with a trombone or similar melodic instrument. You have far more scope with a piano, electronic keyboard or a guitar. No offence to trombonists or the like, but they would be more sensible to choose a melodic motif, unless they have a fairly advanced and versatile technical skill. Do consider the practicality of your main instrument now that you have read through the Boards' requirements above. For many of the categories it is assumed that a chordal instrument is being used.

2 >	CHORD SCHEMES

> A basic proficiency with chords is important.

Let us examine chord schemes first. This is really improvisation from the bottom upwards – a concentration on harmony where any melody used is worked as an afterthought. For this work you will need to have a basic keyboard proficiency, where you are able to think about chords quickly and change them smoothly. You might find suitable chord sequences in any simple pop song.

Question

Improvise for approximately one minute on this chord sequence:

C   Am   Em   F   Dm   F   G   C.

Outline answer

Example 1

Play the chords over with a repeated pop rhythm as in Fig. 11.1

C major

Fig. 11.1

or by giving four beats to each chord (Fig. 11.2).

Fig. 11.2

Does this appeal to you as an eight-bar sentence? Perhaps it can be enhanced by changing some of the rhythm; see Fig. 11.3.

Fig. 11.3   C / / / | Am / / / | Em / F / | Dm / / / | F / G / | C / / / :‖

Example 2

Although it has now been shortened to a six-bar line, the rather predictable 8 × four-bar pattern has been broken up, giving a slight 'kick' to the rhythm. Bar 5 has a similarity to bar 3 which gives a sense of unity. Always try to think musically, even when you are working with simple material. If you play music in a monotonous way it is bound to sound boring; by playing it expressively you will start to bring it alive. Of course you can also vary the dynamics quite substantially to make it more interesting.

These eight or six bars could well be repeated, then you will probably want to change the chords. How can you extend it?

The obvious structure for immediate extension is a ternary, (A + B + A) where you return to your given chord scheme (A) after a new contrasting section (B).

What chords would you choose for your middle section (B)? We could change to the subdominant key for variety, using a shorter pattern:

Example 3:

Fig. 11.4

$$F \;/\; Am \;/\; \big|\; B\flat \;/\; Gm \; C \;\big|\; F \;/\; Am \;/\; \big|\; B\flat \;/\; Gm \; F \;:\big\|$$

This has two good points about it. First of all, there is some similarity in chord progression: B♭ – Gm in the middle has the same interval (that is, a minor 3rd apart) as the opening C – Am in the first pattern. This may seem unimportant, but it gives further unity. Secondly, the placing of a chord on the fourth beat in bars 2 and 4 gives a new rhythmic interest. You might prefer to continue with the rhythm from Example 1 rather than change it just yet.

Fig. 11.5

The first chord pattern can then be played once more, making the standard A A B B A structure with at least twenty-six bars, or as many as forty bars depending on how you used the A section, and how you plan your repeats.

So far so good, but it is rather ordinary. How can you develop it further? Two ways spring to mind:

   i) – carry on using the material we already have, perhaps with some variation: A + B + A + B_2 (varied) +A;

or

   ii) – introduce a new episode (C).

You could even use a combination of both.

   i) First, then, the development of the B section (B_2)
   If you vary the moving quavers in an upward direction it can be made to sound melodic and more positive (Fig. 11.6).

Fig. 11.6

            F   Am   B♭   Gm C

or as in Fig. 11.7 (which is even stronger):

Fig. 11.7

            F   Am   B♭   Gm C

   ii) You can balance the shorter B section by making the new C section longer as in Fig. 11.8.

Example 4

    (Section C)   Am $/$ G $/$ $\big|$ F $/$ G $/$ $\big|$ Am $/$ Dm $/$ $\big|$ Em $/$ $/$ $/$ $\big|$

    Am $/$ G $/$ $\big|$ F $/$ B♭ $/$ $\big|$ Dm $/$ F $/$ $\big|$ G $/$ $/$ $/$ $\big\|$

Fig. 11.8

This is a minor mode, which can add a new dimension without changing the mood. The end of the second half has been contrived to end on a brighter sounding G major chord – the dominant of our original C major. You could make the second four bars of this section the climax of the improvisation by building up strongly to the return of Section A.

With this new material the overall plan could now be played as in Fig. 11.9.

Example 5

Fig. 11.9

A	B	A	B2	A	C	A
(12)	(8)	(12)	(8)	(6)	(16)	(12)

You may decide to miss out some of the repeats on the A section (as above, after B2) to avoid predictability. The model above has approximately seventy-four bars, which is a perfectly acceptable length for this sort of exercise.

EXPERIMENT

'Doodling' is well worthwhile.

The secret is for you to spend as much spare time as you can 'doodling' at the keyboard or guitar, experimenting with chords and rhythms in many different ways and keys. This is the best way to discover new ideas. You will start to evolve your own style and chord clichés before long, and given this sort of chord progression in the examination, you will find you have several musical tricks up your sleeve which you can turn to good use.

Fig. 11.10 and Fig. 11.11 give you two further examples to practise. They are printed as they first appeared.

i)

MEG 1988

Fig. 11.10

C   F   Am   D7   G7   C

ii)

WJEC Specimen Test

Fig. 11.11

I   vi   ii   V

3 ▷ IMPROVISATION ON A GIVEN RHYTHM

Select the main characteristic.

If you are a drummer/percussionist, or have a particularly strong sense of rhythm, you may choose to improvise on a given rhythm, rather than a melody or chord scheme. Make sure that you hear or read the printed rhythm correctly; your improvisation must relate to it closely.

How do you develop the given two or three bars? The secret is to decide which is the main characteristic within the fragment. For example, supposing you were given the motif in Fig. 11.12.

Fig. 11.12

(ULEAC 1989)

You could exploit either the dotted quavers ♩. ♫ ♩. ♫ | ♩ or the semiquavers ♩ ♫♫ ♩, or preferably both. In other words, having played the printed figure, extend it by concentrating on the two elements. The piece should contain dynamic interest to compensate for its lack of melody or harmony. You might decide to work within an arch shape with a climax at the centre as illustrated in Fig. 11.13.

Fig. 11.13

pp —————— ff ————— p

or alternatively, with a climax at the end (Fig. 11.14).

Fig. 11.14

p ———————— ff

The choice is yours, but remember not to play all at the same level, for this would be considered weak.

Fig. 11.15 gives you some more rhythmic figures to work at. The brackets refer to suggested fragments which you might develop.

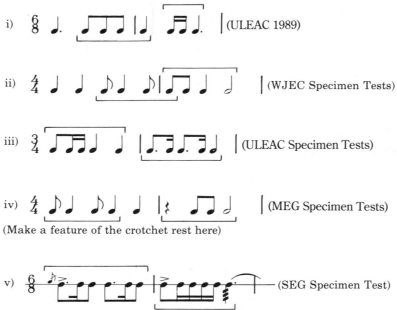

Fig. 11.15   (Make features of the crushed note, the accents and the roll at the end)

Your teacher will be able to give you plenty of examples for practice. In many ways this option goes hand in hand with sight-reading, for it is so important to read the given rhythm correctly.

4 ▷ IMPROVISATION AND MELODIC MOTIF: SINGLE LINE INSTRUMENTS

Here we look at improvisation based on a melodic motif, for single-line instruments. Your way of working here is not dissimilar to that for rhythmic improvisation, except that you have to think melodically at the same time! Extract your fragment for development in the same way, concentrating, besides rhythm, on particular intervals that characterise the motif. One safety tip to ensure fluency in case you dry up in the middle: have an ending worked out so that you can conclude the improvisation convincingly. Your ability to read the given motif must be good; be especially careful with 6/8 examples, where people so often tend to go wrong.

Have an ending worked out.

SEQUENCE

The use of sequence, if not overworked, is a common device in melodic extension. Let us presume that you have been presented with the motif in Fig. 11.16.

Fig. 11.16

Remember to make use of sequence.

First of all, establish the key. It must be in E minor, rather than G major, because of the D#. (It would be calamitous if you played the whole thing in a major key, although you are allowed to transpose).

Secondly, identify the melodic and rhythmic characteristics worthy of development. Melodically, a good choice would be:

⌐a⌐   with its semitonal rise and fall back down again;

and   ⌐b⌐   which is a simple scalic figure. Rhythmically, the two dotted fragments are the same, and equally important.

Useful hints for melodic extension.

Now, how do you extend it? We need an answering phrase to the opening: Fig. 11.17 gives an example of an original phrase/answering phrase.

Fig. 11.17

In this example the rhythm has been repeated exactly to balance the two phrases. In fact $\boxed{a_1}$ is an inversion of $\boxed{a}$, and $\boxed{b}$ has stayed almost the same. By creating this answering phrase we now have three figures to develop: $\boxed{a}$, $\boxed{a_1}$, and $\boxed{b}$.

From now on, you must think quickly! Keep the music flowing with its gentle 6/8 lilt. Instead of coming to rest on a dotted crotchet too often, turn it into ♩ ♪ occasionally, so that you keep a feeling of forward motion. Avoid too many two-bar and four-bar phrases, such as we have at the moment, as it can rapidly become predictable. (You can read more about melodic extension in Chapter 14.)

Sequences are useful, as we have said; **repeating patterns** at a **higher** or **lower** **pitch** is a good method of extension. In Fig. 11.18 you can see a sequence based on the $\boxed{b}$ figure.

Fig. 11.18

The second bar is a rising sequence of bar 1, changed at the end to produce a new figure, a perfect 5th, which we can call $\boxed{c}$. The answering two bars then contain three more references. Perhaps this is beginning to sound very contrived, and more like a written composition where you have the time to think in this way. But actually with practice and applied musicianship you will start to do these things automatically.

In the preparation time before the examination, you could think out material for use as a **contrasting section**. You might take yet another fragment from the given motif, which we will call $\boxed{d}$ and $\boxed{d_1}$ (see Figs. 11.16 and 11.17). In Fig. 11.19 we see this interval of a third used profitably.

Fig. 11.19

Although we are concentrating on $\boxed{d}$, notice that $\boxed{b_1}$ and $\boxed{b}$ have been used as well, creating a real unity. You can extend this middle section in a similar manner, and then return to a version of your first section.

Here are some further melodic examples for you to work at.

Fig. 11.20

In Fig. 11.20 there are two motifs of interest: at $\boxed{a}$ the falling semitones, and at $\boxed{b}$ an angular figure with a steep rise and immediate fall. This example would, therefore, give a good opportunity to create an improvisation based on contrasts between smoothness and angularity.

❝❝Some melodic examples to practise. ❞❞

Fig. 11.21

In Fig. 11.21 notice that there are three figures for development. At $\boxed{a}$ a falling fourth, at $\boxed{b}$ a dotted scalic figure (which could be used in either direction), and at $\boxed{c}$ a syncopated ♪♩ ♪♩ jazzy figure. You should be able to find plenty of scope for extension in this example, even if you choose to use only two of the motifs; it is up to you.

Fig. 11.22

A third example in Fig. 11.22 is a phrase for bass instruments. It is fairly straightforward, with a descending scalic line in C major $\boxed{a}$ and a final rising 4th $\boxed{c}$. The F# – G $\boxed{b}$ is an inessential chromatic note – in other words it is 'extra' to the key. Any or all of these fragments could be developed as above.

5 ▶ IMPROVISATION ON A GIVEN PITCH WITH FREE RHYTHM

Here you are free to create your own rhythm, but the shape of a melodic line is given. This appears to give you freedom, but for a musical result, try to remember your initial rhythm so that you can refer back to it. Be sure to make it an interesting rhythm, too; there is a great temptation, when you see notes without a rhythm, to play them as if they are all equal. Look at Fig. 11.23.

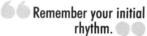

" Remember your initial rhythm. "

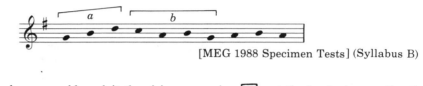

Fig. 11.23

[MEG 1988 Specimen Tests] (Syllabus B)

In this example you could exploit the rising arpeggio $\boxed{a}$ at the beginning, and/or the falling sequence of thirds at $\boxed{b}$.

Fig. 11.24

[MEG 1988] (Syllabus B)

In the second example (Fig. 11.24) there is a falling sequence $\boxed{a}$ based on the interval of a 4th, and an octave figure $\boxed{b}$. Both are well worth developing. You can easily make up your own examples for further practice.

6 ▶ IMPROVISATION AND MELODIC MOTIF: KEYBOARD INSTRUMENTS

Here we look at improvisation based on a melodic motif, for keyboard instruments. The thought processes here are much the same as for single-line instruments, with the added problem of providing an appropriate harmonisation to the melody. Assuming you have a reasonable keyboard proficiency, it should be easier to produce a fluent result than on a single-line instrument. The piano's sustaining pedal will 'hold' for you, and your chords will also give an effect of fullness. With electronic keyboards your chosen sound quality will add novelty value, but don't rely totally on this. It's the musical content that counts!

Firstly, do not assume that everything has to be harmonised. It is quite acceptable for a keyboard to improvise on a single-line if you want to or need to. Work in your own style to the best of your ability. It is a mistake to think that harmonised is 'better' than unaccompanied. This part of the performance section is assessing your musicianship, not your technical prowess on a keyboard.

" It may help to 'play safe'. "

However, if you wish to add the 'correct' chords to your extended melody, the safest thing to do is to limit yourself to chords I, IV and V (that is tonic, subdominant and dominant), until you become really proficient. Most ordinary pieces and songs can be harmonised with these three chords, but for variety and a minor 'flavour' chords II and VI might be added.

Let us work in G major first of all:

    chord I   = G B D
    chord IV = C E G
and chord V7 = D F# A C

Be totally familiar with finding these chords in this key (and eventually all keys up to two or three flats and sharps – although you can choose your own key in the examination).

Fig. 11.25 gives you a starting melody for extension.

Fig. 11.25

Select your chords by deciding which of the three listed above fits the melody most suitably. **Don't attempt to harmonise every note** – this is most important.

The first bar in Fig. 11.25 contains G B D B so the obvious harmony chord is chord I. In bar 2 we treat the middle note of   as unimportant – the C and A belong to chord V7 (D F# A C), and the note B simply runs between them; it is a passing note and does not affect the harmony. Likewise with the quavers in bar 3:  , the A and F# belong to chord V7, and the G passes between them.

The six changes of chord so far are basic harmony, which could be made more interesting by the introduction of other chords, but for the time being be patient! Master the three primary chords perhaps by playing long notes in the left hand at first, until you feel confident enough to vary it.

Fig. 11.26

In the example in Fig. 11.26 we have used the bare minimum of harmony. We have followed the thought process of choosing the appropriate chords, and decided to write them in the simplest way.

The next step (Fig. 11.27) is to find a way of decorating the basic material so that it has more movement. A simple **Alberti bass** would be suitable:

Fig. 11.27

It will take many weeks of regular practice to become adept at choosing chords immediately, and using a suitable broken-chord accompaniment with them. The ear is the ultimate judge with this work, not the textbook; if you find a sound or style pleasing to you, then work away at it until you are satisfied. You will gradually evolve your own style. Working with chords in this way will be beneficial to your composition work and aural skills, as well as your keyboard facility, so it is a very worthwhile exercise. You will probably enjoy **doodling** at the keyboard for its own sake anyway – it is a form of discovery for you.

When you feel ready to move on, the task becomes even more demanding. It is necessary to extend the given fragment of melody and harmonise it at the same time. It would be useful to read the section in this chapter on single-line improvisation once more, to refresh your memory. Your improvisation needs to continue in the given style, and you must not let the process of chord-finding hold you back. The melody must be most prominent. **Remember** – a simple melody that is harmonised effectively with basic chords, and developed musically, is preferable to a more flamboyant piece that is incoherent and unmusical.

7 ▷IMPROVISATION ON A GIVEN TOPIC

Prepare some musical ideas. ❜❜

Here you are expected to improvise freely, creating sounds that suggest the overall mood of the topic you choose. It is a good idea to prepare for this by having a store of musical ideas up your sleeve to help you on the day. For example, if you practise mood painting for water, the countryside, a thunderstorm or the supernatural, you will probably find that something rather similar will turn up!

Keyboard players can produce some lovely effects by using the sustaining pedal – atmospheric effects that are evocative of water or the supernatural. Silences can be very effective too, so there need not be sound all the time. But you should avoid too much effect and too little music: try to give your improvisation some substance, by using repetition and structure. If possible, use the whole range of your instrument and be creative with dynamics, phrasing and tone quality, and aim to make music that is satisfying and charged with feeling. Here are some actual exam questions for you to work on:

a)	Growth	(ULEAC 1989)
b)	Supernatural	(ULEAC 1989)
c)	The river	(ULEAC 1989)
d)	Thunderstorm	(ULEAC 1988)
e)	Busking	(ULEAC 1988)
f)	In a field	(ULEAC 1988)
g)	Carnival	(ULEAC 1991)
h)	Departure	(ULEAC 1991)
i)	Kaleidoscope (changing patterns)	(ULEAC 1991)
j)	Darkness	(ULEAC 1992)
k)	Early Morning	(ULEAC 1992)
l)	Flying	(ULEAC 1992)
m)	A depiction of flowers using a rising scale	(ULEAC 1994 syllabus)

8 > IMPROVISATION TO A GIVEN VERSE

> Look for key words for mood.

You will have probably decided which style of verse you want to improvise to before the examination. Read the extract through slowly and carefully. Look for important words that help to set the mood, in the same way as the motifs or fragments were selected in the musical examples above. Find any imagery that could be *translated* musically, and quickly decide on the style that you are going to use.

This type of improvisation is likely to be quite short, as you are unlikely to repeat too many words. Make sure that your melody is appropriate to the style of the chosen words and that it feels finished at the end of the verse. Repetition may be difficult with a single verse, but more possible, perhaps, in the pop style.

Here is a selection of verses for you to practise:

a) Traditional
O look in the mirror
Set here in my heart
And see that your image
Of me is a part –
Of me is a part.

b) Hymn
Thou art my Father.
Thou art my Mother.
Thou art my Saviour.
Thou art my Friend.
In all places Thou art my Saviour.
What should I fear and why should I repine?

c) Poem
Down in the street there comes the hurdy gurdy man
Cold his fingers, still he plays as best he can.
Shuffling in the snow, he moves with painful gait.
Not a penny piece is laid upon his plate.
Not a penny piece is laid upon his plate.

d) Pop
I was walking down the street
Singin' my melody
Singin' my song to the rhythm in my feet
Rhythm in my feet just
Walkin' singin', rhythm swingin'
Sing along swing along – rhythm in my feet.

(MEG 1988)

e)
Icy winds from the north do blow,
Covering the earth in a blanket of snow.
The blue-veined fingers of winter's hand
Paint and colour this desolate land.   (anon).

For this option you are free to interpret the graphic notation as you think appropriate. Fig. 11.28 is an example from a specimen paper.

Fig. 11.28

(MEG 1988
Specimen Paper)

In this example (Fig. 11.28) volume and pitch are fairly easy to interpret; notice the relative gaps in respect of silence. Silence is often forgotten in improvisation; it can be a most effective part of your piece. Don't forget to have some repetition, and aim for a satisfying structure. You should think out your musical strategy by isolating fragments, in just the same way as in the sections on improvising on a rhythm or melodic motif.

When you have experimented with musical ideas responding to the notation in the given example, decide which fragments you would develop.

A FINAL STATEMENT

In summary, the Improvisation section of unprepared performance needs to be thoroughly prepared! Although you will not know the actual test question until the day, you can spend much time during the course working in different styles, to evolve an individual style of your own. We have stressed the importance of form and structure, but perhaps fluency is even more important – **keep it going**! Remember that you are giving a performance, however short. There must be a feeling of climax and a sense of direction to maintain the listener's interest. Think of your improvisation as if you were performing printed music and learn to value your developing skills in *instant composition*.

REVIEW SHEET

✎ Using chord schemes is

_____ from the bottom upwards.

✎ Improvise for one minute on each of the following chord sequences.

   i) C F   Am G Dm F G7 C
  ii) G Em Bm C G   C D7 G
 iii) C Dm7 F   G   now continue......

✎ Now add a contrasting middle section (B) to each of the chord sequences i) to iii) above.

✎ Use the following chord sequence as the basis for further improvisation.

✎ If you are a drummer/percussionist, try improvising on the following rhythm.

✎ If you play the piano or the guitar try using these chord progressions as the basis for your improvisation.

1) C Am Em D   G7 C
2) G D   Am Em C F   D7 G
3) D C   F   G   Am Em A7 D

✎ Earlier in this chapter you have already improvised on the following rhythmic figures. Now for each one provide a *different* improvisation.

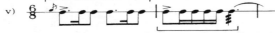

(Make a feature of the crotchet rest here)

v)

(Make features of the crushed note, the accents and the roll at the end)

✎ In this melodic motif, first establish the key.

D.

Now identify the melodic and rhythmic characteristics worthy of development.

Next, think of ways in which you might extend this melody.

✎ Use exactly the same procedure as above for these melodic motifs.

C.

C.

✎ What do you understand by improvisation on a given pitch with free rhythm?

_____

✎ Write out chords I, IV and V for each of the following keys.

Key D major

I _____

IV _____

V _____

Key E flat major

I _____

IV _____

V _____

Key A major

I _____

IV _____

V _____

Now improvise a melody in each case.

✎ Write out chords II and VI for each of the following keys.

Key D major

II _____

VI _____

Key E flat major

II _____

VI _____

Key A major

II _____

VI _____

Now improve a melody in each case.

12

COMPOSING 1: TRADITIONAL NOTATION

HARMONIC EXTENSION FROM A SIMPLE CHORD SCHEME

TUNED PERCUSSION (OR KEYBOARD): 4 PLAYERS

MODEL COMPOSITION I

COMPOSITION FOR FLUTE AND PIANO

MODEL COMPOSITION II

EXAMPLES OF STUDENT COMPOSITIONS

GETTING STARTED

All candidates are required to *compose or arrange music in a traditional or in a contemporary idiom* (National Criteria 3.3). To some students, the thought of composing a piece of one's own is quite frightening. It seems to conjure up an image of solitary confinement for months on end in some freezing attic before dying in your early thirties! Take courage – composing can be a very satisfying activity once you have mastered some basic techniques and gained some confidence in yourself.

This section of the examination encourages you to achieve the satisfaction of making something of your own – a piano piece, a song, or some incidental music for a play perhaps – the satisfaction of discovering something you can say, no matter how modest it may sound. To have invented and moulded musical phrases where none existed before: to select and reject harmonies for a particular context: to agonise over which note should come next: these are all important experiences which can help to shape your musical development and stimulate further creative thinking.

You are probably using this book at the start of an actual GCSE music course, but will undoubtedly have been making up simple tunes, or more extended pieces, for some time. How did you work? Did you compose straightforward melodies and write them down immediately, or did you have a tape recorder handy, so that you could listen critically to a play-back and improve things before committing ideas to paper? Perhaps you are able to hear musical ideas in your head without having to use an instrument to help you, or maybe you prefer to strum a guitar or 'doodle' on a keyboard to stimulate an idea.

ESSENTIAL PRINCIPLES

There is, of course, no correct way to create music. Composing is a process of organising sounds into a form that is aesthetically pleasing. How you choose to work is entirely up to you, but to progress you must be actively involved in the whole process of creating and be very self-critical with regard to any performance of your work. **Imagination** is the secret. Composing helps to train a musician's creative thinking and, of course, most important, it trains the art of listening. A person that once took sound for granted can be shaken from their complacency by this activity, as it demands the continual making of active choices.

> **Composing is a course activity.**

The Groups vary in their requirements for the submission of pieces and their assessment, and you can read about this in more detail in Chapter 3. The material in this chapter, however, is relevant to all Boards. A fundamental point to remember with GCSE is that composing is encouraged as a course activity, and that the final assessment is on a selection of work produced throughout the course.

Composing includes pastiche and experimental work, free composition, melody writing, harmony, part-writing and arranging (National Criteria 4.3). Notice that the activity is quite clearly referred to as Composing, not Composition. In other words, you have the freedom to work with the process of compiling sounds in your own individual way, unhindered by the traditional rules of harmony and counterpoint demanded in music examinations in the days before GCSE. You must be sure to design each of your pieces for a specified medium – for example, solo voice/instrument, vocal/instrumental ensembles. Also, remember that a cassette recording (if required) together with the musical scores and/or commentaries must be available for external moderation by about the end of the Spring Term of the examination year.

In this chapter, we are going to suggest ways of composing using standard musical notation. Four ideas for a composition are given and then five student compositions are presented and commented on for you to see how others have worked. You can read in Chapter 3, in the section on composing, the actual requirements as to the number and duration of compositions for the different Groups. Assume, generally, that it is fully acceptable for your teacher to provide you with any initial material, e.g. a tune for you to harmonise, or a poem for you to set to music. After that, you are expected to continue on your own, and if your teacher makes suggestions during the process of composing, details of this help must be made available to the examiner.

For candidates who have little or no experience of composing, the worst problem can be plucking up the courage to show your teacher your first piece. Most students spend a good deal of time improvising at a keyboard or on a guitar, and this is a valuable way of experimenting with ideas – but do have the confidence to think of your 'doodling' as being worthy of an idea and then you are on the right track. This chapter does not pretend to be a full-scale guide to composition, it presupposes good instruction in school or college and can serve only to stimulate or refine ideas. Space permits only bare guidelines with some of the ideas that follow. They are intended to help you get started on your own pieces, not necessarily for you to work at them as actual examples.

1 ▷ HARMONIC EXTENSION FROM A SIMPLE CHORD SCHEME

IDEA I

Using keyboard or guitar, take a relatively simple chord scheme: C Dm7 F G (Fig. 12.1) and improvise rhythmically by playing it over and over again in a straightforward pop rhythm.

Fig. 12.1

What springs to your mind? Do you wish to add a vocal line? Or an instrumental melody? Or simply extend the rhythmic effect with other chords? For the sake of illustration, let us assume that you decide to extend this initial idea into an instrumental piece by adding on another sequence of chords (Fig. 12.2). Maintain a similar rhythm to your opening:

Fig. 12.2

The second (B) section has more of a minor feel to it through having mainly minor chords, but ends with a (dominant) G chord implying a return to C major. Should this new section be repeated exactly or should it be varied in some way?

Already we can think of the top line as being quite suitable as a melody. If you are not too keen on it, simply change the shape of the chords so that you have a different note from the chord at the top. Perhaps, now, our second section could be rearranged as in Fig. 12.3, in place of a straight repeat.

Fig. 12.3

So far our structure can be thought of as:

    A1   A1   B1   B2

We can think of the  rhythm as being the important part of our **hook**, or the catchy bit that sticks in the mind. It now seems right to bring back the first idea so as to reinforce it. You might consider it necessary to decorate the return of A at this point. It breaks up any feeling of monotony, yet we still feel it as the original idea. There are countless ways that you could use these chord schemes; just carry on improvising in your own style until you are completely satisfied. You will know when it is right.

So far our overall structure works out as a ternary form (A + B + A):

    A1   A1   B1   B2   A2   A2

This is perfectly satisfactory, but rather short. You may well feel that the A1 and B1 sections could be repeated several more times (perhaps with some variation) to give an expanded ternary form, and perhaps a third idea (C) could then be brought in as shown in Fig. 12.4.

Fig. 12.4

Once again, a simple four-chord pattern has been deliberately concocted so as to finish with the chord of G, the dominant of our original C major. It would then make sense to bring back the original idea straight away, thereby producing a simple rondo structure (A + B + A + C + A), or in our case:

    A1   A1   B1   B2   A2   A2   C1   C1   A1   A2.

> **Experiment with chords.**

You can have enormous fun experimenting with chords, and in time you will find that certain combinations of chords will become particular favourites. This simple piece could easily be turned into a song; your lyrics need not be at all complicated. Alternatively you could arrange it for various instruments or even programme it into a music computer. The simplest of ideas can be made to sound exciting when you choose an attractive sound on your synthesizer. **Experiment** – and have the courage of your convictions!

If you are not able to write your piece out using traditional notation you will need to provide a commentary instead. Let us assume that a candidate has decided not to extend the piece further and has found some difficulty in notating it. He has recorded it as an instrumental piece using the school synthesizer and music computer, and has written the following commentary to accompany the recording of the piece.

MODEL COMMENTARY

RELUCTANT RONDO

This piece was given this rather humorous title because I did not really set out to compose a rondo as such. My composition is the result of improvising at the keyboard until I found chords that I felt satisfied with. The overall structure (A B A C A) happens, by chance, to be the same as a traditional rondo, hence the unusual title!

I took a straightforward sequence of four chords: C Dm7 F G and experimented with it until I found a satisfying rhythm.

I was keen for the syncopation ♪♪ ♪♩ to be a strong feature of the piece, so this appears in each of the three main sections. My B section is a minor version of the A section, and answers it in a complementary way. I thought that the minor chords would act as a varied flavour to the strongly major A section.

The final section (C) gives the impression at first of modulating away from the home key, but soon twists itself back so that the original C major is never far away:

F Bflat C G (dominant).

The final return of the opening section is played strongly with a slight rallentando so that we know the end is near; it is a mixture of A1 + A2 to make a strong ending. Throughout, I was aiming at simplicity.

Once I had composed the rondo (using a Yamaha PSR-36 keyboard) I wanted to record my piece using more sophisticated sounds. This I was able to do by using an Atari 1040 ST Music Computer (with C Lab Notator software) and a Kawai K1 synthesiser. I like the strong bass sound (called 'kick bass' on Single 1 D-1) on the K1 synth. I decided not to change this sound at all until I got to section C when I used the contrasting sound 'Reflection' on Single 1 C-5. With careful mixing I arrived at the final version and although it's rather short, I feel quite pleased with it.

This commentary shows fairly clearly how the imaginary candidate has worked – developing and refining the final structure from the basic material of four simple chords. It is written in a clear and unpretentious way, and communicates a feeling of enthusiasm for the task! The technical detail that is included to explain how the piece was recorded is not just waffle to fill up space. It shows that the candidate considered the sounds very carefully (again, with experimentation on the computer) until he arrived at something he felt satisfied with. A point to note here is that the recording is as important as the composing process, for if you select rather ordinary sounds the piece may not succeed. It is rather like a professional composer who writes a good piece and then arranges it in an uninteresting way for orchestra. You really need to be imaginative with both aspects of the task.

Don't neglect recording.

You will find Chapter 11 on Improvisation (especially the section on chord schemes) helpful as well. It deals with much the same work and may be worth re-reading at this point.

2 ▷ TUNED PERCUSSION (OR KEYBOARD): 4 PLAYERS

Keep in mind register, movement and duration.

IDEA 2

This second idea is for four players, but you could easily add more. It limits itself to the notes of the pentatonic scale. The suggested instruments are tuned percussion or keyboards, but you should feel free to use anything available, bearing in mind that instruments must have parts that are suitable for them, in register, movement and duration. Take care to remember this when you are composing or scoring out your first pieces; gradually it will become automatic. For example, bass parts tend to be slower moving than higher melodies and have fewer notes. Do experiment – if it works, and you feel satisfied with it, then it is right!

Let us call the four parts A B C and D rather than specify actual instruments and let us write in the treble clef for now, it can always be adjusted. Our pentatonic scale will be based on the tonic of C, so the notes we shall be working with are C D E G A. Ostinati can be very useful in a piece of this nature; experiment with short repeated patterns to achieve this sort of scoring (Fig. 12.5). In this case A and B each have a two-bar ostinato and C and D have a one-bar ostinato. There are many sorts of scale throughout the world. We have chosen the pentatonic as it is a practical one to use for tuned percussion, but you could quite well use a harmonic minor scale, the whole tone scale, or even a 'home-made' one. Experiment with different scales and see what you can come up with. The pentatonic can easily sound Japanese, Chinese or Scottish depending on how you use it – it doesn't really matter as long as you like the way it turns out.

Fig. 12.5

You could then be rather clever by trying to organise a dialogue between A and B by staggering their entries. The original A part has been dropped; A now plays the same music as B – but two beats later, as a simple canon. Perhaps you could also create more interesting C/D parts as in Fig. 12.6.

Fig. 12.6

You may decide to score your quartet without a prominent melody, in which case the character of the piece will depend on the perpetual movement of the ostinati and the timbres of the chosen instruments. If you work this way, make sure that you concentrate on the other musical ingredients – *dynamics, tempo, nuance* etc – to compensate for the lack of melody in the traditional sense. Be musical about it, don't just work away thinking that the right notes in the right place make a good performance! Aim for subtlety: perhaps a very quiet beginning, building to the loudest part in the middle and fading out at the end. This arch-shape is a common and satisfying way of building a piece.

> **Remember dynamics, tempo and nuance.**

Extending the piece

How can this sort of idea be extended? After all, ostinati can only be played so many times before they become monotonous. Listen to some music by Steve Reich, Philip Glass or John Adams. These minimalist composers (so-called because they exploit a minimal amount of musical material) are expert in their use of ostinati, and can make pieces lasting half an hour sound interesting, by subtle and almost imperceptible changes every now and again. These composers are cited as masters of ostinati, but you may want to try creating some minimalist music yourself. If composers such as Glass have written pieces as long as opera using minimalist techniques, it is obviously possible at GCSE level to use simple instruments for very short pieces. (For example, listen to Steve Reich's Music for Pieces of Wood, or his Clapping Music – they are both very effective.)

If you find this subtle changing of ostinati too difficult (and it is a skill that needs a lot of practice,) try to make a piece in ternary or rondo form. Your episodes could be in a different pentatonic key, perhaps based on G (G A B D E), or F (F G A C D). You might find a motif (a short rhythmic or melodic figure) from your opening section which can become the basis of your new episode. This will help to give some unity, avoiding the prospect of separate sections all tacked on to one another.

How about making the ending of your piece a round? This could be done either by rewriting your first section, or producing an entirely new section as a coda. Here is a suggested round which is based on the original material from Fig. 12.5.

Fig. 12.7

The asterisks indicate the point of entry for each of the four instruments. The first bar of the round derives from the C part of Fig. 12.5. The rhythm has been simplified and the octave jump is inverted. Notice how the quaver rhythm in bar 3 of the round occurs again at the end of bar 7; this will sound effective when all four parts are playing.

SOME GENERAL CONSIDERATIONS

Here are some musical considerations which you should apply to all your composition work:

> **Apply these principles to all your compositions.**

- It is generally accepted as good practice not to make your melodies too angular and jumpy. Don't be frightened of repetition in melody writing. With beautiful tone and a well chosen accompaniment a melody can have surprisingly few notes. Sibelius in his second symphony has an oboe melody that commences with nine repetitions of the same note, B flat, before it actually moves. It is in a lento tempo marking, and it sounds marvellous! Having said that, of course, there are obvious exceptions. The serialist composers (Schoenberg and Webern being the more 'severe' exponents of this genre) deliberately set out to compose their 'melodies' with no repetition at all until all twelve notes of the chromatic scale had been used once.

- Music is usually written in even numbers of bar – phrases of four, six and eight bars are the most common. This gives a balance between phrases, and helps to give shape to melodies.

- You may find it easier at this stage to commence and finish your melodies on the home note, or certainly one of the notes from the tonic chord (chord I of the scale). Also a long note at the end of a melody or piece gives a satisfying sense of finality.

These three points are a summary of average practice, but there are always exceptions. We have mentioned the serialist composers who avoided repetition and smoothness: similarly, modern jazz is often very angular and irregular. Even Haydn in the eighteenth century was fond of using a five-bar phrase to avoid any sense of squareness.

> **3** **MODEL COMPOSITION I**

IDEA 3

You may like to compose a song by setting some well known words. Shakespeare has always been a favourite, as his words are so versatile; they withstand a variety of musical styles. 'Under the Greenwood Tree' is from Act II scene V of *As You Like It*. This idea is presented as a **model** composition to demonstrate two very different ways of treating the same melody:

a) in a simple rock style
b) in a more traditional style as an art song.

Here is an outline of some of the thought processes involved.

> **Read the text several times.**

First of all, you must read through the chosen text several times. It is necessary to become familiar with the rhythm of the words and absorb the style, noticing any imagery or repetition:

Under the greenwood tree,	Who doth ambition shun,
Who loves to lie with me,	And loves to live i' the sun
And turn his merry note	Seeking the food he eats.
Unto the sweet bird's throat,	And pleas'd with what he gets
Come hither, come hither,	Come hither, come hither,
come hither:	come hither:
Here shall he see	Here shall he see
No enemy,	No enemy,
But winter and rough weather.	But winter and rough weather.

'Greenwood tree' and 'lie with me' suggest a Pastoral (countryside) and somewhat lazy mood. It is also a good idea to read the play to gauge the mood in context. The extract is sung by the character Amiens, so we should preferably use a male voice. Our choice of key is purely arbitrary, but a major key seems more appropriate. We'll use G major.

Space prevents us from describing every step involved; Fig. 12.8 is the resulting melody which, with some contrivance, will fit the second verse as well.

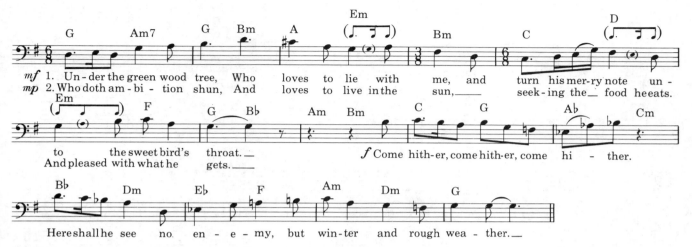

Fig. 12.8

The 3/8 bar is really only half a bar of 6/8 time. This was dictated by the rhythm of the words: it would be rather weak to wait on the word 'me' for a full bar, and the 3/8 provides a rhythmic interest in itself. The 'come hither' harmonies, which veer sharply away from G major, provide harmonic variety before the return to the tonic key. The F natural on 'rough weather' is a mild concession to sixteenth century modality as the flattened leading-note gives a period flavour.

Having composed the melody, here are two ways of presenting it:

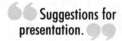
Suggestions for presentation.

a) The simple rock style uses the straightforward chords as in Fig. 12.8. You will need to provide an interesting introduction, where the colour is provided by an unusual progression of chords which returns between the two verses. This is shown in Fig. 12.9.

Fig. 12.9

b) The second version, Fig. 12.10, uses a piano accompaniment to create an art song. Here the piano part is more than a harmonic accompaniment – its music derives from and enhances the melody itself. The harmony chosen is deliberately simple, with a few mild dischords to add flavour, and the accompaniment aims to capture the lilting character of the melody. The quick notes of 'turn his merry note' (♩. ♫♫♩) have been 'borrowed' in bar 1 of the introduction. The piano part is built over a tonic pedal (drone) in bars 5 – 10. Notice how the gap after 'sweet bird's throat' hints at the introductory figure. The 'come hither' accompaniment doubles the melody in the bass with simple chords above. The introduction for verse 2 is identical to the opening, and also serves as a short postlude (closing section) to finish the song. You are not expected to copy either version of this; it is included as an example and serves to show what different results can be achieved by using different styles. Both versions are equally successful. You will probably want to work in a different way, but try to make your accompaniment as interesting as your melody, especially with a piano part.

Here are some famous Shakespeare songs that you may like to set in your own style:

1   Oh, mistress mine, where are you roaming? (see 'Twelfth-Night' Act II scene III)

2   It was a lover and his lass.   (see 'As You Like It' Act V scene III)

3   Blow, blow, thou winter wind.   (see 'As You Like It' Act II scene VII)

Under the Greenwood Tree

R. J. LAMBERT

Fig. 12.10 'Under the Greenwood Tree'

IDEA 4

This piece is submitted by the author as a 'model' composition. The objective in composing it was to write a lively piece for flute and piano and illustrate many of the points that have been mentioned earlier in this chapter. The musical intention was to use a light-hearted 'vamping' piano style, and a jig-like melody for flute (redolent of an Irish piper). The piece is quoted in full in Fig. 12.11 and a commentary is given as a further example for you to absorb. It is by no means an easy piece, and would require an excellent flautist and no mean pianist to perform it.

Fig. 12.11 'Abigail's Jig' – for flute and piano

Abigail's Jig

R. J. LAMBERT

MODEL STUDENT COMMENTARY

ABIGAIL'S JIG

This piece was especially written for the school flute teacher. It was recorded by him and the Director of Music as both parts are too difficult for any of the pupils to play! I tried to capture the atmosphere of an Irish jig as played by a piper, with a harmonically straightforward piano part using a mixture of 'vamping' and melodic imitation of the flute part.

The introduction is intended to be humorous and rather musically misleading. It starts in F minor but is immediately contradicted by the chords of A, A flat, E flat and Cm7. It openly parodies the 'cowboy' music of Aaron Copland, and uses flattened leading note chords (instead of a dominant) throughout. This modal harmony helps to create the mood of pseudo-folk music.

The main theme starts in the flute in the unexpected key of D minor. The piano has simple vamping chords until figure B, where it has an answering theme in F major interrupted at regular intervals by the flute. The main theme returns, forte this time, with a similar answering theme in the piano four bars later.

At figure C the introductory figure returns, but for variety a flute counter-melody is added this time. This four-bar phrase serves as a link into the second main theme which is presented by the piano.

This theme is also in D minor and is based largely on arpeggios and
scales. Two or three bars before figure D the harmony modulates
sequentially and builds up in volume to a key change to E minor at
figure D. I decided to suddenly drop the volume on the actual key
change in keeping with the humour of the piece. The main theme is
played by the flute but within four bars the second theme appears, as
before, in the piano with flute interjections. The climax of the
piece is at figure E where the flute plays decorative triplets
against a strong statement of the main theme which is played in
augmentation (in this case, double value). The last two bars of the
piece are a fortissimo statement of the introduction with the added
flute-counter-melody. The piece finishes with a demisemiquaver rush
up the scale on the flute.

The piece took me about a week to complete from the initial
keyboard improvising to the completion of the scoring, and I
thoroughly enjoyed working at it. My teacher suggested the key
change to a higher key to raise the tension a little, but the actual
notes are all my own work.

TEACHER ASSESSMENT

**Make everything
relevant.**

This commentary is deliberately detailed as an example of the sort of analytical information
you could include. Do make it all relevant and avoid unnecessary waffle. This particular
commentary was included as an example, but a commentary for a piece that has been so
carefully notated is probably superfluous. If you wish to include a brief explanation of how
your piece came about that will be quite sufficient.

ANALYSING COMPOSITIONAL TECHNIQUE

The rest of this section describes the piece in greater detail, this time with the purpose of
analysing compositional technique. It may help to trigger off some thoughts for your
compositions, and it also provides extra practice in analysis as required for some Set
Works. It must be emphasised that this music stemmed from doodling at the keyboard.

Improvisation is a pleasurable activity in itself. Even though much of what you play at
this stage will probably be scrapped, the time spent is never wasted; improvisation is really
a sort of unwritten composition and the technique you develop in working at it can be
drawn upon later.

The opening four-bar phrase sets the mood of the whole piece. Its rhythm is as
important as the deliberate 'wrong' chords. It took a fair bit of time at the keyboard before
the unusual sequence of (normally) unrelated chords arrived:

Fm A A♭ E♭ Cm7 | Fm A E♭ F | Fm A C E♭ B♭ | Fm A E♭ F(major) |

Notice how bars 2 and 4 are identical – this cadence is deliberately strong because the
other bars are so unusual. Bar 3 has a repeated rise of a similar interval (a third).

You may like to experiment with these unusual groupings of chords: decide on your tonic
key and juxtapose this with chords that are not closely related. For example, still in F
major you might try: F – D – A♭ – E♭ – F. Notice how the two final chords here and in the
Jig make the same cadence, E♭ – F. The E♭ major chord (the flattened seventh chord) acts
as a substitute for the more usual C – F, and the effect is very similar to a perfect cadence.
It therefore has the power to bring the short sequence back to the original tonic.

Once the tune arrives the accompaniment is kept extremely simple, to give full attention
to the flute melody. The overall key of D minor is not so very far away from the F
minor/major of the introduction – it is part of the humour of the composition to use a
different key for the introduction. The tune is played twice but notice small differences in
the flute part this time, and that the piano part changes its rhythm slightly to avoid
predictability and to add interest.

Figure B grows naturally out of figure A. It centres around the tonic of F, and has some
connections with the chord sequence of the introduction: (F A♭|F Cm|F A♭|F Cm7 F) but
this is a subconscious choice – it was not planned. It allows the pianist the opportunity for
some dialogue, although the flute does its best to join in whenever it can. Because the basic
melody is rather four-square, every opportunity to 'seal over the cracks' is taken. Here the

flute interrupts at bar 16 with a semiquaver run into a return of the main theme. A variant is offered at 21–24 to break up the obvious pattern of repeated tunes. It is based on the falling 5th motto (as at the beginning of bar 5), but develops into a harmonic reference (in bar 22) to the introduction.

Figure C again uses the same chord sequence as the introduction, but this time the flute joins in with a counter-melody. This tune is partly determined by the underlying chords but dotted rhythms are introduced to give something new after the smooth-running semiquavers. This brief reference to the rather strange opening serves as a link to the second theme which the piano introduces five bars after figure C. In many respects it is a similar melody to the first theme, and was in fact designed not to change the mood. It is presented by the piano, but the flute enters with the arpeggio figure (see bar 33). We can see that the opening of the second theme is an inverted version of the first (Fig. 12.12):

Fig. 12.12

(It could be argued that this sort of detail is either over-contrived or purely coincidental; however, it is considered to be good compositional style when there is a unity of ideas, themes and figures. Don't always attempt to produce a completely new idea for its own sake – endeavour to draw out a secondary idea from the preceding material.)

> **Don't always try to be too original!**

The end of this section is a modulatory passage leading to a new key at section D. One of the easiest ways of changing key is by means of a sequence (a repeated pattern of notes or chords) F .. (down 4th) ..C; Gm .. (down 4th) .. D (see bars 43–44). Above this the flute is decorating somewhat fussily to create a feeling of climax.

The upward key change is a common cliché in a short piece of this nature. Instead of developing the material further, or introducing new ideas, it is not unusual to repeat the main theme and end the piece in a higher key – higher of course, to increase the effect of brightness or tension. In this particular case the approach to the change of key is quite a dramatic build-up, but when the E minor arrives at figure D the volume drops immediately; the sense of humour is still there! The main melody is played only once (four bars) before the second idea is brought in – emphasising the compatibility of the material. Four bars later, however, the 'correct' theme (corresponding to that at letter B) is brought in but with 'wrong' harmony, similar to the introduction:

G (tonic) B♭ | Am Dm | Bm B♭ | G B♭ G |

Figure E is the loudest and most dramatic part of the piece: the flute is playing decorative semiquaver triplets arranged sequentially (in a similar pattern) against the main theme played at a lower register in the piano part, while a feeling of breadth is created by an octave-rolling bass beneath. The tune is written here in double the original note values (augmentation), which is another fairly common and useful compositional 'trick'. At the same time the flute semiquavers give a feeling of decoration by using the opposite effect of half values. The short coda, four bars from the end, uses two ideas: firstly the arpeggio figure (from bar 33), now still in augmentation in the piano, and finally, at figure F, the original introductory figure with added flute counter-melody which rounds the piece off with a lively scalic flourish. The final chord is E major, a conventional minor – major ending where the G# has a brightening effect. This is called a *Tierce da Picardie* (Picardy Third) and is a device which has been used by composers for hundreds of years!

5 ▷ MODEL COMPOSITION II

This is another piece submitted by the author as a 'model' composition. Play it over, or try to hear it through and this time, instead of discussing it bar by bar or writing a model commentary on it, answer the following five questions. The answers are given at the end of the piece.

Q1 The composer has tried to capture a 15th century 'flavour' in this piece. How has this been achieved?

Q2 Comment on the use of repetition in the piece.

Q3 How are dynamics employed?

Q4 If the male chorus parts are intended to be prominent, how does the composer write for the female voices?

Q5 Comment on the ostinato figures in the organ accompaniment.

Adam lay ybounden

for Royston Parish Church Choir

Words anon, 15th cent.

R. J. LAMBERT

1. A - dam lay y - boun - den, Boun - den in a bond; ____ Four thou-sand win - ter Thought he not too long. ____

Answers to the questions on 'Adam lay ybounden':

1 By prominent use of bare consecutive fifths in the voice parts, by the chant-like use of male voices, by employing ostinato patterns in the drum part and by persistant use of drone notes in the organ accompaniment. The oboe is instructed to play like a shawm, so would produce a harder tone than usual. Finally, the words are 15th century!

2 The reiterated oboe counter melody is actually slightly different on each hearing, but has the feeling of being the same each time. Apart from the last two bars, the drum part has two simple ostinato figures which are highly repetitive. Repeated ostinato bars are prominent in the organ accompaniment, and the opening choral figure is used, with slight variation, in each verse.

3 The oboe is kept forte most of the time to maintain its solo prominence against the organ, which is kept mostly mf except where it takes the counter melody either with, or instead of, the oboe. The second verse at figure C, is set at a contrasting mp volume until it approaches figure D with a crescendo. The final section, from figure H, is sung with a strong fortissimo.

4 The female voices enter first in verse 2 with a simple unison scalic counter melody. When the alto part becomes too high, the harmony (where possible) matches the male voices by using the interval of a fifth.

5 The organ part up to figure A is derived entirely from the oboe melody, and extends itself increasingly. The one-bar ostinato from figures A–C, and D–E is simply the first bar of the oboe tune. This figure tries to re-establish itself from the seventh bar of figure F, but it is mixed in with other accompanying harmony.

Now you try to write a piece with straightforward ostinato patterns, or with slightly varying counter melodies. Good luck!

6 EXAMPLES OF STUDENT COMPOSITIONS

To conclude this chapter here are five examples of student compositions, all of which were submitted for examination in 1988 or 1989. It is a pity that you can only see the pieces and not hear them; music often comes alive when played well even if it sometimes looks uninteresting on paper. Two of these compositions had commentaries attached which are also included here for you to think about. These compositions have not been selected on grounds of merit, although they certainly contain some creditable ideas; they are presented with examiner's comments with the following aims in mind:

> How you will benefit from seeing the work of other students.

a) to improve your own standard of presentation and accuracy of notation;
b) to see how others develop their initial ideas;
c) to consider the importance of commentaries when added to a score.

MARCH FOR TRUMPET AND PIANO

Candidate's commentary (submitted with the composition)

> As I used to play the trumpet and now play the piano, I had a fairly
> good idea what a march for trumpet and piano should sound like.
>   I decided to write it in ternary form and in the key of C major (the
> trumpet being transposed up to D major).
>   Firstly, I wrote the trumpet's tune and then I composed the piano
> accompaniment. I did not directly record the tune, but programmed it
> into a Yamaha CX5 Music Computer. I used a trumpet sound and an
> electric piano sound. When I finished programming it into the
> computer, I played it back, recording it onto a cassette.

Candidate's score

The March for Trumpet and Piano is reproduced as Fig. 12.13. The piece itself is only 24 bars long.

Examiner's comments

This short piece works quite well, and is cast in an effective ternary form. The melody for trumpet is satisfactory, although more use might have been made of the triplet figure which appears only once. There is no real sense of climax to the piece; this might have been achieved with a higher range of trumpet notes towards the end, instead of repeating the first section exactly. The use of dynamics is rather unimaginative: the piano part is simply marked mf all the way through, and the instructions for trumpet are only marginally more interesting. The ⟨ ⟩ marking in bar 10 is likely to produce a strange 'ballooning' effect, and should be reconsidered.

The candidate is perfectly correct in stating that the B♭ trumpet is a transposing instrument, but there is no need to provide both C and B♭ parts here. A score normally contains one or the other, and it proves confusing to see both. Apart from that, the notation is very clear with only minor inaccuracies (in bar 1 the piano quavers should not be under the minim but on the fourth beat and in bar 11 the C trumpet part has the semiquaver indication missing).

The commentary is perfectly adequate considering that it is in addition to, not a substitute for, a notated score. It gives a clear explanation of how the candidate went about creating and recording the piece.

Fig. 12.13 **March for trumpet and piano**

SCHERZO FOR PIANO

Candidate's score

The Scherzo for piano is reproduced as Fig. 12.14.

Fig. 12.14 Scherzo for piano

Examiner's comments

This is an effective piano miniature. I am not sure that 'Scherzo' is the right title for this piece – apart from the fact that historically, composers wrote their Scherzos in a quick 3/4 time with one beat to a bar, it actually implies something light-hearted; literally a 'joke', which is not the case in this piece. Perhaps the title could be reconsidered.

The piano writing is well thought out in both hands, with effective imitation as in bar 2. The piece is interesting rhythmically, and the semiquaver figure (♩♩♩♩) helps to give the piece some movement. The sequence in bars 9–12 is treated well: bar 12 has a sense of forward motion instead of waiting, as in bar 10.

A + B + B is an unusual structure for a piece. Is this satisfying as it stands? Should the A theme return to finish off the piece? Details of phrasing are good at the beginning but seem to dry up after bar 10, and it must be admitted, too, that the dynamics are rather uninspired. The notation itself is clear, but care should be taken to align the beats accurately between the hands. Avoid placing a ♪ above a ♩ as in ♩ ♪ ♩ ♩ (bar 12). (The quaver being shorter should be moved along.)

Five more minutes spent on notation to check the final details and markings would have improved this written score considerably.

PUCK'S LULLABY

Candidate's score

Puck's Lullaby is reproduced as Fig. 12.15.

Fig. 12.15 'Puck's Lullaby'

A commentary was added which explains the reasons for its composition.

The school did a production of *A Midsummer Night's Dream* and we were asked to compose the incidental music for it. This piece is written for Puck, end of Act Three Scene Two. The play was set in the 60s, mini skirts and hippies all the fashion, so the music had to be appropriate.

It is written for keyboard synthesiser with drum beat, flute and voice in the style of a 60s pop song. I chose C minor as the key to give the piece a dramatic and eerie quality because Puck is, in fact, casting a spell.

I wrote the accompaniment first. It is very simple chords with slow quaver repetition in the right hand. The melodic range was restricted by the singer (a non-trained fourth former). The phrases can be sung in short breaths again as dictated by the singer and Shakespeare's metrical verse. For variety in the texture I placed a flute above the main melody which is sometimes imitative.

Its function in the play is to put right the mischievous antics of Puck. I tried to put this across in the music and the tension is maintained until the last two bars. I wanted an unusual cadence and used the minor version of the leading note as a variant on the dominant.

Puck has been playing with the emotions of the four lovers throughout the play and only now is putting things right, Lysander, Hermia, Demetrius and Helena falling in love with the right people. During the piece there is a slight use of dissonance but always resolving harmonically.

Examiner's comments

This was submitted in beautifully clear notation; it is a very well written piece and there is a clear explanation as to its construction. This is a good example of how a piece can grow from its improvised accompaniment. The rather narrow-ranging vocal line is understandable when one reads the commentary. There is a sensitive imitation between flute and voice in bars 10–11; this is treated very musically, for the vocal line does not copy it exactly, and the flute goes on to another figure, so avoiding predictability. The dynamics are used sensibly throughout.

The candidate mentions the use of dissonance in the commentary – is bar 6 correctly notated with the E flat in the vocal line against E natural in the accompaniment? This does work perfectly well; or is it a simple error?

One small point: the low flute B natural in bar 2 is not possible on a real flute (middle C is its lowest note). Be careful with instrumental ranges when you are using synthesisers to help you.

> **Take care with instrumental ranges.**

A MOVEMENT FOR CLARINET TRIO

Candidate's score

A Movement for Clarinet Trio is reproduced as Fig. 12.16.

Examiner's comments

This is an example of a piece that looks rather dull on paper, but comes to life with a good performance. It uses the full range of the clarinet well between the three players, and the dynamics are employed intelligently, providing a good contrast within the movement. The second clarinet figure (commencing at bar 18) subtly grows from the ornamental figure in bar 16. This may be subconscious, but is good compositional technique. Perhaps a modulation (key change) somewhere would have added more colour.

Are those phrase marks written over the tops of the bars? If so, it would be better to indicate a legato mood with an instruction at the top of the piece, rather than use these markings which imply slurring, instead of tonguing for wind players.

Do you mean F♯ – E♭ in bars 27/29/31/33 etc? It is by no means wrong, but many pieces avoid this interval from the harmonic minor scale and use F♯ – E natural or F – E♭ instead. It may be useful to indicate both notes with accidentals to clarify this.

Clarinet Trio

Fig. 12.16 Clarinet trio

PSALM 134

Candidate's score

Psalm 134 for four-part choir is reproduced as Fig. 12.17.

Fig. 12.17 Psalm 134

Examiner's comments

This candidate, who openly expresses a love for the choral music of Rachmaninov, achieves here a fine pastiche of the dark Russian vocal style. The Psalm is one of a set of three, all of the same high standard of musical thought and clarity of notation. The candidate thoughtfully includes a piano part which would prove invaluable in rehearsal, as the vocal lines are difficult to score-read. The use of E♭ minor and the deep bass notes add to the lugubrious atmosphere. This piece requires a very good choir to give the fine performance it deserves. The score is beautifully clear and written in conventional vocal style with separated quavers.

A FINAL STATEMENT

When assessing your compositions, your teacher will judge your work according to established criteria; your work will not be compared with the work of other candidates, but assessed on your own ability. Work is then moderated by external examiners to ensure a uniformity of standards.

It is expected that your compositions may imitate other styles at this level; in no way will this penalise you, for traditional styles can be compiled creatively. Arrangements of other work are encouraged, although this seems not to be a popular option. Successful arranging requires as much imagination as a free composition; avoid any tendency to merely transcribe the chosen tune for other instruments or voices. If you think of your arrangement as if you were writing variations, then you might be more creative. Consider adding counter melodies or fresh harmonies; change the key perhaps, or modulate more freely.

66 **Quality not quantity.** 99

Do not assume that 'difficult is best', or that your pieces must be lengthy. Marks awarded for composition are likely to be for quality rather than for length or the number of pieces submitted. The examiners are looking for evidence of **expressive ability**; twenty-four bars of **clearly written**, **sensitive music** with a **satisfying structure** is preferable to pages of incoherent note-spinning. Now over to you, and enjoy yourselves!

R E V I E W   S H E E T

✎ Take the following simple chord scheme. Then try some or all of the following suggestions.

          C   F   Am D7   G7   C

i) Add a vocal line.

ii) Add an instrumental melody.

iii) Add on another sequence of chords to make a second (B) section.

iv) Repeat part iii) but this time making the rhythm more interesting (if you have not changed the rhythm from the chord scheme provided).

✎ Here is a simple melody with chords indicated underneath. Use this as a starting point for a composition involving any instrument(s) you choose.

      I ——————— V7 —— I   IV— V7 —— I———————

✎ Write a commentary below on your composition.

✎ Compose a song by setting these well known words from 'As You Like It', Act V, Scene III, by William Shakespeare. Use any style you feel appropriate.

> It was a lover and his lass,
>   With a hey, and a ho, and hey nonino,
> That o'er the green corn-field did pass,
>   In spring time, the only pretty ring time,
> When birds do sing, hey ding a ding, ding;
> Sweet lovers love the spring.

Now write a commentary below on your composition.

_____

_____

_____

_____

_____

_____

✎ Now compose a song by setting these well known words from 'Daffodils' by William Wordsworth. Use any style you feel appropriate.

> I wandered lonely as a cloud
>   That floats on high o'er vales and hills,
> When all at once I saw a crowd,
>   A host, of golden daffodils;
> Beside the lake, beneath the trees,
> Fluttering and dancing in the breeze.

Now write a commentary below on your composition.

_____

_____

_____

_____

_____

_____

✎ Here is another opportunity to practice composition. Compose a song by setting this verse from 'Piano' by D. H. Lawrence in any style you feel appropriate.

> Softly, in the dusk, a woman is singing to me;
> Taking me back down the vista of years, till I see
> A child sitting under the piano, in the boom of the tingling strings
> And pressing the small, poised feet of a mother who smiles as she sings.

Now write a comentary below on your composition.

_____

_____

_____

_____

_____

_____

✎ Write a piece of music for any musical instrument you are familiar with. Now write a commentary below on this piece of music.

_____

_____

_____

_____

_____

_____

COMPOSING 2: GRAPHIC NOTATION

COMPOSING 3: ELECTRONICS

GRAPHIC NOTATION

WORKING WITH ELECTRONIC INSTRUMENTS

GETTING STARTED

In Western music, a thorough knowledge of *notation* has long been regarded as a prerequisite for composers and performers alike. It is easy to forget, however, that a great deal of music around the world is not written down. Popular music, folk, jazz, and Indian music are among the styles which are either improvised or committed to memory. Staff notation is a well understood and useful tool, but it is by no means the only way of recording sounds on paper.

Even the most detailed and complex traditional score can indicate only a portion of the information required for a satisfactory performance – we still depend on the interpretation of the conductor, performer and the taught tradition for these signs and symbols to be fully realised, or brought alive, according to the composer's intentions.

During the last few decades there have been tremendous improvements in music education, including a movement away from an exclusive use of staff notation. Traditionalists might argue that the existence of alternative notation is necessary simply because staff notation has not been learnt properly. This may be partly true, but forms of graphic notation actually became necessary for some of the different styles that have evolved this century.

ESSENTIAL PRINCIPLES

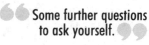

GRAPHIC NOTATION

A graphic score is one where the notation is invented by the composer for a particular piece; the signs and symbols (which may, of course, include traditional ones) are devised to represent ideas where approximation is appropriate. It can never be as accurate as staff notation, but is to be encouraged for GCSE if you take pains to record your intentions for performance.

A graphic score is certainly useful for those candidates who find staff notation difficult, and should not be thought of as inferior; contemporary composers such as Stockhausen and Berio have used graphic notation for their compositions where some degree of choice is desirable or necessary. This could be just the thing for you if you wish to explore textures of sound and spatial concepts, rather than melodies and rhythm in the traditional sense.

Once you have considered the sounds you wish to explore and the overall structure of your piece, you will need to select or devise suitable **signs** and **symbols** for the notation. The next important step is to work out a *key* so that you can clarify the interpretation of your symbols. You will need to consider the following criteria:

> ❝❞ **Questions in working out a key for notation.** ❝❞

- How long or short do you wish the notes to be and how will you notate this?
- How will you notate pitch?
- How will you notate harmony? Are you keen to explore clusters of notes or do you prefer more conventional chords?
- Will you specify instruments or permit any combination that is available?
- Will you invent your own symbols for expression or retain the traditional ones?

There is an important maxim with all composition, that you should **hear the sound before you use the sign**. In other words, notation itself is not music, even though we use the same word, 'music', for the written sign as well as for the sound. **Notation** is merely an accepted way of **representing** sounds on paper. Only when these symbols are realised can we consider it to be music.

Ask yourself these questions when composing a piece using graphic notation:

> ❝❞ **Some further questions to ask yourself.** ❝❞

- Which instrument is playing the important part? Does it remain so, or does another instrument take over?
- How can I ensure that this instrument is heard to full advantage, and not swamped by the other parts?
- Should I choose a sound or instrument which contrasts with the other parts and therefore becomes conspicuous?
- Should I make it louder than the other instruments? Or is it easier to make the other parts quieter?

How would you interpret the signs in Fig. 13.1? In the notation in Fig. 13.1, no indication of duration (length) of notes has been indicated, so freedom is implied if not indicated on the score.

In a) you need to relate the sizes of the boxes to each other – in terms of height (which can represent pitch) and width (which can represent duration). Could the boxes be used for blocks of chords? If so, the notes will be arbitrary because no pitch has been indicated.

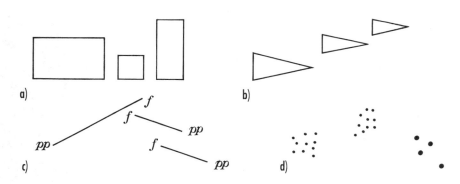

Fig. 13.1

In b) we could think of the sounds as becoming quieter and each one higher than before, but are these sounds single notes, or chords? The key at the beginning of your piece would have to indicate this.

In c) we have some traditional Italian dynamics, and it is good to use these. Why discard signs for the sake of it? The lines imply a glissando (or slide) up and down a scale. The length of the line gives an approximate duration of the glissando, and their position indicates fairly clearly when they should be played. Notice the overlap between all three. The notes used in the glissando would obviously depend on the particular instrument being used.

In d) the series of dots would imply a cluster of single notes played at random, and in close proximity. The second cluster would be proportionately higher, depending again on the instruments being used. The final grouping of four dots is slightly bigger. Could this mean louder notes or longer notes? This needs to be made quite clear in the key to your piece.

The four groups of symbols carry a fair amount of information, some implied and some to be explained more fully in the key. Let us now consider ways of employing signs in a piece which explores textural and spatial effects.

KEY

The height of each square on the grid represents the total range of the instrument. The conductor is to indicate by means of a down-beat where each ten seconds has elapsed. This timing is to be regarded as approximate.

The signs are more or less self-explanatory:

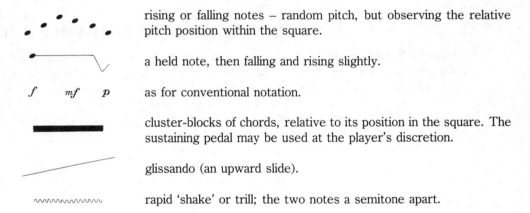

rising or falling notes – random pitch, but observing the relative pitch position within the square.

a held note, then falling and rising slightly.

f　mf　p　　as for conventional notation.

cluster-blocks of chords, relative to its position in the square. The sustaining pedal may be used at the player's discretion.

glissando (an upward slide).

rapid 'shake' or trill; the two notes a semitone apart.

The graphic score in Fig. 13.2 illustrates the first 40 seconds only of a piece.

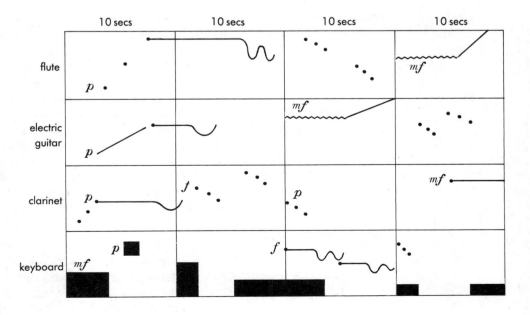

Fig. 13.2

You can see that by including the ten-second time-spans as 'bars' and also some traditional dynamic markings, it starts to take on some of the characteristics of staff notation. With careful thought, this sort of notation can convey a considerable amount of precision while retaining a certain element of freedom which provides a sense of spontaneity.

Given these suggestions, and the brief example above, could you experiment with this style of composition and notation to create an inventive piece? **Remember, the sound** comes **first, then** the **sign**. Don't fall into the unmusical trap of drawing meaningless lines and squiggles on paper and kidding yourself that it is music. Allow the instruments or parts to relate to each other, as if you were notating imitation or counterpoint more conventionally.

A final point: ensure that your performers give a first-class account of your piece, or it may sound a little pretentious. If a piece sacrifices a melodic content in the traditional sense, then more importance must be given to timbre and nuance (tone colours and subtle shading) to compensate.

2 ▷ WORKING WITH ELECTRONIC INSTRUMENTS

When GCSE Music was introduced, pupils had the opportunity to acquire a broad base of practical skills and the chance to explore a much wider range of musical styles than ever before. Pupils were able to use, for the first time, electronic keyboards, synthesisers and music computers as composing tools, in whatever genre they chose to explore; the keyboards and synthesisers could also be used for the performing elements of the course.

This short section will be of most benefit for those candidates who have not, as yet, worked with electronic instruments; it introduces them briefly, and then sets out to encourage you to use these new instruments. Most importantly, it suggests ways of using them more musically.

DIFFERENCES BETWEEN SYNTHESISER AND KEYBOARD

> Know the difference between synthesiser and keyboard.

First of all, the words 'synthesiser' and 'keyboard' are often used as if they are interchangeable. There are, however, important differences between them. In a nutshell, the many varieties of portable keyboard with their banks of automatic accompaniments are aimed at the home musician – and great fun they are too. The synthesiser, however, is much more versatile; it is essentially a professional musical instrument capable of multi-timbral sounds, which are altered or created yourself. It has a wide range of sounds, rhythms, pitches and durations. Developed over thirty years ago, it is now a much-used instrument with rock musicians and modern composers (This is not the place to go into electronic details – you can read elsewhere of oscillators, mixers, filters, envelope shapers and so on. It is a very complicated piece of machinery).

MIDI

> MIDI is an important consideration.

There is one technical detail that must be mentioned, as it is an important musical consideration. When choosing an electronic instrument for use in composition (or performance) try to obtain one that is equipped with MIDI (Musical Instrument Digital Interface) – you will find that most keyboards produced recently have this facility built in.

The digital system is widely used in electronics, and is used here so that everything you play on your keyboards or synthesiser is encoded as a series of numbers.

MIDI is a universal language which is utilised now on all makes of hi-tech equipment. If you connect a MIDI lead to your synthesiser's MIDI OUT socket and link it to the MIDI IN socket of another MIDI keyboard, information can be transmitted from your synthesiser to the other keyboard. For example, if you move the pitch bend wheel on your synthesiser, or play a note, this will then be duplicated on the keyboard. In this way several interconnected keyboards will produce a great variety of complex blends of timbres. This facility is used to good effect in the rock business where keyboard players use these layered sounds to good advantage by means of MIDI – listen to Jean-Michel Jarre's *Oxygène* album, for example.

RECORDING

If you choose to work with a portable keyboard with built-in rhythms, do make sure that you don't resort to simple 'button-pushing'. The pre-recorded sounds can be great fun to play with, but are so inflexible; you should be in full control of the instrument as a performer, and should select the different sounds inventively. An incessant rhythm on a keyboard is as relentless as a drum machine: vary it and think of a contrast in speed or dynamics if you can.

Both of these instruments are invaluable as composing aids; you can experiment with chords and melodies until you are satisfied with the result. Then, on completion of the piece, the point to consider is, how do I record my composition? Will I be content with the rather limited sounds of my keyboard for a recording? Could I bring my composition alive with more sophisticated equipment?

When submitting your scores or commentaries, you may have to include a recording. If so, the examiner will want to assess your work alongside the recording. Although the quality of the recording itself is not assessed, it will make a more favourable impression if it is clear and well-balanced. Do you have access to a computer with music software at school?

USE OF COMPUTERS

The Hybrid Music System was designed with education in mind. Its software 'environment' is called AMPLE, and can be used in two options: staff notation or AMPLE's own music language which is comparatively easy for pupils to learn – even for those without musical training. Based around a BBC microcomputer, a compatible disc-drive, monitor and printer, and utilising your own hi-fi system (or the Hybrid one) it can be linked up to the Music 5000 synthesiser and the Music 4000 keyboard. There is also a Music 2000 interface for use with MIDI instruments. This is an ideal work-station for composition. You may wish to work by improvising on the keyboard first; you can then spend time recording, editing and adding in extra parts in the AMPLE notation using the 'Notepad' in word-processor fashion. Your piece can easily be converted to staff notation and printed out that way, or retained as AMPLE notation. Any further details of expression, tempo, instrumentation and even stereo positioning can all be calculated and worked out as the computer plays the music.

The sounds are created by machine, but the selection process is made by you. The ingenious mixing desk allows you to experiment with timbres and blends of sound, saving and synthesising each one until you are satisfied with the end product. All your compositional work is stored onto floppy disc, and you can easily pick up where you left off.

There are other software packages available – some perhaps more complex to master initially – but very worthwhile as an aid for composing. C–Lab Notator software for use with the Atari computer is an excellent example; a highly sophisticated piece of equipment – Beethoven would have loved one!

Your school will probably have equipment like that mentioned so far. If so, do ask if you can have some hands-on experience; it may be just the thing for your compositions. Try out a drum machine; could it be used for your piece?

Many of you will be familiar with the above, and some of you may even own some of the equipment. But if this is new territory for you, and yet there is an opportunity to try it out, be adventurous – **have a go**! It may be just the thing that you are looking for.

USEFUL THEORY

G E T T I N G   S T A R T E D

You may not find this section the most interesting, but music theory needs to be learnt thoroughly if you are to be sure of a top grade in GCSE. If you wish a) to give a good account of yourself in the written papers; b) to interpret your ensemble and performance pieces intelligently; and c) to notate your compositions accurately – you should make sure that you are familiar with the following theoretical knowledge:

KEY SIGNATURES

The seven sharps and seven flats are always used in a fixed order:

You may not actually use a key with all of the sharps or flats, but you should learn them just in case – it may turn up in a written paper, or in a performance piece. The order of the flats is quite easy to remember with a simple phrase:

British **E**uropean **A**irways **D**o **G**ood **C**harter **F**lights (or you can easily make up your own).

For the order of the sharps simply reverse this, into:

F C G D A E B – or make up a nonsense line to help you remember, as with the flats. (**F**armer **C**harles **G**ets **D**runk **A**t **E**very **B**arndance…?)

You will need to know which scales contain these sharps or flats. The relative minor scales, which share the same key signatures are given in brackets:

C	major has no sharps or flats	(A minor)
G	major has 1 sharp	(E minor)
D	major has 2 sharps	(B minor)
A	major has 3 sharps	(F# minor)
E	major has 4 sharps	(C# minor)
B	major has 5 sharps	(G# minor)
F#	major has 6 sharps	(D# minor)
F	major has 1 flat	(D minor)
B	flat major has 2 flats	(G minor)
E	flat major has 3 flats	(C minor)
A	flat major has 4 flats	(F minor)
D	flat major has 5 flats	(B flat minor)
G	flat major has 6 flats	(E flat minor)
C	flat major has 7 flats	(A flat minor)

Thus, if you are asked to enter the key signature for A major into the correct place – check first which clef you are in, then enter the necessary number of sharps (in this case 3 = F C and G sharps) after the clef and before the time signature:

It is worthwhile practising some of these to help you remember. You should certainly know up to four sharps and flats very well indeed.

ESSENTIAL PRINCIPLES

1 > RELATIVE MINOR SCALES

When you are working with minor scales you can work out the correct minor key signature from that of the major. (This may save you having to learn the minors by heart, but you will need to know all the major key signatures!) Take a minor scale and count up three semitones to find its relative major. They will share the same key signature. For example: A (minor) – count up through B flat and B natural to arrive at C (major) = no sharps or flats; or E (minor) – count up through F and F# to arrive at G (major) = one sharp (F#). Try some of these for yourself and check your answers with the above table of key signatures. Similarly, of course, you can count down (three semitones) from a major to a minor key.

2 > MINOR SCALES

There are two types of minor scale, the *Harmonic minor* and the *Melodic minor*. Harmonic minors usually have the seventh note (leading note) raised a semitone by means of an accidental. So A minor, for instance, will have the same key signature as C major but the seventh note is G# and not G natural. Also, the scale is similar ascending and descending (see Fig. 14.1).

Fig. 14.1 A harmonic minor

The melodic minor scale (Fig. 14.2) has some of the difficult intervals ironed out, and is used more when writing smooth minor-key melodies. The 6th and 7th notes are raised on the way up, but flattened (that is, the key signature is applied) on the way down.

Fig. 14.2 A melodic minor

Again, you should practise some of the easier harmonic and melodic minor scales – up to four sharps or flats, perhaps.

3 > PENTATONIC SCALE

This five-note scale (see Fig. 14.3), which omits the 4th and 7th degrees of our major scale, is used by many different cultures around the world. Chinese, Japanese, American Indian, American Negro and Scottish folk music have it. There is an illustration in Fig. 14.4.

Fig. 14.3 Pentatonic scale

Fig. 14.4

(You could experiment with this scale, and perhaps use it as the basis for a composition or improvisation. The piano black keys form the pentatonic scale – use F# as your home note.)

4 > WHOLE-TONE SCALE

Here there are no semitones at all, and the scale creates a nice feeling of vagueness (Fig. 14.5). So suitable for Impressionistic music!

Fig. 14.5 Whole-tone scale

Play the scale over several times until you are really sure of its sound, and then use it within a short composition of your own. Of course, you do not have to include whole-tones all of the time, just when you think it is appropriate!

5 RESTS AND NOTE VALUES

Silences in music must be indicated as accurately as actual sounds. Many students get the semibreve and minim rests confused, and note groupings are often incorrectly written. The table in Fig. 14.6 should help.

> A table to help your accuracy with rests and note values.

Name	Note	Rest	Value (when a beat = ♩)
semibreve	o	▬ *	4 beats
minim	♩ (𝄽)	▬	2 beats
crotchet	♩ (𝄽)	𝄽 (or 𝄽)	1 beat
quaver	♪ (𝄽)	𝄾	½ (♫ = 1 beat)
semiquaver	♬ (𝄽)	𝄿	¼ (♬♬ = 1 beat)
demisemiquaver	♬ (𝄽)	𝅀	⅛ (♬♬♬♬ = 1 beat)

Fig. 14.6 Silences in music   * This rest is also used to denote an empty bar (or complete bar's rest,) whatever the time signature.

By adding a dot after a note, it can be made to last half as long again:

♩. = a dotted minim (1½ minims, or three crotchets)
♩. = a dotted crotchet (1½ crotchets)
♪. = a dotted quaver (1½ quavers, or ¾ of a crotchet)

Likewise with rests, we can lengthen by use of dots:

1½ crotchet beats rest = 𝄽·   or we can use two rests: 𝄽 𝄾

Fig. 14.7 gives an example in 4/4 time:

Fig. 14.7

In 6/8 time (where the pulse is two dotted crotchets = 2 × 3 quavers) it will be written as in Fig. 14.8.

Fig. 14.8

> A table to help with time signatures and their correct groupings.

The table (Fig. 14.9) should remind you of time signatures and their correct groupings. Be especially careful of 6/8 time which is often incorrectly grouped as 3 × 2 quavers, which is actually 3/4 time.

Fig. 14.9

Many modern composers use different time signatures from the above. 5/4 and 7/4 are very common now, but should not cause too much trouble for you. 5/4 is often thought of as 2 + 3, or 3 + 2, for example, and soon feels natural with practice. It gives a freer form of rhythm, and can be very effective when time signatures are changed within a single piece. Try composing a piece in an unusual time, or a mixture of time signatures.

6 › INTERVALS

An interval is the distance between any two notes. Think of the lower note as one, then count on up through the lines and spaces to the higher note, thus a) 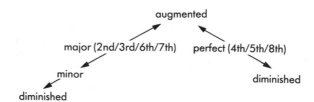 is an interval of a 5th, and b) is an interval of a 7th. If both notes are contained in the major scale of the lower note, it will be a **major** interval (for 2nds, 3rds, 6ths and 7ths) or a **perfect** interval (for 4ths, 5ths and octaves). So then, a) will be a perfect 5th, and b) is a major 7th.

If, however, the top note does not belong to the major scale of the lower note, another name has to be given, see Fig. 14.10.

Fig. 14.10

The arrows in Fig. 14.10 represent a rise or fall of a semitone. Thus, an interval with the upper note a semitone higher than a major 6th, for example, is an augmented 6th, and a semitone less than a major will be a minor, etc.

Fig. 14.11   (c) Major 3rd   (d) Minor 3rd   (e) Augmented 3rd

In the three examples in Fig. 14.11, we are using the scale of C major because the lower note of each interval is a C. In c) both notes are present in C major, so the interval is a major 3rd; in d) the upper note is a semitone lower than the 'true' note E, so the interval is a minor 3rd; and in e) the upper note is a semitone higher than the correct note, so is an augmented 3rd.

QUICK TEST

For practice, describe the intervals illustrated in Fig. 14.12. The answers are given at the end of this chapter.

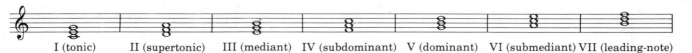

Fig. 14.12   (a)   (b)   (c)   (d)   (e)   (f)   (g)   (h)   (i)   (j)

For your compositions, and perhaps keyboard improvisations, you will probably be working with chords. You should become familiar with all the common chords of the scale. Fig. 14.13 gives you the chords of C major.

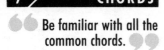

  I (tonic)   II (supertonic)   III (mediant)   IV (subdominant)   V (dominant)   VI (submediant) VII (leading-note)

Fig. 14.13

7 › CHORDS

> Be familiar with all the common chords.

Harmony is the application of suitable chords to a melody, and the three most important chords in traditional Western music are the tonic (chord I), the subdominant (chord IV) and the dominant (chord V). With these three chords alone, it is possible to harmonise many pieces – from pop songs and twelve-bar blues, through to hymn tunes or a simple *lied*. The remaining chords, however, are frequently used in addition, to add flavour to the harmonisation, particularly chords II and VI.

8 > CADENCES

A cadence is a full or half *close* in music, two chords at the end of a phrase or section to round things off. There are four types of cadence:

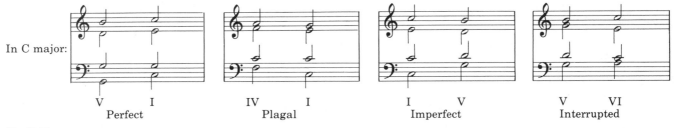

> The four types of cadence.

- **Perfect cadence**   chords V and I   Strong, and final.
- **Plagal cadence**   chords IV and I   Final, but 'softer' like a church Amen.
- **Imperfect cadence**   chords I (or II or IV) and V   Incomplete because it goes away from tonic.
- **Interrupted cadence** chords V and VI   Unexpected as its name suggests; needs a continuing phrase to finalise.

The four cadences are shown in Fig. 14.14.

In C major:

V   I   IV   I   I   V   V   VI
Perfect   Plagal   Imperfect   Interrupted

Fig. 14.14

9 > ORNAMENTS

Ornaments are decorations in music. They have been used at all times to embellish a melody line, but in the Baroque and early classical times especially, spontaneous ornamentation was expected of a performer, even if it was not actually indicated in the music. Ornaments may be written as special signs, or as small notes against a larger one. You may find ornaments in your chosen performance pieces and set works, or you may wish to use some in your compositions. Fig. 14.15 gives some of the more common ones.

Mordent (note, note above, note)

Inverted mordent

Turn (4 notes – note above, note, note below, note)

Inverted turn

Arpeggio (a quick-spreading chord)

Appoggiatura (lean into the main note by taking ½ of its value, or ⅔ if it is a dotted note)

Acciaccatura (crushed quickly into the main note)

Trill (or shake)

or in quick time:

Fig. 14.15

A trill over a short note, played at speed, may be thought of as a mordent (see Fig. 14.16).

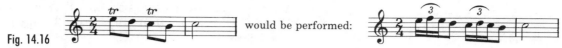

Fig. 14.16

Ornamentation is a detailed topic. If you require further information, consult a good textbook, or ask your teacher for advice. For GCSE , a working knowledge of the more common ornaments is perfectly satisfactory, but bear in mind that your interpretation of them, strictly speaking, should take into account the period in time of composition, and the overall speed of the piece – you cannot 'trill' as many notes in a fast piece as in a slow one.

10 ▷ FORM

Form is **structural shape** in music. Much of 'classical' music shows easily identifiable forms, but nothing is fixed in format, and many variants can be found. Composers write their music as they feel, not to suit descriptions in text-books! We can only describe the average structures that composers have evolved, and must realise that there will always be diversity.

When young students start to think seriously about musical analysis, many think at first that a good composition is one where there is a wealth of good tunes, or ideas, one after the other. It is only through experience, good teaching and copious listening that they come to understand that repetition and contrast of a minimal amount of musical material is what helps to make a satisfactory composition. (Think of this when you work on your own compositions!) Themes are important, but so too is a contrast of key. Changes of key (especially in Classical times) mark out the significant landmarks in a work.

> **Changes of key are important.**

Before we consider whole movements and how they are structured, we must not forget that melodies and even phrases should be constructed in a careful way. A typical musical sentence (from a simple song, perhaps) might consist of 2 × 2-bar phrases, for example with a cadence in the middle and at the end. (See the section on Cadences earlier in this chapter). But composers try to avoid a feeling of 'squareness' (that is, predictable numbers of phrases and bars) by sometimes extending a bar. This will help to break up a monotonous pattern.

> **Extending a bar can help.**

AN EXAMPLE

Look at the 21-bar melody in Fig. 14.17, and play it through if you can. How has it been composed? Is it just a random collection of bars which 'happen to fit' together? Look in detail at the way each bar is part of the whole.

Fig. 14.17

The melody has been written in F major.

Bars 1–4   A four-bar sentence dividing into 2 × 2-bar phrases.
Bars 5–9   This time a five-bar sentence (immediately avoiding any predictable pattern). The extra bar (bar 8 really) is created by repeating bar 7 in sequence a third higher.
Bars 10–13   2 × two-bar phrases, both passing through new keys (G minor 10–11, by means of the F# leading note, and B flat major at 12–13). This is a straightforward example of sequential modulation – the changing of keys by means of a simple repetition at a different pitch.

Bars 14–21   An eight-bar sentence. The interrupted cadence (chords V–VI in bars 16–17) demands an extension; notice how the last few bars make use of the very opening phrase. Bars 15 and 16 are a variant of bars 2–4; 18 = bar 1 (rearranged) and 19 = 2 and 3 in quicker notes (which is called diminution).

This may all sound rather complicated and rather pompous for a simple tune in F! However, it all serves to show how composers think and work – although many do all this automatically, of course. You should try to create melodies in a similar way. (See also Chapter 15: (2) Baroque Period – Things to Do No. 1) Don't over-do the use of sequences, it can itself be very predictable. The great skill is in making a sculpted composition sound as if it has been conceived spontaneously.

THEME AND VARIATIONS

This is a common and popular form with composers of all periods and you may enjoy working with this yourself, in any style whatsoever. The simplest way of using this structure is for a theme (either original, or openly 'borrowed' from another composer) to be followed by several variations. There is never a set number of these, it is left to the discretion of the composer. Variations are different presentations of the rhythmic, harmonic and melodic structure of that theme.

A good example of early Variation form is the so-called 'Harmonious Blacksmith' for harpsichord by Handel, or more properly, 'Air and Variations in E major'. The theme is stated simply, in a singing style (cantabile) (Fig. 14.18).

Fig. 14.18 Theme

The first variation (Fig. 14.19) has more movement, but barely disguises the theme.

Fig. 14.19 Variation I

Whereas in the second variation (Fig. 14.20) the melody is (almost) absent but the chords remain unchanged:

Fig. 14.20 Variation II

The third variation (Fig. 14.21) retains the chordal framework and presents a flowing top line. Notice the very unusual time signature.

Fig. 14.21 Variation III

Variation four (Fig. 14.22) uses the triplet figure (the running quavers) from the previous variation, but employs them here as a bass part.

Fig. 14.22 Variation IV

Finally, to make a flamboyant ending, Handel writes rapidly moving ascending and descending scales above the original chords for Variation Five (Fig. 14.23).

Fig. 14.23 Variation V

In later periods the theme was merely a starting point for varying mood pictures, albeit loosely linked to the theme in some way to give a feeling of unity. You may already know Andrew Lloyd Webber's 'Variations'. This is based on a popular Paganini violin tune in A minor; several composers, including Rachmaninov ('Rhapsody on a Theme of Paganini') have used the same theme for their variations. Try to get to know them, listening carefully all the time for references to the original melody. Note which variations you enjoyed the most. Were they the ones which contained the theme clearly, or the ones with clever changes of harmony or rhythm? You will find this sort of analysis automatic with practice, and you will probably enjoy your listening all the more for knowing what to listen out for.

Generally speaking, composers use the following devices to create their variations:

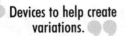 **Devices to help create variations.**

a) Changing speed or time.
b) Varying the rhythm.
c) Transferring the theme (or fragments of it) to another line.
d) Decorating the melody.
e) Changing key.
f) Using counterpoint, imitation or fugue.
g) Isolating a fragment from the Theme and developing it into something new.

These are only a few of the many ways that variations can grow from the original theme. You can probably think of several more. They can be combined, of course, so that for example, a) + b) + d) + f) + g) might all be part of one variation – the possibilities are endless. The whole concept is one of **development**, that vital ingredient of all serious composition.

RONDO FORM

A rondo is a structure which alternates a recurring theme (which we shall call A) with contrasting episodes (B and C etc). The number of episodes can vary, but a typical eighteenth century Rondo might run as follows:

A B A C A + coda   or   A B A C A D A + coda

You can see how the A section keeps on 'coming round' as its name implies. With Haydn and Mozart a Rondo was often found as the final movement of a Sonata or Concerto, and the theme was usually rather high-spirited and tuneful. You will probably know the rondo theme from the last movement (finale) of Mozart's 'Eine Kleine Nachtmusik' (Fig. 14.24).

Fig. 14.24

Could you write a rondo? It need not be too complicated; make a strong A theme as it has to be heard several times, and give variety by putting your episodes into a different key.

BINARY FORM

As its name suggests, this form is built in two sections, both of which are usually repeated:

Section A :||: Section B :||

Section B is sometimes longer than section A, and there is often a modulation to a new key towards the ending of section A. The original key will return before the end of the piece.

TERNARY FORM

This is built up in three sections: A   B   A

The middle section provides a contrast, and the composer may decide to vary the second A section, but it will be based on the same music.

Some melodies are constructed in a simple ternary form, such as the tune 'All Through the Night' (Fig. 14.25).

Fig. 14.25 'All through the Night' – trad. Welsh tune

GROUND BASS

Sometimes also called Passacaglia, this is where a musical figure (the *ground*) is repeated many times over in the bass part while *harmony* and *melody* are added above. Purcell was a notable exponent of this structural device; his most famous example is 'Dido's Lament' from his opera 'Dido and Aeneas'. An extract is given in Fig. 14.26.

Fig. 14.26

In the extract, the bass part appears twice but the whole song contains nine consecutive statements of it. (Notice the figured bass – a musical shorthand for the harpsichordist.)

THE SUITE

A suite is a collection of dance movements. It was popular from the sixteenth to the eighteenth centuries, although the word is still used occasionally today by composers. Bach is regarded as one of the greatest composers of Suites. The most common movements with most early composers were the Allemande, Courante, Sarabande and Gigue. Between these last two movements were sometimes added a variety of other dances, such as a Gavotte or Polonaise, Bourrée etc. Most of these dance movements were in Binary form, and the same key was almost always used for each movement, with modulation within movements to provide variety.

You might consider writing a collection of short contrasted pieces, which you could group together as a suite. Any group of instruments will do, or it may be composed for just keyboard. Individual movements you might cast in Binary or Ternary Form, or you may like to try a set of short variations.

SONATA FORM

Sonata form is explained in Glossary 2 (Musical Words) and is illustrated in Chapter 15: (3) The Classical Period – Things to Do, No. 3. This is a most important musical form and you should try to understand it thoroughly, and apply this understanding by listening very carefully to symphonic movements that use Sonata Form. Try to note when musical subjects within the structure reappear – in the *Development* and *Recapitulation*.

---

11 ⟩ GENERAL SIGNS AND SYMBOLS

❝❝ Use appropriate markings in your compositions ❞❞

Most of the common Italian terms that you are likely to encounter are included in Glossary 2 at the end of this book. It still seems to be the custom to use Italian (although some composers prefer to use their native language). You should try to use appropriate markings in your compositions, so that you are communicating your intentions as clearly as possible in your notation. It is also important that you understand thoroughly the meanings of such words and terms when performing your solo and ensemble pieces.

Besides Italian, there are many signs that are useful in music. Some of the following you will probably know and use already, but it is a useful list for reference.

♩ = 120	A metronome marking, for measuring the speed of a piece. If ♩ = 60 represents one beat per second, then 120 must be two beats per second, and so on. Maelzel was the inventor of this clockwork device in the early nineteenth century. If you use a metronome for checking the suggested speed of your performance pieces, make sure that you read it correctly! Is it ♩ = 120 or ♪ = 120?
(crescendo hairpin)	A crescendo marking; get louder.
(diminuendo hairpin)	A diminuendo marking; get softer.
Op. 66	Opus 66 – the sixty-sixth work in a composer's catalogue of compositions.
𝄐	Pause. (Written over a note: 𝄐) Prolong the note at your discretion.
G.P.	General Pause. All performers must stop playing until indicated otherwise.
‖: :‖	Repeat marks. Play the passage between the dots twice.
Ped. (or 𝄰)	Use the right (sustaining) pedal on a piano.
V	Up bow for string players.
⊓	Down bow for string players.
(notated note)	Repeat this written note as eight semiquavers:
= *(notated passage)*	(More musical shorthand.)
(notated bar with repeat sign)	⁒ = repeat the previous bar.
(notated passage with 8ve / loco)	Play an octave higher. The word 'loco' indicates a return to the ordinary pitch.

A double bar-line. Used to indicate the end of a piece or section. Also used when time signatures are changed e.g.:  etc.

Staccato. Short, detached notes.

Staccatissimo. Very short notes.

Mezzo staccato. Half staccato, with a slight accent.

sf or fz

Sforzando. A short, forcefully accented note ( ).

gliss. or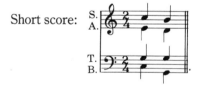

Slide quickly from the lowest to the highest written notes. (For harp, trombone, piano etc.)

A slur. Play the notes smoothly and connected.

A tie. When two identical notes are joined, hold the second for its value without actually playing it.

Alto   Tenor
clef   clef

Alto and Tenor clefs – sometimes known as C clefs. The alto clef is used by the viola while the trombone, cello and bassoon occasionally use the tenor clef. The line indicated by the clef is middle C, so:

C   C   C   C

are all the same pitch.

S.A.T.B.

Choral music can be written out in two ways. The short score uses two staves, so that sopranos and altos share a stave, and the same with tenors and basses:

Short score:

(Notice how the usual way of drawing stems on notes has to be changed so that they fit clearly on the music.)
The more normal way is to use full score, that is, four staves:

(Notice how the tenor voices use the treble clef. They sound an octave lower.)

12 > GUITAR CHORDS

Some of you may wish to teach yourself guitar so that you can join in the Ensembles. Fig. 14.27 gives you some of the common chords that you are likely to encounter. The small 'm' indicates that it is a minor chord; so that Em = E minor chord. The dots represent a finger position on the strings, and the cross indicates that you should not play on that string.

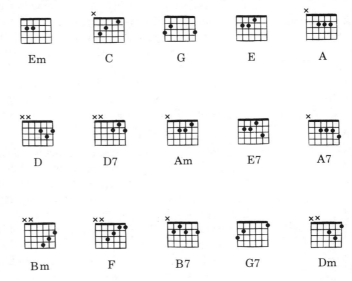

Fig. 14.27

CHORD SEQUENCES TO PRACTISE

Beginners could try these as useful practice. More advanced players may find them helpful as chord progressions for a possible composition or improvisation:

1) C Am Em D G7 C

2) G D Am Em C F D7 G

3) D C F G Am Em A7 D

13 > TRANSPOSING INSTRUMENTS

If you have used an orchestral score when studying your set work you may have wondered why some instrumental parts have different key signatures. Here (Fig. 14.28 overleaf) is how Elgar sets out the instruments for the opening of his Symphony No.1 in A♭ major (1908).

You will notice that the majority of instruments, whether treble or bass, use the 'correct' key signature of four flats for A♭ major. These instruments are said to be in Concert Pitch. The remainder are called transposing instruments; in other words, the notes seen and played sound at a different pitch. For example, a clarinet in B♭ reading 🎼 will actually sound the note 🎼 .

The part is written one whole tone higher than it actually sounds.

Why is this the case? Surely it would be easier for all concerned if they were all the same? It stems from the early days of woodwind instruments when it was virtually impossible for clarinettists to play music with many sharps and flats. To make things easier for them, instrument makers produced clarinets in different sizes, which transposed into different keys. There are three types of clarinet in use today, the orchestral B♭ and A clarinets, and the smaller E♭ clarinet which is used mainly in military bands and occasionally in the orchestra.

You will read in Chapter 5, how brass players, in the days before valves had been invented, had to use the natural notes (harmonics) on their brass tubing. If they wished to change key, they had to insert 'crooks' of different lengths to raise or lower the overall pitch of their instrument. They always read in the key of C; if the music was in the key of D, they inserted a D crook. This is why brass parts of that time are based on a limited series of notes; players could not easily change crooks until the end of a movement. Today we have the fully-chromatic valved trumpet, but it is still a transposing instrument as it is usually built in B♭.

> A golden rule for transposing instruments.

The golden rule with transposing instruments is that **written C sounds the letter name of the instrument** and you can then adjust all other notes accordingly.

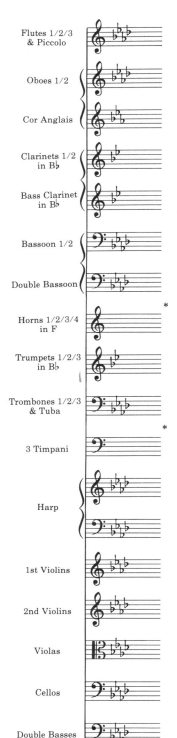

So for the A clarinet, for example, written C sounds the A a minor third below: sounds

This is certainly confusing for the young musician confronted with this concept for the first time, but is something that experienced musicians get used to. Clarinet players in an orchestra usually take their A clarinets with them as well as their normal B♭s, so that they can swap over before a piece with awkward fingering. Trumpeters, however, are quite used to transposing at sight – so that they might well be using a B♭ instrument in a piece in E major and have to put the music up into F# major (a tone higher, and now into six sharps!). It is a skill which players of transposing instruments acquire with practice.

Here is a list of the main transposing instruments:

Piccolo:	sounds an octave higher than actually written
Clarinet in B♭:	written a tone higher than it sounds
Clarinet in A:	written a minor 3rd higher than it sounds
Bass Clarinet in B♭:	written a major 9th higher than it sounds
Cor Anglais in F:	written a perfect 5th higher than it sounds
Alto sax in E♭:	written a major 6th higher than it sounds
Tenor sax in B♭:	written a major 9th higher than it sounds
Horn in F:	written a perfect 5th higher than it sounds
Trumpet in B♭:	written a tone higher than it sounds
Double bass:	written an octave higher than it sounds

PRACTICE QUESTIONS

These are not examination questions as such. They are given so that you can test yourself once you have studied this theory chapter. Remember that you will probably apply this knowledge with a real piece of music in any section of the exam. If you find any part of this difficult, be sure to ask your teacher to help you sort it out.

1 Key signatures

Fig. 14.29

a) Name the major key that uses this key signature.
b) Name the minor key that uses this key signature.
c) Where would you write the same key signature into the bass clef?
d) What major key has (i) 4 flats; (ii) 3 sharps; (iii) 2 flats; (iv) 3 flats?
e) What minor key has (i) 3 flats; (ii) 2 flats; (iii) 3 sharps; (iv) 4 flats?
f) What is the relative minor scale of: (i) E flat major; (ii) F major; (iii) D major?

2

Fig. 14.30

a) How fast should this tune be played?
b) How many beats in a bar?
c) What type of rests are used in bars 3 and 4?
d) What key is the piece in? (**Remember**: key signature first, then look for any accidentals)
e) Explain how the ornaments in bars 1 and 4 are to be played.
f) What intervals are used between the two notes marked at 1, 2, and 3?

* It is the custom not to use key signature with horns and timpani.

Fig. 14.28

3

Fig. 14.31

a) Name two instruments capable of playing this music.
b) What key is it in? How do you know?
c) How fast would it go?
d) How many beats in a bar here?

4

Fig. 14.32

a) What instrument is likely to play this?
b) How fast should it go?
c) Explain 'con sord'.
d) Describe the interval formed between the lowest and the highest notes of this short tune.
e) What major key is it in? How do you know it is not a minor key?
f) Using some manuscript paper, write it out in the treble clef at the same pitch.

5

Fig. 14.33

a) Copy this out on to some manuscript paper four times.
   Complete the melody using notes from:
   i) the pentatonic scale based on C,
   ii) C major,
   iii) A minor,
   iv) the whole tone scale based on C.
   Make sure that you use the given 6/8 time correctly, and that you end all four examples on the appropriate tonic.

6 Look at Fig. 14.34 and then complete it with the correct rests.

Fig. 14.34

7 Put in the correct time signatures in Fig. 14.35.

Fig. 14.35

8 Fig. 14.36 gives some further examples of intervals for you to describe. (Be careful to note changes of clef.)

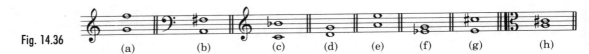

Fig. 14.36

9 Transpose the melody in Fig. 14.37 so that it would be suitable for: i) B♭ clarinet; ii) Horn in F; iii) B♭ trumpet; iv) Cor anglais; v) Clarinet in A; vi) Alto sax in E♭

Fig. 14.37

ANSWERS

1 a) D major

b) B minor

c)

Fig. 14.38

d) i) A♭ ii) A iii) B♭ iv) E♭

e) i) C minor ii) G minor iii) F# minor iv) F minor

f) i) C minor ii) D minor iii) B minor

2 a) ♩ = 96 crotchets per minute. Use a metronome to check different speeds.

b) 𝐂 = 4 ♩ beats in a bar.

c) ꞇ = a quaver (½ beat) rest.

𝄽 = a crotchet (1 beat) rest.

d) A minor (because of the G#).

e) The turn would be played as four semiquavers:

The inverted mordent is played like this:

f) 1) Perfect 5th 2) minor 6th 3) minor 3rd

3 a) Piano or harp, because of the wide range of notes requiring bass and treble clef.

b) E minor, because of the accidental D#.

c) ♩. = 120. 2 dotted crotchet beats per second.

d) 2 dotted crotchet beats in a bar.

4 a) The viola because it is the only instrument to use the alto clef.

b) ♩ = 84. Use a metronome to check the speed.

c) Use a mute. (in full: con sordino)

d) B♭ – F = a perfect 5th.

e) B♭ major. There is no F# – the leading note for the relative key of G minor.

f)

con sord.

Fig. 14.39

5 The bar given was designed to contain notes common to the four scales. Obviously, there are many ways of completing a melody, but remember the following:

i) Pentatonic: use only C D E G A, ending on C;

ii) C major: use C D E F G A B C, ending on C;

iii) A minor : use A B C D E F G# A, ending on A;

iv) Whole tone scale: use C D E F# G# A#, ending on C. This version will sound the most unusual with only four bars in the given exercise, but try experimenting with the scale. You may like to extend this one.

6

Fig. 14.40

7 1) 6   2) 2   3) 4   4) 9
     8   4   4   8

8 a) Minor 7th   b) Major 6th   c) Minor 7th
   d) Perfect 4th   e) Perfect 5th   f) Major 3rd
   g) Major 6th   h) Major 3rd.

9 To transpose a line of music higher or lower you must change the key signature as well. For example, if a melody in C major needs to be raised a tone into D major, you should first write in the appropriate key signature of two sharps and proceed to raise each note of the tune by one tone. Any accidentals will need to be altered so that the line remains parallel to the original. Don't assume that accidentals remain the same: e.g. B♭ raised a tone becomes C natural and C♯ lowered a tone becomes B natural.

   i) This needs to go up one whole tone, so our original key of G major now becomes A major with 3 sharps (Fig. 14.41).

Fig. 14.41

   ii) This needs to be written up a perfect fifth into the key of D major (see Fig. 14.42).

Fig. 14.42

   iii) the same as i)
   iv) the same as ii)
   v) This must be transposed up a minor third because that is the interval between A and C. B♭ major with 2 flats is a minor third above the original G major (see Fig. 14.43).

Fig. 14.43

   vi) Alto saxophones are written a major 6th higher than they sound, as that is the interval between E♭ and C. E major with 4 sharps is the key a major 6th above the original G major (Fig. 14.44).

Fig. 14.44

Answers to the QUICK TEST intervals given on page 139 earlier in this chapter:
a) Perfect 5th   b) Minor 7th   c) Minor 6th
d) Augmented 4th   e) Major 3rd   f) Minor 3rd
g) Major 6th   h) Major 6th   i) Minor 3rd
j) Major 7th.

REVIEW SHEET

✎ Do you know all your key signatures? Test yourself with these, and write them into the correct place on the stave:

(a) A major has _____ sharps   (b) D major has _____ sharps

(c) F major has _____   (d) A minor has _____

(e) E minor has _____   (f) G major has _____

(g) B flat major has _____   (h) G minor has _____

(a) (b) (c) (d) (e) (f) (g)   (a) (b) (c) (d) (e) (f) (g)

✎ For those of you doing arrangements which use orchestral instruments, have you learnt all your transpositions?

(a) The french horn is written _____ than it sounds.

(b) The B flat clarinet sounds _____ than it is written.

(c) The alto saxophone is written _____ than it sounds.

(d) The double bass is written _____ than it sounds.

✎ Are you confident with all the forms and structures?

(a) Rondo Form might run as follows: A + _____

(b) Binary Form is simply _____

(c) A + B + A is called _____ Form.

✎ Remember your knowledge of intervals is only really useful if you can *hear* them. Using a keyboard, test yourself with the more common intervals, such as major 3rd, major 6th, octave, minor 3rd, perfect 4th, perfect 5th etc. (Don't forget to count the bottom note as *one* when you count up to the top note.)

✎ Similarly with cadences. Play the cadences over that are given in section 8 of chapter 14 until you are really familiar with the sound. Remember, when you are asked to recognise a cadence, that you should decide whether it is a final-sounding effect (perfect, plagal) or unfinished (imperfect, interrupted) before you reach your final answer.

✎ Are you sure of all your scales?

(a) the melodic minor scale raises the _____ and _____ on the way up, and lowers the same notes on the way down.

(b) the harmonic minor scale has a raised _____ in addition to its key signature.

✎ Have you learnt all your rests?

(a) this is a crotchet rest _____ and this is a quaver rest _____ .

(b) 7̄ is a _____ rest and ═══════ is a minim rest.

✎ Are you sure of the names of the Suite? _____ and _____ and _____ and _____ are the more common dances. They were usually composed in _____ Form.

✎ Sonata Form is the most complex of the normal musical structures. The three main sections are called Exposition, _____ and _____. In the Exposition, the first and second _____ are linked by the _____ Passage. The first subject is in the tonic key, whereas the second subject is usually in the _____ key.

HISTORY OF MUSIC: 1550 TO THE PRESENT DAY

1550–1600

**1600–1750
THE BAROQUE PERIOD**

**1750–1830
THE CLASSICAL PERIOD**

**1830–1900
THE ROMANTIC PERIOD**

**1900 ONWARDS:
THE MODERN PERIOD**

JAZZ

**THE WORLD OF POPULAR
MUSIC**

GETTING STARTED

This brief outline of the history of music starts in 1550. This is a date of convenience really, for by that time composers were writing music that is still widely heard today, and available in recorded form. Of course, there was a great deal of music before 1550 but notation was primitive, and not all musicians were able to write their compositions down. You may like to listen to some earlier music, for more and more is becoming recorded, but examination syllabuses rarely go much before our chosen date.

ESSENTIAL PRINCIPLES

1 > 1550 – 1600

In the sixteenth century music was considered to be a highly important art. After the uncertainty of the so-called Dark Ages there was a rediscovery of culture and learning that had not been seen for many centuries. During this new period of Renaissance there was a burst of creativity in all the arts, and the music of this time attained a refined beauty and polish that make it a peak of artistic achievement of the last thousand years.

If you are only used to hearing music from later times, you may at first find sixteenth century music hard to understand. It tends to be *contrapuntal* and full of *imitation*; it was constructed with the old *modes*, for our more recent system of major and minor scales was as yet undeveloped.

Listen to some sacred (religious) music by *Palestrina* or *Byrd*.

Palestrina was a master of contrapuntal composition, composing *masses*, *motets* and *magnificats*. He was chosen as a 'model' composer by the Council of Trent (1545–63), a committee convened by the Catholic Church to improve the state of church music. The Council considered that music was becoming too ornate and the words unintelligible as the voices were too interwoven; it was too worldly, as popular songs were often used as a 'theme' running through these interweaving parts. Only music of pure clarity was allowed; 'pure' implying that it was free of secular connections.

Byrd was a founder of the English school of *madrigal* writers, and also composed pieces for the *virginals*, but his church music perhaps represents his finest work. Try one of his three masses for unaccompanied voices, and notice how the vocal lines all merge beautifully with one another, and how the Latin words appear all mixed up together – but to glorious effect.

Besides church music, music in the home began to flourish. Madrigals by *Morley*, *Weelkes* and *Lassus* (to name but three) were sung in the wealthier homes, and *consorts* of instruments, such as recorders and viols had contrapuntal music written for them, as well as playing madrigals as instrumental pieces. Composers such as *Dowland* were beginning to write *art songs* with *lute* accompaniment. Keyboard instruments, such as the *virginals* and *spinet* became increasingly popular, and had attractive pieces by *Byrd*, *Gibbons*, and *Bull* composed for them.

Try to hear some early music – don't just read about it!

THINGS TO DO

1 Listen to some sixteenth century religious music by Palestrina or Byrd – it doesn't really matter which piece you choose:
  a) Is the tempo (speed) of the piece fast, moderately fast or slow? Does this tempo vary throughout the piece?
  b) Can you understand the words? Are they sung in English, Italian or Latin? Find out what the words mean.

2 Listen to any madrigal from this period (preferably in English so that you can understand the words):
  a) What is the mood of the madrigal? Is it bright and cheerful, relaxed or melancholy?
  b) Is it about love? How does the composer express the words?

3 You may like to join a group of singers and try some madrigals. Some of the simpler ones can be performed with one singer to a line or part.

'Since singing is so good a thing,
I wish all men would learn to sing.'

(Byrd)

Try the simple *part-song* 'Farewell, dear love' with a few friends. The music and words are in Fig. 15.1. It is for SATB, and though less contrapuntal than many of its contemporary English and Italian madrigals, it provides a good, simple example of the madrigal idiom.

The second verse is printed below.

2 Farewell, farewell! since this I find is true;   Shall I bid her go? What and if I do?
  I will not spend more time in wooing you,   Shall I bid her go, and spare not?
    But I will seek elsewhere   O, no no no no no, I dare not!
  If I may find her there.

Farewell, dear love

ROBERT JONES (1600)

Fig. 15.1 'Farewell, Dear Love' – Robert Jones (1600)

Note that the second verse uses exactly the same music. This is known as *strophic form*. Do you like the final chord? The B natural in the tenor part makes it a (brighter) major chord – this is called a *Tierce de Picardie*, or Picardy Third.

4   Extract the chords from the first line of the printed choral piece 'Farewell, dear love'   Gm D B♭ F Dm Gm C D.   Now use them as the harmonic basis for your own song in G minor. You need not change chords as quickly as Robert Jones, the original composer. For example, you could rearrange them like this:

$$\frac{4}{4} \text{Gm} \diagup \diagup \diagup \mid \text{D} \diagup \diagup \diagup \mid \text{B♭} \diagup \diagup \diagup \mid \text{F} \diagup \diagup \text{Dm} \mid \text{Gm} \diagup \text{C} \diagup \mid \text{D} \diagup \diagup \diagup \; :\parallel$$

and then invent some new lyrics in a more modern style. You could soon have the basis of an attractive song – all grown from another, nearly four hundred years old!

5   Alternatively, use the Jones chord scheme as a recurring ostinato for an improvisation. Use spread arpeggios over the chords to maintain a sense of movement. You will need to finish with the tonic chord of G minor. Try an improvisation (i) exploring a feeling of sorrow, or (ii) entitled 'Farewell' – you may like to use these chords as the basis for a second section: F B♭ F Dm Gm D – G (major or minor).

6   Read up about the instruments of this period, and listen to further examples of consort music. Can you tell the difference between the sound of viols and the modern string family? Can you differentiate the various recorders? How does a lute differ from a Spanish guitar? Try to see inside a harpsichord and examine how the mechanism differs from a piano. When you listen to this early music, a live performance will be the most helpful as you can see everything that goes on, such as the frequent tuning of lutes and theorbos, for example. Failing this, choose the ensembles or choirs that specialise in the period. Here are some examples:

- **Vocal:**
  The Clerkes of Oxenford, director David Wulstan
  The Hilliard Ensemble
  Pro Cantione Antiqua
  The Sixteen (choir and orchestra) director Harry Christophers
  Monteverdi Choir (and orchestra) director John Eliot Gardiner

- **Instrumental:**
  Consort of Musicke, director Anthony Rooley
  Jaye Consort of Viols
  Musica Antiqua Koln (Cologne), director Reinhard Goebel
  The New London Consort, director Philip Pickett
  The Parley of Instruments, co-directors Peter Holman and Mark Caudle
  Taverner Consort and Players (also with voices) director Andrew Parrott
  Trevor Pinnock – solo harpsichord
  The English Concert, director Trevor Pinnock.

7   For those who enjoy the music of this period and would like to find out more, try to find out about the following:
(a) Broken Consort;   (b) the meaning of the word 'Renaissance';   (3) Fitzwilliam Virginal Book;   (d) Viola da gamba;   (e) Monteverdi (try the opening of his 'Vespers' 1610).

8   Obtain a copy of Byrd's motet 'Ave Verum Corpus', (which was set by NISEAC in 1991), and try to hear a performance of it. You probably think all composers have the freedom to write whatever music they wish, but William Byrd was a recusant; a Roman Catholic living in a Protestant land. It was considered unseemly to write music for both religious factions, although Byrd suffered no real persecution for writing Latin music for the Catholic church, and he was permitted to retain his joint position with Thomas Tallis as organist of the Chapel Royal.
    The *motet* uses the Aeolian mode (A B C D E F G A – a sort of A minor without the G sharp). It starts in a serious style, moving *homophonically* (all parts moving more or less together) to begin with, but some imitation is used on the words 'in cruce pro homine'. There is a marvellous poignancy on the words 'O dulcis, O pie', notice how there seems to be a conflict between C sharps and C naturals which all adds to the expressive effect. Remember that any phrasing, dynamics or bar lines are the work of a twentieth century editor as Elizabethan composers did not include them. Some

editors place their barlines according to the stress of the text, and this sometimes results in bars of irregular length. These barlines should not be thought of, however, as implying accented first beats. One does not need to understand Latin, or be a religious person to be moved by this sort of music. Allow yourself to enjoy it!

PRACTICE QUESTIONS WITH ANSWERS

Question 1

Which is the most important voice part in this motet?

Answer 1

None. Composers of this period treated the voice parts equally. Often several melodies were combined and this style of writing is called *polyphonic*, meaning 'many sounds'.

Question 2

The motet ends with a chord made up of A C# and E. What do we call it when we end a minor piece with a major chord?

Answer 2

A Tierce de Picardie or Picardy Third. Do you find this expressive, or would you rather the piece ended in its original key?

Question 3

How does Byrd treat the words 'miserere mei' (have mercy upon me) just before the repeat?

Answer 3

He treats them imitatively. The altos and tenors state the figure initially, while the others rest, then the order of voices which follows is Bass – Soprano – Alto – Tenor – Alto – Soprano – Bass – Tenor: nine times may look monotonous, but the entries are varied in pitch, and not set out predictably. When sung beautifully, this is a very moving section of music, continually unfolding and full of feeling.

9   Get to know Thomas Weelkes' madrigal 'As Vesta was from Latmos Hill Descending'. (This was also set by NISEAC in 1991.) This is written for S.S.A.T.T.B. (a six-part choir). It is one of the set entitled 'The Triumphs of Oriana', all of which end in a similar way praising the fictional Oriana, supposedly Queen Elizabeth I, who was then deceased, although some scholars suggest it was Anne of Denmark who might have been crowned Queen of England: 'Then sang the Shepherds and Nymphs of Diana: Long live fair Oriana'.

The madrigal is built primarily in the mixolydian mode (which is the same as G A B C D E F G – that is no F# as in G major). Don't be put off (when listening) by the many repetitions of the words – it is great fun to sing when the parts all seem to chase each other. The words are typical of the period: the nymphs and shepherds of the goddess Diana join those of Oriana in singing the praises of the young queen.

PRACTICE QUESTIONS WITH ANSWERS

Question 1

Can you spot the word painting in this madrigal?

Answer 1

Words like 'descending' and 'ascending' are composed with quavers moving in the appropriate direction. The vocal parts are used in appropriate groups for the words 'first two by two', 'then three by three', 'together', and finally 'all alone' for first sopranos only. The entry of second tenors and basses is delayed until the arrival of the 'shepherd's swain', which reinforces the sense of masculinity. A swain is Old English for a rustic lover.

Question 2

How does Weelkes use his six-part choir?

Answer 2

The composer does not use his six voice parts all the time. Indeed, the first twenty-two bars are for four parts alone. Using more voice parts allows greater variety in the compositional texture. The full choir is used to good homophonic effect with 'Then sang the Shepherds and Nymphs of Diana' in contrast to the preceding polyphonic writing.

Madrigals were through-composed; it was quite usual for the first line of the words to be repeated several times, often with imitative entries before using a different imitative figure for the second line and so on. Composers rarely returned to the opening theme, and this may sound strange to us at first.

2 > 1600–1750 THE BAROQUE PERIOD

The word 'Baroque' is borrowed from architecture, where it suggests the elaborate twisting of the sometimes excessively decorated buildings of that time. Similarly, Baroque music is often full of ornaments and decorations.

This was a time of great change in music. By about the end of the seventeenth century the outdated modes had been replaced by our familiar major and minor scales, and harmony, as we know it, had started to develop. The viols became obsolete, and the more versatile violin family took their place. The great violin makers, *Stradivarius*, *Amati* and *Guarneri* flourished at this time.

Music was written to order in those days and composers all worked for a patron. This might be the church, where they were employed to provide all the music for church services; or a wealthy nobleman, where they were paid to entertain him and his guests at important social functions. King Louis XIV of France, for example, employed the composer *Lully* as his court composer.

There was a distinct move away from the sort of vocal music that Palestrina and Byrd had written in earlier times. Gradually, the melodic interest moved up to the top vocal line, and there was an effort to make the words become more distinct in themselves, and to write music which illustrated their meaning more dramatically.

The composer *Giovanni Gabrieli* and his uncle *Andrea Gabrieli* were, in their time, both organists at St Mark's in Venice. The splendid acoustics of this spacious building were exploited by these composers when they divided up their vocal and instrumental forces to form *antiphonal* effects. (This had a direct influence on the development of the later concerto principle, where forces were separated, instead of having one body of sound. This started with the concerto grosso and moved to the solo concerto in the late Baroque and Classical eras. This also had major implications for the concept of drama in music, in both vocal and instrumental spheres.)

A new invention, to be known as *opera*, started in Florence about the year 1600. The first operas were very different from the large-scale spectacles of modern times. They were largely recitative, with some arias and choruses. Although first produced in private homes, the first public opera house opened in Venice in 1637. The first audiences came to prefer the arias, for these were expressive and often showy pieces; people were drawn by a particular performer rather than the plot or even the music itself. A basso continuo was played throughout the opera by a harpsichord player, often supported by a cello. To save the composer from writing out every note, the harpsichordist would read from a figured bass.

Monteverdi is regarded as the first great composer of opera. He is accredited as the first composer to use *tremolando* on the violin as a dramatic effect, and he used a variety of instruments to accompany his operas – not yet the orchestra as we know it today, but certainly the foundation, a mixture of different tone colours, was being laid. Later in the century, *Alessandro Scarlatti* was the chief Italian composer of operas, but they are not often performed today, as they contain many arias in the lengthy *da capo* form and the plots are unacceptable to modern audiences.

The French composer *Couperin* wrote suites for the *harpsichord*, which gradually superseded the virginals and spinet. These suites contained stylised dances, often in binary or rondo form. Like *Corelli*, the English composer *Purcell* wrote trio-sonatas for two violins and the obligatory continuo (cello and harpsichord). Besides much church music, keyboard pieces and music for plays, he wrote only a single opera, 'Dido and

Aeneas', as opera took longer to establish as a form of entertainment in England than on the continent.

The two great composers of the later Baroque period were undoubtedly *Bach* and *Handel*, both born in 1685 in Germany. You should familiarise yourself with as much of their music as you can – it is often strong and strident music, and if you are able to play or sing Bach or Handel you will realise how beautiful and enjoyable it all is. Notice how the Baroque principle of 'one movement, one mood' applies here, it is certainly expressive and full of feeling, but far less changeable than the music of, say, a hundred years later.

BACH

Coming from a large extended musical family, Bach lived and worked all his life as organist and kappelmeister in a narrow area of Germany. A devoted family man (he was the father of twenty children!), he combined a strong and simple religious faith with a no-nonsense approach to life. After several organist posts he settled in Leipzig in 1723 as Cantor (head of music) at St Thomas' Church, where he taught and trained the choirboys, and provided music for the church services. His vast output includes the six Brandenburg concertos, four orchestral suites, the forty-eight Preludes and Fugues for keyboard, the Mass in B minor, the 'St Matthew' and the 'St John' Passions, the Christmas Oratorio, various concertos and sonatas, and over 200 church cantatas. His organ music continues to form the basis of the organist's repertoire.

HANDEL

Unlike Bach, Handel was a well-travelled, and worldly-wise man, but most of the pieces for which he is remembered today were composed in England. He studied in Italy, mastering the art of writing operas, before settling in England in 1712 as the foremost composer of Italian operas of that period. However, Handel was forced to turn his attention to the composition of oratorios when the public demand for Italian opera declined. His most famous example of this form is the ever-popular 'Messiah', composed in just three weeks, and first performed in 1742. Other examples of this genre include 'Samson', 'Israel in Egypt', 'Saul' and 'Judas Maccabaeus'. Everyone knows the 'Water Music' and the 'Royal Fireworks Music', but you should try to hear some of Handel's *concerti grossi* and organ concertos. Although he was the composer of many fine fugues, Handel's music tends to be rather less contrapuntal than Bach's, perhaps reflecting his obvious interest in the art of writing operatic melody, where the attention is focused on the top melodic line.

SCARLATTI

Yet another composer was born in the same year as Bach and Handel – Domenico Scarlatti, the son of Alessandro. A travelling keyboard virtuoso who furthered the development of keyboard music, he is considered to be the greatest of harpsichord composers, producing more than 500 one-movement sonatas in binary form, paving the way for the piano sonatas of the Classical period.

THINGS TO DO

1 The melody in Fig. 15.2 is the main theme to the first movement of Bach's third Brandenburg Concerto. Play it several times. How many times does this rhythmic figure appear in the extract: ♪♪ ♪♪♪ ? And this one ♪♪♪♪ ? Why does C sharp appear in the second and third bars? (It denotes a brief modulation (key-change) to D major, the dominant). Now listen to a recording of the whole movement, noting how often the two figures are used. Notice that the mood does not change ('one movement, one mood').

Fig. 15.2

You might like to compose your own melody (or fuller piece) using the minimum amount of musical material. Try to keep your piece flowing as Bach does, and maintain your opening mood. Fig. 15.3 gives you some short figures to get you started:

Fig. 15.3

Listen to other Baroque pieces and note how similar figures are developed. Examples: a) Bach 'Concerto for Two Violins' (third movement). See Fig. 15.4.

Fig. 15.4

b) Handel 'Concerto Grosso' Op.6 No.1 (first movement). See Fig. 15.5.

Fig. 15.5

Again, notice with these two pieces how the mood stays constant once established.

c) Bach – Brandenburg Concerto No 2 in F major (set by SEG in 1994). In the slow movement, the solo instruments (violin, oboe and flute) all take it in turns to develop this figure:

Fig. 15.6

and in the third movement, the high Baroque trumpet joins them in this rhythm:

Fig. 15.7

Try working out a theme of your own with similar rhythms.

2 You should be aware of the main types of Overture prevalent in the Baroque period: the *French Overture* and the *Italian Overture*.

a)   Listen to the Overture to Bach's Suite No. 2 in B minor (see No. 4 later in this section), or the Overture to Handel's oratorio 'Messiah' (which will be especially useful to you if you are following the ULEAC syllabuses 1994/5 where extracts for this work are set – see Chapter 5, analysis 2). These two are examples of the so-called *French Overture*. There are usually two main sections. There is firstly a dignified slow section, characterised by dotted rhythms, often played as double dotted notes (see Fig. 15.8) although rarely written in this way. This is followed by a faster main section which is often in a fugal style (see No. 3 in this section for a better explanation of *Fugue*). Occasionally there is a brief restatement of the slow, dotted music to round off the Overture. The composer Lully, who was court composer to Louis XIV at Versailles, is associated with the early use of the French overture.

Fig. 15.8

b) The *Italian Overture*, alternatively named 'Sinfonia', has three main sections:

I a quick (*allegro*) section, which was often fugal;

II a slow section (*adagio*);

III another quick, dance-like section (*presto*).

The composer Alessandro Scarlatti is credited with the introduction of the Italian Overture, and used it in his many Italian operas. (With much development the Italian Overture led on to the Classical Symphony, as its 'quick – slow – quick' plan became enlarged into separate movements, and the Minuet was introduced as an additional movement. For a good example, try to listen to some of the short symphonies by *Thomas Arne*: No. 2 in F major recorded by Cantilena, conductor Adrian Shepherd, is an excellent one.

The Italian Overture developed into the Classical Symphony.

3   Make yourself familiar with the texture of fugue. Listen to any Bach Fugue for organ to see how it is composed. What exactly is fugue?

A fugue is a contrapuntal piece where the parts (always called voices, even in instrumental works) are highly imitative. It is a texture rather than a form, because no two fugues are alike after the opening (*exposition*).

A strand of melody (the *subject*) is played or sung unaccompanied in the tonic key. It is then imitated by a second voice, but in the dominant key this time (the *answer*). This answer can be 'real' if it imitates exactly, or a 'tonal' answer if it is an imitation with some slight changes. Likewise the third and fourth voices enter, tonic and then dominant. The entry of the voices may be in any order, the composer may choose. Fig. 15.9 is a plan of the start of a four-part fugue.

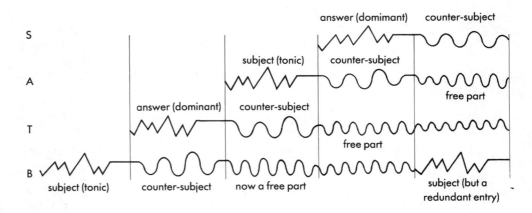

Fig. 15.9 Fugal exposition

Once a voice has stated its subject or answer it continues immediately with another contrapuntal melody, known as the *counter-subject*, if each voice uses it. If not, it is generally known as a *free part*. Sometimes composers begin to state the subject, for example, when the fourth voice has reached its answer, and it then 'dries up'. This is called a *redundant entry*, and it gives the fourth voice the opportunity to state the counter-subject.

Everything so far is part of the fugal exposition, as in sonata form where all the main themes are stated at the outset in the exposition. From this point on the composer is free to develop as he wishes. In the middle section of a fugue the composer may introduce the subject in related keys, usually avoiding the tonic; or he may introduce new ideas, which we call episodes, as a varied contrast to the subject. These episodes are often devised from a fragment of the original subject or counter-subject.

To round off the fugue satisfactorily, the subject will return again in the tonic key. The composer may decide to present it only once, or in several voices. After the last statement is made the coda brings the fugue to its conclusion.

4   Obtain a good recording of Bach's Suite No. 2 in B minor for orchestra, and listen to the whole Suite carefully. It opens with a French Overture, which we used as an example in (2) above, and is followed by a set of shorter, stylised dances. The word *Suite* today implies a set of short pieces, but Bach originally gave his four Suites for Orchestra the name *Ouverture*. He wrote No. 2 in Leipzig towards the end of the 1730s and scored it for flute, strings and harpsichord continuo. All seven items in this Suite are in the tonic key of B minor. Notice how the mood of each dance, once established, does not alter substantially. You may like to familiarise yourself with the whole Suite, but here we shall cover only the Overture, Rondeau, Menuet and Badinerie.

PRACTICE QUESTIONS WITH ANSWERS

Question 1

How does Bach construct his Overture?   (3)

Answer 1

It is a French Overture, and has three sections: a) slow with dotted rhythms in a solemn

> **Always bear in mind the number of marks available for a question.**

mood b) a faster fugal section in four parts and c) a return to the slow section, again with dotted rhythms, which serves as a coda to the Overture.

(**N.B.** It is important to notice that this question is worth only three marks, and so demands a fairly brief answer and you should not spend too long on it. If there were more marks available you should go into more detail, using information from 2 and 3 above. For an excellent analysis of this Overture see *Musical Forms I* by Roy Bennett, published Longman 1987.)

Question 2

Is the Rondeau (the second movement) a typical Rondo? *(8)*

Answer 2

We normally think of a Rondo structure as A + B + A + C + A, where the main theme A is in the tonic key, and the contrasting episodes B and C are thematically different as well as being in keys other than the tonic. In Bach's *Rondeau*, the episodes contain references to the main rondo theme, which is rather unusual (see Fig. 15.10).

Fig. 15.10   opening of A   bars 12-14 of episode B   bars 36-38 of episode C

The contrast in this Rondeau is one of key more than one of melody. Episode B is in E minor, and episode C passes through the keys of A major, D major and F# minor. In answer to the question, therefore, this is a Rondo, but not a Rondo as in the later Classical style where the episodes would be thematically different.

Question 3

What form does Bach use for the Menuet? *(2)*

Answer 3

It is in binary form (A + B).

Question 4

Give a brief account of the Badinerie from Bach's Suite No. 2 in B minor. *(5)*

Answer 4

This lively piece in B minor acts as the finale to the seven movement Suite. The French title implies a frivolous and happy mood. The flute part is difficult – there are a lot of notes and the mood must remain light. The piece is constructed in binary form, where the basic dancing arpeggio figure is used in both sections (Fig. 15.11).

Fig. 15.11

The second half of the movement commences in F# minor (the dominant) and the tonic key returns finally in bar 32. There are only forty written bars, but each section is repeated, making a total of eighty bars in all. This fast-moving piece has something of the atmosphere which Mendelssohn perfected a hundred years later in his music to 'A Midsummer Night's Dream'.

You would enjoy listening to Bach's Suite No. 3 in D for orchestra. Whereas No. 2 is intimate in character, the third is more pompous and extrovert.

5   Listen to Handel's anthem 'Zadok the Priest' (set by WJEC 1994) and study the following questions and model answers. Notice the mark weighting and how the length of answer relates to this.

PRACTICE QUESTIONS WITH ANSWERS

Question 1

Why and when did Handel write 'Zadok the Priest'?   (3)

Answer 1

Handel composed a set of four Coronation Anthems including 'Zadok the Priest' for the coronation of King George II in Westminster Abbey in 1727. It was the tradition for Composers of the English Chapel Royal to provide music for such occasions, and Handel had been appointed to that position in 1723.

Question 2

How does Handel make the opening choral statement so exciting?   (3)

Answer 2

He has a long, steady orchestral build up of twenty-two bars, with constantly repeated upward arpeggios. Starting quietly and gradually building up, this creates a tension which is released with a fortissimo choral entry reinforced by trumpets and timpani. The seven-part homophonic choral writing to the words 'Zadok the Priest and Nathan the prophet anointed Solomon King' bursts out in a magnificent wealth of sound, giving an impression of strength and grandeur.

Question 3

Why did Handel choose the key of D major for this anthem?   (2)

Answer 3

When Baroque composers wanted to include trumpets which were in those days valveless and generally pitched in D, they wrote in that key.

Question 4

What instruments does the composer use in the orchestra for 'Zadok the Priest'?   (2)

Answer 4

The anthem is scored for two oboes, three trumpets, timpani, strings and continuo.

3   1750 – 1830
THE CLASSICAL
PERIOD

The word 'classical' is often loosely used when describing any music that is not pop or jazz but applied strictly, it refers to this short period of musical history which was dominated by Viennese composers. Indeed, Vienna was so important that we sometimes refer to this time as the Viennese period. *Haydn, Mozart, Beethoven* and *Schubert* were all concerned with Vienna, which was then undoubtedly the musical capital of Europe, and remained so for about a hundred years.

Composers were now using less counterpoint in their music; fugues were occasionally written, but far less than in Baroque times. *Sonata form* evolved in this period, and the *symphony* and *concerto* (not to be confused with the concerto grosso which phased out), *string quartet* and *piano sonata* were developed, and the modern *symphony orchestra* was born. Continuo parts were less used, and the *piano* eventually superseded the harpsichord. Schubert composed many art songs (*lieder*) and *Weber* created the first German operas.

This seems a lot to happen in a short time, but things evolved gradually, rather than appearing overnight. Haydn and Mozart perfected the new sonata form in their symphonies, climaxing the work of earlier, overshadowed composers. Classicism in music emphasises **order** and **form**, **gracefulness** and **beauty**, and it avoids the excessive emotion that was to be so apparent in music later, in the next century.

HAYDN

Haydn and Mozart had great respect for each other's work, and were good friends, despite the age difference, but led very different lives. Haydn, from a humble background, sang as a choirboy at St Stephen's Cathedral in Vienna, and spent most of his working life in the service of the wealthy Esterhazy family. There he composed, and even dressed to order, and directed the orchestra and singers. In later life he travelled around Europe, thanks to his employer's generous pension, composing prolifically and enjoying his deserved success. Listen to some of the later symphonies (there is a grand total of 104 altogether), or part of his oratorio 'The Creation'; his string quartets are rewarding to listen to, and everyone enjoys the Trumpet Concerto.

MOZART

In contrast, Mozart was much more of a free spirit. Having been taken all over Europe as a child prodigy by his father, Mozart found it hard to settle down as an adult. As a young man he had worked in the service of the Archbishop of Salzburg, but came to hate the system of patronage, which he equated with slavery. Once he was dismissed, in 1781, he became completely freelance and found it very difficult making ends meet. He wrote an enormous amount of music in his short life (he died at thirty-five), but was not really appreciated until after his death. You should listen to extracts of his operas: 'The Marriage of Figaro' perhaps, or 'Don Giovanni', which are certainly operatic masterpieces. You are sure to enjoy his concertos – for piano, or violin or french horn, and you should get to know the last three symphonies (nos. 39–41), which were composed in less than six weeks in 1788. Remember when you listen to some of his late music, that it was composed at a time of great insecurity for him, and financial struggle, yet it shows tremendous calm and beauty.

BEETHOVEN

❝❝ Try to note any similarities and differences when you listen to these great composers. ❞❞

Beethoven and Schubert were to link the Classical period of music to the *Romantic*. Their early music shows the strong influence of Haydn and Mozart, as you might expect, but they developed their own ideas and styles as they matured, their works increasingly showing their innermost feelings. Beethoven's so-called 'middle period', from about 1800, was a time of developing mastery. His works became more majestic (listen to the 'Eroica' Symphony, No. 3, or the famous fifth symphony and the beautiful E flat major 'Emperor' Piano Concerto). You will recognise his love of nature in the 'Pastoral' Symphony, No. 6. Beethoven had settled in Vienna by this time, leaving his native Bonn for good. Although he was never directly employed by the aristocracy or church, he had many wealthy acquaintances and survived by teaching, giving concerts and dedicating his music to his patrons.

Increasing deafness was a major problem for him, forcing him to give up his piano-playing in public and eventually his conducting, but he continued to compose. His last period of composition, from about 1820, produced some incredibly personal works, demanding enormous concentration of the listener. It includes the last five string quartets, the magnificent Mass in D and his ninth and last symphony, the 'Choral', with its innovation of using voices in the last movement. This was a setting of Schiller's 'Ode to Joy', and expresses a striving for the heights of happiness.

It had been Haydn who added the Minuet as a regular third movement in sonatas and symphonies; Beethoven later substituted the faster, and often lighter Scherzo for the Minuet. He often expanded the coda compared to Haydn and Mozart, and made it an important feature of the composition. Beethoven would deviate from the usual four movements in his sonatas – there are examples in two, three, four and five movements. He would sometimes add a slow introduction, and at other times link movements together. Instruments in his lifetime were continually being improved, so he experimented with re-groupings within the orchestra, which has not radically changed to this day.

SCHUBERT

Schubert was twenty-seven years younger than Beethoven, and lived in the great man's shadow in Vienna all of his short life. He was a very prolific composer – he wrote nine symphonies, keyboard pieces, and much fine chamber music, but he is best remembered for his development of the art song, or *lied*. Six hundred examples exist: many with fine melodies, but they are particularly satisfying because the piano accompaniment was by now regarded as an equal counterpart to the voice, often capturing the intimate atmosphere of the poem being set. Listen to 'The Erl-King', for example, where the piano represents the galloping of the horse, yet at the same time encapsulates the sinister mood of the poem.

WEBER

Weber wrote piano and chamber music, and some orchestral music including three clarinet concertos, but is important for his German operas. 'Der Freischutz', first produced in Berlin, is considered to be the first romantic opera and contains chivalrous and supernatural elements based on an old German legend. 'Euryanthe', first heard in Vienna, had a weaker libretto and is less often heard. Finally, 'Oberon', composed for performance in London (where he died at the early age of forty in 1826) depicts fairyland, based on 'A Midsummer Night's Dream' by Shakespeare.

THINGS TO DO

1 Get hold of a collection of Mozart and Haydn Piano Sonatas – it doesn't matter which ones you choose. Examine the sort of accompaniments that are used by these Classical composers. They are rather fond of the so-called 'Alberti Bass', a recurring broken-chord (*arpeggio*) figure, such as in Fig. 15.12.

Fig. 15.12

Alberti bass does not always need to be in the bass clef, as you can see from the first two examples, it simply provides a flowing part to which a melody was added. Fig. 15.13 shows an example by Mozart.

Mozart: Piano Sonata in C (2nd movt.) K.279

Fig. 15.13 Mozart: Piano Sonata in C (2nd movt) K. 279

2 Perhaps you might compose a keyboard piece (in your own style) using broken chords as part of your accompaniment. Remember, it can become very tedious if you are not careful. Mozart was clever in the way that he subtly changed the shape of the figure, perhaps also passing it from one hand to the other, thus avoiding monotony and dullness. Make sure that you do the same!

3 Listen to the first movement of Mozart's 'Eine Kleine Nachtmusik'. Meaning literally, 'A Little Night Music', this is his most well-known serenade – a set of four movements in relaxed mood for string orchestra.

This first movement is in Sonata Form, and is a useful movement to help you understand the workings of this important Classical structure.

Exposition: Fig. 15.14 is the first subject in G major, a vigorous theme made from arpeggios (broken chords), as was common with Mozart.

Fig. 15.14

The bridge passage, or transition (see Fig. 15.15) leads from the tonic key of G major into the dominant key, (notice the C sharp, which confirms D major).

Fig. 15.15

Fig. 15.16 is the 2nd subject in D major.

Fig. 15.16

Notice the contrast in style and mood this makes with the first subject. A *codetta* (a short rounding-off section) completes this exposition. The repeat of the exposition may be ignored – it is left to the discretion of the conductor. *Development*: At first Mozart uses the strong opening of the first subject, but then develops the second part of the second subject (Fig. 15.17).

Fig. 15.17

As is quite common with Mozart this is a fairly short development section, and soon leads into the *Recapitulation*: First subject as in Fig. 15.14. The bridge passage starts the same as Fig. 15.15, but changes this time (Fig. 15.18) so that the second subject will start in the tonic key of G major, as was the custom.

Fig. 15.18   (compare this with Fig. 15.16a))

> **Sonata Form applies to several forms – not just sonatas.**

The *coda* is made to be rather longer than the codetta, and brings the movement to a very lively end. When you have read this carefully, listen several times to the movement to let it all sink in. **Remember**, *Sonata Form* is a structure used in symphonies, sonatas, concertos and chamber music. You should understand it thoroughly.

4 Listen to some String Quartets by Haydn, Mozart, Beethoven or Schubert, and familiarise yourself with the texture of this important Classical medium. Choose later works by Haydn and Mozart where all four stringed instruments are treated equally.

5 Listen to Schubert's Piano Quintet in A major (The Trout): 1st and 4th movements: Theme and Variations (SEG 1994).

If you have read through the preceding history sections and taken heed of the suggested things to do, you will be familiar by now with a wide range of music, from early madrigals and church music up to the standard classical structures. You will probably have heard some other chamber music before you listen to this work by Schubert, so it should not feel too 'new' for you. Do listen to the whole work, so that you can place the two movements into context.

Instead of an analysis of this movement, here are some ideas for your own research which will help you to understand the piece and something of its background:

a) Why is this Piano Quintet called the 'Trout' (or 'Die Forelle' in German)?

b) Do you find the combination of piano, violin, viola, cello and double bass a satisfactory one for chamber music? It is actually an unusual grouping of instruments; which is the 'intruder' into chamber music? Is this unfounded? Should this instrument be used more often in this way?

c) Which is the most common ensemble of instruments for chamber music?

d) You are told the form of the 4th movement; how many variations does Schubert compose here?

e) How does Schubert treat each variation in this 4th movement? Consider each one separately. Is the theme present in each? Does he change key, or time, or speed? Which instruments are prominent?

f) Does Schubert use much counterpoint in these variations? If so, where?

g) Find out briefly, about Schubert's life. Be aware of his life and times and the type of music writing and music making prevalent in that period.

h) Was Schubert an originator (devising new musical styles and ideas); or was he a perfecter (summing-up or perfecting existing ways of composition)?

i) What sort of music did Schubert compose? Have some idea of his output and where the 'Trout' Quintet appears – early, middle or late in his career.

j) Can composers be more expressive when writing for only a few players? If so, why and how?

PRACTICE QUESTIONS

Having worked out your own ideas about chamber music, and listened carefully to these movements of the 'Trout' Quintet several times, answer the following GCSE-style questions:

1 Name the instruments that are required for this quintet. *(2)*
2 How many variations are there in the 4th movement? *(1)*
3 Which variation is played in the minor key? *(3)*
4 Write a brief commentary on the last variation, explaining how Schubert makes use of the 'Trout' theme. *(6)*
5 Write a programme note for the 1st movement. In your answer refer to keys, textures and anything that is of interest to a listener who may be hearing it for the first time. *(12)*

1550–1830 – A FINAL STATEMENT

This concludes only the third of the seven historical sections in this chapter, but before you proceed, it might be a good idea to reflect for a moment. Factual information of this sort has no value for its own sake. You are not a good musician just because you can remember intricate details of composers, pieces and dates. The main purpose in studying in this analytical and historical way is to gain a further insight into a piece so that we might understand it better and enjoy it more. Ideally, music should not have to be 'translated' into words; but once we have accepted that music is an examinable subject, we have to assess your responses to music by using words – we cannot measure your feelings.

> Factual knowledge serves only to increase your understanding and enjoyment of music.

Many people enjoy learning facts about music and there is nothing wrong with that. However, don't lose sight of the fact that music is all about sounds and expression and was never composed to give examination candidates something to study! It is a good thing that the GCSE boards recognise that an acquaintance with Italian terms, staff notation and so on, are only ways of increasing our awareness of how music works. The ability to express ourselves satisfactorily as a performer, or to respond sensitively as a listener must come from within ourselves.

4 **1830 – 1900 THE ROMANTIC PERIOD**

In this period, composers showed less interest in the formal, or structural side of music, and began to emphasise the imaginative, and more emotional side. Art often reflects life; as Europe became more democratic, and power was removed from the aristocracy, so composers were influenced by this new belief in freedom. The Romantic composers were inspired by things outside music: landscape, literature, and the supernatural, for instance. Their music became more descriptive (see *Programme* music), often with unusual titles; the orchestra grew much bigger throughout the century as instruments were developed and improved.

MENDELSSOHN

We have seen how Beethoven and Schubert straddled two periods; some later composers wrote pieces that seemed Classical in outlook. Both *Mendelssohn* and *Schumann* certainly had Romantic attitudes, but composed in Classical forms. Mendelssohn helped to develop the concert overture – an overture that stands on its own. His 'Hebrides' Overture (set by NISEAC in 1994) is a good example for you to listen to. This sea-picture is cleverly suggestive of swell, storm and calm – yet is composed in traditional sonata form, where the rippling calm is the exposition and the storm is the development section. His oratorio 'Elijah' (still very popular with choral societies today) was written at a time when composers wishing to write religious music were concentrating on large works for the concert hall rather than small-scale vocal pieces for use in church services.

ROSSINI

Rossini was the most outstanding opera composer of the earlier Romantic period. You might listen to parts of 'William Tell' or 'The Barber of Seville': the overtures to these are particularly exciting.

THE LATER ROMANTICS

As the century progressed, Romantic music became more complex and abundant, and different styles emerged. The more conservative 'Classical' Romantics, such as *Brahms, Dvorak, Tchaikovsky* and *Bruckner* continued to write symphonies; the forward-looking Romantics – *Berlioz, Smetana, Liszt, Rimsky-Korsakov, Mussorgsky*, for example, turned to the *symphonic poem* (or *tone poem*), where they were unconstrained by the normal sonata form expected of a symphonist. Although there was not a great deal of religious music written, much fine chamber and piano music appeared. Nearly all of *Chopin*'s works were for piano, and Liszt wrote extremely difficult piano music to show off his prodigious technique.

There was a development of musical nationalism at this time. *Glinka, Borodin*, Mussorgsky, *Balakirev* and Rimsky-Korsakov in Russia, the Norwegian *Grieg*, and Smetana and Dvorak in Czechoslovakia – all tried to express the spirit and character of their own country by using its folk tunes and dances, and rhythmic idioms in their music.

Wagner was a sort of nationalist, using the old German legends of gods, heroes, giants and dwarfs as the background to his music dramas (as he preferred to call his operas). For Wagner, the ideal work of art had an equal unity between music, words, costume and set; he even wrote his own libretti. His vast 'Ring' cycle of four operas took a period of nearly twenty-five years to complete, and with the generous patronage of King Ludwig II of Bavaria, Wagner was able to build his own opera house in Bayreuth, Germany. Wagner used the *leitmotiv* – a continually recurring theme which is associated with a character, object or event. He also increased the size of the orchestra and was to be very influential as an orchestrator for a long time to come.

Another highly successful opera composer was the Italian *Verdi*, who was born in the same year as Wagner, 1813. Whereas Wagner was an operatic innovator, Verdi continued, at first, on the same Italian-style lines as his successful predecessors – Rossini, *Bellini* and *Donizetti* – approaching opera through the voice, with a more subservient orchestra; this was the converse to Wagner, who conceived opera as being, in musical terms, a union of voice and orchestra.

You should try to hear an opera by Verdi or Wagner – preferably in the opera house! It will be a very memorable experience.

QUESTIONS, NOTES AND ANSWERS

Here is a question on Wagner's Prelude to his opera 'The Mastersingers of Nuremberg', which is a set work for general study by WJEC for 1994.

Question

Outline how Wagner's Prelude to 'The Mastersingers' establishes the mood for the opera which follows.

Notes

a) By now it should be apparent that you need to know your chosen work very well indeed; you must be prepared to answer a wide range of short questions on it.

b) Read the question several times noting the exact wording. Here you are only instructed to 'outline' so avoid expanding your points too fully. Two or three well written paragraphs will be quite sufficient – it is not an essay. It will be necessary to include some relevant information on the opera itself (the plot and setting, and Wagner's use of the *leitmotiv*), as well as the required detail on the Prelude, but the answer should not become an unnecessarily detailed description of the Prelude.

c) List the points that you want to include in rough before you begin your answer. This will help you to decide on the content and how you can best arrange it into paragraphs.

> **Work out key points before you write the answer in full.**

    Introduction/background to opera
    Use of *leitmotiv* themes
    The Prelude
    Conclusion

Now read the question once more. Keep the key words 'establish the mood' in mind as you write your answer; this is the angle you need to concentrate on. Finally compare your answer with the model answer that follows.

Tutor's Answer

Richard Wagner (1813–83) composed 'The Mastersingers of Nuremberg' during the years 1862–7. He sets the opera in sixteenth century Nuremberg in Bavaria, where there is to be a Song Contest attended by the whole city. The prize is the hand in marriage of the beautiful Eva.

The Prelude (which is Wagner's term for Overture) was completed long before the rest of the work, which is unusual. Wagner obviously had his operatic themes planned well in advance or he would not have been able to deploy them in this opening Prelude. He creates musical cohesion by using a short theme, called a *leitmotiv*, to represent each idea or person in his music dramas (as he preferred to call his operas).

In this way the themes from the opera are actually incorporated in the Prelude. The strong opening theme in C major represents the Guild of the Mastersingers. Then there is an E major theme associated with the young knight Walther, which is used as his prize song in Act 3. We hear a theme representing Walther's impatience and a more jeering version of the opening theme represents the Apprentices mocking their elders in the Guild. Wagner brilliantly combines three of these melodies towards the end by adapting their speeds to allow them to fit together. This is a fine example of his contrapuntal skill and ability as an orchestrator. The Prelude is brought to a rousing conclusion by triumphant brass flourishes.

By becoming familiar with the themes and their varying moods in the Prelude, an audience is cleverly prepared for the operatic scenarios that are to follow.

THINGS TO DO

Listen to the Symphonic Poem 'Vltava' by Smetana (set by NEAB History and Appreciation of Music for 1994 and 1995). Use the advice given at the beginning of Chapter 2, and listen constructively to it several times. Are you able to analyse it for yourself yet? Some people can feel the structure of a piece by just listening with concentration; if you can obtain a score of the piece so much the better. If you are still finding set work analysis rather difficult, here is a brief description of 'Vltava':

Smetana composed a set of six symphonic poems between 1874 and 1879, and they were published as a cycle entitled 'Ma Vlast' (My Country). The six pieces each describe a different element of Bohemian history: (1) 'Vysehrad' is the castle of mythological kings of Bohemia (now Czechoslovakia) which overlooks the river Vltava. (2) 'Vltava' depicts the river. (3) 'Sarka' portrays a Bohemian Amazon leader. (4) 'From Bohemia's Fields and Groves'. (5) 'Tabor' is an epic of Hussite warriors and (6) 'Blanik' is a legendary resting-place of dead Hussite heroes – the piece is a description of Czech knighthood.

You may, of course, like to hear some of the others in the cycle, but in this country 'Vltava' is by far the most popular. We are not too familiar with Bohemian history, and this may well be the reason; 'Vltava' is a highly effective description of the course of a river.

The opening represents the source of the river, and characteristic 'water music' is shared by the two flutes (Fig. 15.19).

Fig. 15.19

The clarinets enter at bar 16 (representing a second stream). (Might the intermittent violin pizzicato chords be representing light reflecting off the stream – or is it a splashing effect? You must decide). The river is growing – with added instruments and a general crescendo – and the main Vltava river theme arrives at bar 40 (see Fig. 15.20).

Fig. 15.20

This is an appropriately majestic theme in E minor for the river, and its accompaniment has plenty of flowing semiquavers to give it movement. At bar 80 the river passes a hunt in the woods, which is suitably depicted by the use of horns and trumpets playing typical hunting calls (Fig. 15.21).

Fig. 15.21

This section is written in the key of C major, a necessary change after seventy-nine bars centred on the tonality of E. It all continues until Smetana calms it down in both volume and speed, returning to E major in bar 102.

The river now enters a populated district, and we hear a polka (a traditional Czech dance; this one is Smetana's own composition) which represents the music for the dancing of peasants at a village wedding. Clarinets and bassoons double the violins in the G major melody (Fig. 15.22).

Fig. 15.22

This dance section of 'Vltava' lasts for sixty-three bars. As with the 'Hunting' section, Smetana allows the music to wind right down as if the river has flowed on past the event. He writes a bass (tonic) pedal on G from bar 161–186, and effects a marvellous modulation from the key of G major into A flat major, a semitone shift which is a good example of Romantic writing; this would have been considered too 'daring' in earlier periods. He uses the long-held G as part of the new chordal link into A flat (Fig. 15.23).

Fig. 15.23

This new section is perhaps the most Romantic of the piece. It depicts water nymphs bathing and playing in the moonlight. Flutes, clarinets and harp are prominent as the flowing river accompaniment, and high muted divided strings play an ethereal melody in slow-moving minims representing the water nymphs (Fig. 15.24).

Fig. 15.24

Gradually more instruments are added as the river becomes more turbulent. A dominant pedal of the original key (i.e. the note B) arrives at bar 229 and after ten bars of orchestral crescendo – again with flutes and clarinets prominent as at the very beginning – we have a restatement of the main 'Vltava' river theme in the home key. It leads on this time to the climax of the whole work, the St John Rapids, where the composer brilliantly depicts the foaming cascades and rushing torrents. Listen out for the shrieking piccolo at the height of the musical furore. (With all the richness of this music, it is an amazing fact that Smetana was totally deaf when he wrote it.)

Finally, at bar 321, again over a dominant pedal (on B) a fortissimo (fff) climax suddenly drops right down to pp, and then scurries up the scale to the last statement of the main theme of the piece, this time in a triumphant E major, portraying the broad flow of the Vltava as it reaches Prague, the capital (Fig. 15.25).

Fig. 15.25

At bar 359, we hear the brass and woodwind play the 'Vysehrad' (castle) theme which is also used in the first symphonic poem of the set. (Fig. 15.26).

Fig. 15.26

Smetana remains in E major until the end of the piece. For the last time, he allows the volume to decrease to ppp and rests with just the violins on a pause. The work ends with a *fortissimo perfect cadence*.

QUESTION AND STUDENT ANSWER

Here is a pupil's answer to a set work question with examiner's comments:

Question

Write a paragraph on the musical ways in which Smetana describes the river in 'Vltava'.

Student answer

66 Good. Concise use of relevant detail. 99

66 Good. You start to answer the questions straight away. 99

66 Good. Clear, short answers. 99

Smetana establishes his water effect immediately by using flutes and clarinets in a persistent semiquaver movement. This is to represent trickling mountain streams which later form the river itself. He cleverly orchestrates this section with pizzicato and punctuated chords to give the effect of light reflecting off the water, or of splashing water against rocks. The main theme for the river is suitably majestic and has a flowing movement as an accompaniment; this theme returns later. The climax to the work is where the orchestra plays fortissimo for the St John rapids. All the instruments here have turbulent rhythms, and the combined effect would be good for a film where people shoot the rapids in a canoe. The work has a long coda all based on one chord before it finishes with a loud perfect cadence. Some imaginative harp writing is used as a reminder of water during the water nymphs section.

5 › 1900 ONWARDS: THE MODERN PERIOD

The compositions that have appeared this century reflect rapidly-changing times. Two horrific World Wars, and enhanced awareness of the world around us through television and radio have raised our social conscience; artists aim to reflect life, and comment on it far more than ever before.

In 1900 there were two main groups of composers: those who continued the Romantic tradition (the *Neo-Romantics*); and those who were inspired by *Impressionism*.

NEO-ROMANTICS

Elgar, Vaughan Williams, Holst, Bax, Mahler, Richard Strauss and *Sibelius* all developed Romantic writing further from the styles of Brahms and Wagner. They all had their different characteristics of course – some continuing the nationalist movement with the collection and use of folk-music – but did not radically change the nineteenth century symphonic tradition.

IMPRESSIONISTS

Debussy, however, was greatly influenced by the developments of the Impressionist painters, such as Cézanne and Monet. By using unconventional harmony, *overtones* and *whole-tone scales* he produced many pieces with atmospheric, shimmering effects. (Notice the dreaminess in his piano prelude 'The Submerged Cathedral' or the orchestral 'Prélude à l'Après-midi d'un Faune', for example). His music felt very different and new at the time, yet was still basically tonal (see *tonality*). *Ravel, Falla* and *Delius* were others to be inspired by Impressionism.

ANTI-ROMANTICS

Some composers became decidedly anti-Romantic, however.

Prokofiev composed lively and often discordant music, until commanded by the Russian authorities to revert to 'easier', more lyrical music. *Stravinsky* used contrasting styles in his long composing life. Having assimilated the colourful nineteenth-century symphonic style from his teacher Rimsky-Korsakov, he produced several successful ballet scores, including 'The Rite of Spring' and 'The Firebird', which broke new ground with their driving, complex rhythmic structures and general move away from anything approaching conventional 'sweetness' of melody and orchestral sound. Continuing to reject all things romantic, he experimented with *polytonality* and with rhythm and melody, none of which was very popular with audiences at the time. In fact, 'The Rite of Spring' caused about the biggest riot from an audience ever known when it was first performed in Paris in 1913. In contrast to this forward-looking work, Stravinsky also looked back to the eighteenth century: he would combine the simpler forms of that time with the flavour of modern music. This we now call *neo-classicism*. (Listen to his 'Pulcinella' ballet suite: he is avoiding emotional intensity, re-producing the calm and clear textures of pre-Romantic times).

Bartók in Hungary had been influenced by Wagner and Strauss, but he also gradually changed his style, choosing to absorb the rich resource of Hungarian folk-tunes into his work.

Schoenberg had also started his career as a neo-Romantic. His 'Verklärte Nacht' (Transfigured Night) sounds as if it might be a late work by Brahms. In time, however, he came to feel that the use of tonality was no longer valid as a vehicle for expression, and after much soul-searching, devised the strict twelve-note method known as *serial composition*. Key sense was now abandoned, and all chromatic notes became equal to one another. His followers were *Berg* and *Webern* who treated this new *atonal* method in their own individual ways.

JAZZ

Jazz was a strong ingredient in American music, especially with *George Gershwin*. Listen to excerpts of his opera 'Porgy and Bess', or the well-known 'Rhapsody in Blue'. *Charles Ives* used *polytonality* in some of his pieces, as he remembered from childhood the clashing sounds of rival marching bands. *Copland*, in his ballet scores especially, managed to capture the Wild West flavour. Try 'Billy the Kid' or 'Rodeo'.

MUSIC SINCE 1945

Since the end of the second world war there has been an incredible development in *electronic technology*. We can all now listen to and enjoy high-quality music at the touch of a switch, and come to know music that we may not otherwise encounter. In all ages there have been both innovatory composers and reactionary composers. The reactionary ones prefer to work within an existing and accepted style, perfecting as best they can the current musical language. Others, however, are rather more revolutionary. The so-called avant-garde composers are continually seeking new ways of expression, new instruments and new structures.

Since 1945, *Britten, Tippett,* Stravinsky, *Shostakovich,* Vaughan Williams and *Walton* are among the most important names in the traditional methods of composition. They are all individuals, of course, but nonetheless, they can be grouped within the mainstream of twentieth century music. The avant-garde composers are also diverse in style, and space permits only the mention of a few. The Italian *Berio* sometimes gives the performer a choice of actual notes to play. Originally a serialist, he has written electronic as well as orchestral music. The Polish composer *Penderecki* has written notable religious music with voices used in strange new ways – whispering, chanting, murmuring, whistling and so on – besides normal singing. *Stockhausen* has written many electronic works and sometimes allows choice to the performer as to where and when he should play. *John Cage* has written for the prepared piano, and *aleatoric* pieces based on random sounds. He is notorious for his 4'33" piece, which consists of absolute silence from the performer! *Messiaen*, from France, has used birdsong and complicated Indian rhythms in much of his work, which is strongly religious.

OPERA

Opera is much the same today as ever – a mixture of art, stagecraft and business wrangling. Financial problems are always dominating opera houses, and those in charge of them are often unwilling to try new works that may not sell tickets! Opera-goers tend to be very conservative anyway, not always giving a chance to something new. Despite all this, there have been some operatic masterpieces this century. Berg's 'Wozzeck' (produced 1925) and Britten's 'Peter Grimes' of 1945 are notable examples. The latter was an instant success in an artistically-deprived post-war Britain, but Berg's opera, with its dissonance and *sprechgesang*, met with initial hostility. 'Wozzeck' is now well established in the repertoire; new music always takes time to become accepted!

Television, with all its modern technology, allows great opportunity for dramatic effect, and composers have been composing operas specifically for this medium. *Menotti*'s 'Amahl and the Night Visitors' was the first example in 1951, and more recently Britten composed 'Owen Wingrave' for TV in 1971.

Listen intelligently and try all styles.

This century has seen an extremely wide range of techniques and styles in its 'classical' music, and it is often very hard for the listener to feel any sense of unity or continuity between the countless schools of thought. It is impossible to speculate on the future of serious music; there will always be experimentation – and much will fall by the wayside – but it will be interesting to see in years to come whether or not composers eventually 'lighten' their music by introducing elements that will be more immediately appealing for the ordinary listener. You must try all styles. Some will probably be not to your taste, but give it a chance! Listen intelligently, and think what feelings the composer might be trying to express, even though the language may be strange to your ears.

THINGS TO DO

1   Make up a composition in Impressionist style, using chords that have a feeling of timelessness about them. Aim for a relaxed atmosphere if you can by avoiding chords that are too 'definite'. Try chords like the ones in Fig. 15.27.

Fig. 15.27

It may be helpful to have a picture in your mind as you are working, even if you don't acknowledge this in the eventual title. 'Fog' or 'mist' perhaps might get you thinking of the right atmosphere. If you are using the piano, you can obtain some marvellous foggy effects with the sustaining pedal; with a synthesiser you can experiment until you find the right sound.

2   *Stravinsky: Symphony of Psalms*
         and *Petrushka* – The Shrove-Tide Fair

Stravinsky is a most important composer of this century, and you should become familiar with some of his work. He was born in 1882 near St. Petersburg (once called Leningrad), where his father was a bass singer at the Opera House. Although his parents persuaded him to study law, he was a keen musician. In 1902 he showed some of his compositions to Rimsky-Korsakov and was taken on as a pupil by him. At about this time he met Diaghilev, the director of the Ballet Russe, and went on to compose ballets for the company: 'Firebird' in 1909, 'Petrushka' in 1910–11, and 'The Rite of Spring' in 1911–13.

The 1917 Revolution forced Stravinsky to leave Russia and he settled first in Switzerland, then France and finally America at the beginning of the Second World War. He became a nationalised American and made Hollywood his home until his death in 1971.

His music seemed to change as often as his life. His early ballet scores had Romantic influences, notably from his teacher Rimsky-Korsakov. Then followed his radical works of the First World War, his lengthy neo-Classical period, and finally in his last years, he turned to serialism, where he was working in note rows, thirty years after Schoenberg and Berg had first created the process.

Listen to his Symphony of Psalms (1930) which bears the strange dedication: 'composed to the glory of God and dedicated to the Boston Symphony Orchestra on its 50th anniversary'. At least God came first! All his life Stravinsky was a sincere member of the Russian Orthodox Church.

Question 1

What words does Stravinsky use for the 'Symphony of Psalms'?   (2)

Answer 1

He uses verses from three Psalms and they are set in Latin. 1) Psalm 38: 13–14; 2) Psalm 39: 2–4; and 3) Psalm 150 (complete). The three movements are performed without a break.

Question 2

How does Stravinsky's orchestra for the 'Symphony of Psalms' differ from a normal symphony orchestra?   (8)

Answer 2

The most obvious difference is that upper strings (violins and violas) are not required at all. Other sections are large. In the wind there are four flutes and a piccolo doubling on fifth flute, four oboes and a cor anglais, three bassoons and a double bassoon, but clarinets are not required. In the brass there are four horns, four trumpets in C and a D trumpet, three trombones and a tuba.

In the percussion section he writes for timpani and bass drum. There is also a harp and two pianos. The average symphony orchestra would not use as many flutes, oboes or bassoons, and would require clarinets. The trumpet section would be smaller (probably three), and the piano, if used, is not normally doubled. Stravinsky has selected a different series of timbres in composing this work.

Question 3

Write a commentary on the first Psalm in 'Symphony of Psalms'. Consider the use of vocal and instrumental textures in your answer, rather than keys.   (*10*)

Answer 3

Stravinsky writes quite a long introduction for orchestra – twenty-five bars of irregular time signatures with flowering semiquavers punctuated unpredictably by chords. The French horn and solo cello hint at the first choral melody which is then stated by the contraltos. Stravinsky requests that children's voices be used where possible in preference to adult sopranos and contraltos. This first melody has seven bars written on only two different notes! The full choir answers with a single homophonic phrase, then a four-bar link of semiquavers leads to another seven-bar phrase for altos using the same two-note melody. Stravinsky is aiming for understatement here, avoiding the emotional impassioned sound that characterised much choral music prior to his time.

A single punctuated chord leads to a tenor line, joined later by sopranos (or trebles), who sing a four bar phrase on only one note. The accompaniment all through consists of the semiquaver figure, and spiky woodwind writing, often in fairly low registers, especially for oboes. The build-up commences at Fig. 10 when the altos and basses begin a more conventional choral statement, joined three bars later by the other voice parts. The climax is reached at Fig. 12 with bare, homophonic chords marked ff. The Psalm ends in a stark, unemotional way. The work finds its power from understatement; its austerity seems to underline the importance of the text: 'Hear my prayer O Lord and consider my calling with thine ears'.

When you have become familiar with this first Psalm, try to analyse the other two yourself. Do you find the work expressive? Does it have the power to move us in the same way as more openly emotional works, and if so why do you think this is?

Now turn to some of Stravinsky's Ballet music. Listen to 'Petrushka' and study the following question and answer.

Question 4

How does Stravinsky capture the mood of the 'Shrovetide Fair'?   (*4*)

Answer 4

The very opening suggests the hustle and bustle of a fairground with its sideshows and crowds of spectators. Stravinsky composes with several things going on at once, and uses a perpetual motion within the orchestra to convey an excited atmosphere. Apparently Stravinsky had heard a barrel-organ while working on this score and orchestrated the very tune, cleverly suggesting a creaky old barrel-organ by his skilful writing for woodwind instruments. Similarly, he borrowed another tune, a French dance melody this time, and used it to suggest a wandering musician with a music box playing for his dancer. This is interrupted immediately by the syncopated theme of the opening, again implying many things all going on at once.

3   Get to know *Bernstein's 'West Side Story'*
    The following numbers from Act 1 are set by SEG for 1994:
    America; Cool; Ballad – One Hand, One Heart (Tony and Maria); Ensemble – Tonight; The Rumble (Instrumental)
    ULEAC sets the following for 1994 and 1995: 3 Something's Coming (Tony); 4 The Dance at the Gym (Instrumental); 4 Blues; 4(a) Promenade; 4(b) Mambo; 4(c) Cha-Cha; 4(d) Meeting Scene; 4(e) Jump; 7 America (Anita, Rosalia and girls); 10 Tonight (Ensemble – Maria, Tony, Anita, Riff, Bernardo); 14 Gee, Officer Krupke (Jets)
    IGCSE uses the West Side Story Song Album published by Chappell and sets all the songs included in DG415963–1 LP DG415963–2 CD DG 415963–4 Cassette.
    'West Side Story' is an updated version of the 'Romeo and Juliet' story. It is set in the slums of west-side New York and the time is the 1950s. The Montagues and Capulets of Shakespeare's play are updated to become two teenage rival gangs, the Jets and the Sharks; Romeo and Juliet are modern young lovers called Tony and Maria. Their

drama is enacted in the violent city backstreets and *choreography* (dance routine) is a vital element. The musical show opened on Broadway in 1957 and ran for three years. It was equally successful in London when it arrived in 1958. You may have seen the film version which was released in 1961.

You should try to hear the excellent recording of this musical and/or see the film; another way of being introduced to it is to listen to the composer's 'Symphonic Dances from West Side Story' which captures the overall atmosphere and presents several of the songs in clever arrangements for orchestra.

Question 1

What mood does Bernstein capture in the song 'America'?   *(1)*
Is it: a) ☐ Sad and lonely
       b) ☐ High-spirited, energetic
       c) ☐ Angry

Question 2

What is the main musical characteristic used in 'America'?   *(1)*
Is it: a) ☐ Use of dynamics   c) ☐ Syncopation
       b) ☐ Changes of key   d) ☐ Changes of tempo

Question 3

Do you know of another well-known composer who wrote a piece based on the same Shakespeare play?   *(2)*

Points to think about:

- Will 'West Side Story' last, or is the 50s setting already out of date?
- Which is your favourite song from the musical and why? Is it the words or the melody you like best, or something else?
- Is it a good thing to bring Shakespeare stories up to date? Or is it preferable to think up new ideas for musicals?

If you are interested in the life and work of composers and conductors, *Leonard Bernstein* is a colourful character to read about; there are several good biographies available which are very readable. He was born in 1918, the son of Russian immigrants, in Massachusetts. He studied with *Koussevitsky*, the conductor of the Boston Symphony Orchestra, and was appointed assistant conductor of the New York Philharmonic Orchestra in 1943. His big break came that year when he deputised at short notice for the conductor who was taken ill; lucky for Bernstein it was a concert which was broadcast throughout America! He was famous as a conductor, composer (serious works as well as musicals), broadcaster and lecturer. He died in October 1990.

Answers to questions   1 = b);   2 = c);   3 = Tchaikovsky: 'Romeo and Juliet'.

1550 TO THE PRESENT DAY – SOME IDEAS

To conclude our look at 'serious' works written between 1550 and the present day, we shall take just one more piece and present you with a series of points to ponder over. These are not the sort of questions that you will encounter for your exam, but they aim to encourage you to develop opinions and ideas of your own. The danger of reading analytical information in the form of study notes, questions and answers, is that it can all become over-technical and can gloss over the most important element of any work of art – that of feeling. Here we can only be subjective; in other words, there is no real right or wrong, only personal opinion.

Ask yourself:

❝ Value your own opinions and responses. ❞

- Do I like this piece? If not, why not? Is it because I shouldn't like it – or my friends won't like it?

- Is it because I've never heard it before?
- Have I really understood the 'message' or emotion behind the music?

Listen to Penderecki's 'Threnody to the Victims of Hiroshima' (WJEC 1994). Here you must find out your own background information; we shall say nothing technical about this piece whatsoever, except that Hiroshima was the Japanese city where the first atomic bomb was dropped in 1945. Assuming that you know that anyway, and are familiar with the historical consequences of that horrific event, the very title conveys its emotive content before you even hear a note. This is not intended to be armchair listening – you will realize that immediately! Ask yourself what the composer is trying to do, and decide whether the experiment is a success. Above all, keep an open mind when you are listening, then consider the following. (Answers will not be provided).

1   Has Penderecki managed to create a mood, or range of moods, appropriate to that suggested by his title? Do you find the piece moving?
2   Listen to the instrumental effects the composer has used. Are the musical ideas appropriate? If so why? Do you think the sounds are effective or just gimmicks? Indeed, is there a future for this type of serious orchestral composition in our age of new sound technology?
3   Should the piece have more melodic content?
4   Can you see this style of music 'surviving' in the sense that other composers could use it for less emotive pieces?
5   Is the sole purpose of music to entertain or please? Do you consider it a good thing that composers should disturb the listener, by rousing a social conscience? In your opinion is music a suitable vehicle for making serious comment?

6 ⟩   JAZZ

At the time when modernist composers in Europe and America were evolving a different musical language, another very different type of sound-world was born. This was to be known later as jazz. This is not the place to give a detailed history of jazz. It is such a diversified area of music that space permits only a concise introduction to the background, its styles and musicians.

With so many different styles to listen to, it is actually rather difficult to define what jazz actually is. Improvisation is a major ingredient, and strong feeling and high energy are nearly always present. For a long time jazz was categorised as just another section of popular music, not to be taken too seriously. But this is no longer the case, for although a novelty in 1900, it was firmly established as an important musical genre by around 1930, and given serious attention by major composers such as Stravinsky and *Kurt Weill.*

You will probably know that during the eighteenth and nineteenth centuries the slave trade transported thousands of Africans to America. It takes little imagination to picture the incredible hardship that those people endured -- the claustrophobic journey, the humiliation of slavery auctions and the cruelty of perpetual work.

Music to the African is a natural part of life. Small wonder that it was used to express sorrow and grief. Work songs were, as the name implies, sung in time with work; the regular beat of these songs was timed to fit to hammer blows, or whatever. When they were not working, simple instruments were fashioned from everyday objects to beat in time with the songs.

There were differences, obviously, between African music and American (which was basically white European anyway). The African music tended to use pentatonic (five-note) scales (see Chapter 14), whereas the American used the seven-note major and minor scales. Strong rhythm and drumming was a vital ingredient of African music, and everyone would want to join in the performance – with clapping, singing or dancing. This was very different from the European way of doing things, where a composer would write for certain players, and the audience would only 'join in' by applauding at the very end. During the course of time, black and white music was to mix. The slaves heard around them European tunes, and military band pieces. When slavery ceased in 1865, with the ending of the American Civil War, many white bands split up and there were cheap instruments around for the blacks to play: trombones, cornets and clarinets. Before long, there were black bands in most southern American towns. Their music 'jazzed up' the spirituals (religious hymn-like songs – the slave-owners had tried to convert their slaves to Christianity) and the 'white' marches in an exciting way – by adding 'blue' notes (see *Blues*) and bending notes slightly out of true pitch. Many of the freed slaves found work on the railways and made up more worksongs, often in a 'call and response' style. They were free from slavery, but still faced enormous hardship and racial persecution. Their sadness still found expression in their songs – 'singing the blues' was a way of releasing their feelings, and it was often primitive and emotional. The so-called 'blues scale' includes the flattened or 'bent' 3rd and 7th (see Fig. 15.28).

Fig. 15.28

The twelve-bar blues was later to be a standard jazz chord progression, see Fig. 15.29.

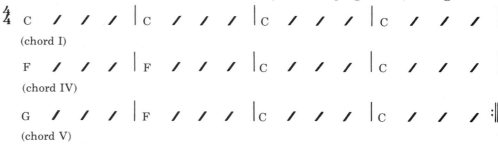

Fig. 15.29

This familiar chord scheme is a framework upon which a song or improvisation can be built.

BIRTH OF JAZZ

New Orleans was the city associated with the birth of jazz. Bands would play in the dance-halls, bars and on the Mississippi river boats. There were usually six players: clarinet, cornet, trombone, piano or banjo, string bass and drums and these bands are generally referred to as 'Dixieland' or 'trad' jazz bands. When there was no room for a band, a pianist would play, and a favourite style at the turn of the century was *ragtime*. Much of this music, by *Scott Joplin* and others, was written down and published. It was the first black music to really be accepted by the whites, who went on to write rags themselves. (This, of course, has a similarity to 'classical' music, where music is written down accurately.)

In 1918 the American navy closed down most of the bars in New Orleans and many of the jazz players were forced to travel north to find work. In this way, the popularity of jazz was to spread, and with the help of gramophone recordings and the development of radio, jazz was soon to be heard all over the world.

In the 1920s, *boogie-woogie* was a popular piano style. This was a fast-moving bass part in a twelve-bar blues framework (see 'Things To Do' (2) at the end of this section).

SWING

An economic slump put many jazz musicians out of work and it was some time before jobs could be found. When things did improve (by about 1933), a new style of jazz appeared, known as swing. It used 'blue' notes (see *Blues*) as before, and the old 'call and response' from the worksongs, and sometimes a boogie bass, but somehow it sounded new because it was played by larger bands – as many as thirteen players, instead of the usual half dozen. Now things had to be written down. Band leaders such as Benny Goodman and Paul Whiteman made careful arrangements for big band and the players now had to be able to read their parts or learn everything by heart. The arranger usually scored for four instruments in the saxophone section, five in the brass section, and four in the rhythm section. A feature of swing was the use of short, repeated figures, called *riffs*. They were passed around the band in a 'call and response' way. Sometimes a soloist would change the riff, to avoid monotony, by adding an idea of his own, but Goodman always kept a tight control on his players – the parts had to be played as written!

BE-BOP

Swing was superseded by a new style in the 1940s – be-bop (or bop for short). Some musicians (such as Dizzy Gillespie and Charlie Parker) were tired of using riffs and working from arrangements. The be-bop bands were smaller, so that the soloists became more prominent. The rhythms used were far more sophisticated than in swing, often using Cuban-style rhythms (such as the *cha-cha, conga* or *rumba*), and the drummer played in a 'cooler' way, mainly on cymbals. The bass line was a perpetually-moving pizzicato string bass part. Be-bop music was often based on popular songs, but the melody was replaced by a highly chromatic decorative line, with complicated chords – to such an extent that the original song could easily become unrecognisable!

MODERN JAZZ

Modern jazz dates from about 1950. Musicians like Gerry Mulligan, Miles Davis and Gil Evans came to prefer simpler harmonies and rhythms to those of be-bop. The West coast of America became the focal point for modern jazz. Some players began to use instruments not formerly associated with jazz: flute, horn and cello, for example. The Modern Jazz Quintet (MJQ) used classical pieces arranged in a jazz style in their concerts, and included vibraphone. This style of marrying classical to jazz was called *Third Stream* music.

Jazz today is very much a mixture, because some players prefer to revive earlier styles – Kenny Ball and Acker Bilk in this country have worked in the traditional (trad) jazz style based on the New Orleans 1920s bands – while others pursue modern jazz or swing. The National Youth Jazz Orchestra is a good example of a band which plays swing. Jazz trios are fairly common – the pianist Oscar Peterson is probably the most well-known musician to work mainly with string bass and percussion. Free-form jazz is where the music contains no common chords or obvious melodies, it all being based on free improvisation. Finally, bands such as Chicago and Blood, Sweat and Tears use a mixture of jazz and rock.

JAZZ TO LISTEN TO

The following alphabetical list of names is but a selection of great jazz musicians for you to get to know and enjoy. There is no need to learn the given dates; they are given only for your general interest. You may like to find out about some of these colourful characters. They certainly make interesting reading, as well as listening!

Louis Armstrong (1900 – 1972)	trumpet and vocals
Count Basie (1904–1984)	band leader/piano
Bix Beiderbecke (1903– 1931)	cornet and piano
Big Bill Broonzy (1893– 1958)	blues singer and guitar
Dave Brubeck (1920–)	piano/composer
Kenny Clarke (1914–1985)	drums
John Coltrane (1926– 1967)	multi-instrumentalist
Miles Davis (1926–1991)	trumpet
Duke Ellington (1899– 1974)	composer/band leader
Ella Fitzgerald (1918–)	singer
Stan Getz (1927–1991)	tenor sax
Dizzy Gillespie (1917 – 1993)	trumpet (notice his 'vertical' trumpet)
Benny Goodman (1909–1986)	clarinet/band leader
Woody Herman (1913–1987)	clarinet/alto sax/band leader
Earl Hines (1905– 1983)	piano
Billie Holiday (1915– 1959)	singer
Scott Joplin (1868–1917)	ragtime piano and composer
Glen Miller (1904–1944)	trombone/band leader
Charles Mingus (1922– 1979)	bass/composer
Thelonious Monk (1917–1982)	piano
Jelly Roll Morton (1885– 1941)	piano
Gerry Mulligan (1927–)	baritone sax, composer and arranger
Charlie Parker (1920– 1955)	alto sax/composer
Oscar Peterson (1925–)	piano
Bessie Smith (1894– 1937)	blues singer
Art Tatum (1910–1956)	piano
Fats Waller (1904–1943)	piano
Muddy Waters (1915–)	guitar/singer

THINGS TO DO

1   Listen to some Scott Joplin piano rags, and see if you can write one of your own. A rag usually has four main themes (each sixteen bars long) = A B C and D.
   The plan then should be: A A B B A C C D D which makes it quite a lengthy piece. Yours can be much shorter, of course, the structure is entirely up to you. You will

probably need to improvise at the keyboard first. Work out an 'oom-pah' bass part for the left hand first, using simple chords, then add a catchy melody above it, with syncopation.

2 If you are a keyboard player practise a boogie style. You will need to master the left hand part first, and there are all sorts of variations to it. Try the simplified version in Fig. 15.30 first.

Fig. 15.30

When you feel happy with this rather tricky bass part add on the suggested chords with the right hand. It is really a twelve-bar blues with a decorative bass.

3 Listen to some Swing music by Benny Goodman or Count Basie. Can you hear the riffs? Now listen to some 'trad' jazz played by Kenny Ball or Acker Bilk. Which do you prefer – swing or trad? Why?

4 Try to compare Be-bop with Swing by listening to some appropriate Dizzy Gillespie and Count Basie.

5 Try using simple chords and then adding some 'foreign-sounding' notes to them. For example in Fig. 15.31.

Fig. 15.31

C chord + F♯   D minor chord add C♯

How do you like the sound of these? Experiment at the keyboard as often as you can, noting which chords you particularly like, and why.

6 Can you think of ways in which worksongs could be used today? Make up one for a particular job, making sure that it has a very strong rhythm. Perhaps you could use the pentatonic scale (C D E G A only) as the African slaves did. You may like to include some harmony, and a 'call and response' pattern. Fig. 15.32 shows two well known spirituals which are good examples of 'Call and response' – you may find them useful as starting points for your worksong.

Swing low sweet char - i - ot, comin' for to car-ry me home.

Fig. 15.32

When Is - rael was in Egypt land, let my peo-ple go!

7 The marching band was very popular in nineteenth century America (and indeed, still is). Try writing a march tune, using either 2/4 or 4/4 time. Write it for keyboard first, and if you are satisfied, you may like to arrange it for instruments.

We started our brief guide to the history of music with the year 1550. With a similar convenience, this outline of the main developments in pop music will start in 1950. There has always been 'popular' music, of course, that is, music for ordinary people to sing and dance to, but pop music, as we know it, is an industry based on the selling of records, and more recently, pop videos. This quick-moving world goes hand in hand with fashion and dance crazes; some lasting for only a matter of weeks, others for rather longer periods. This is a very different tradition to the world of 'classical' music, although sometimes the two cultures come very close to each other. Some pop composers use styles that invoke serious composers (e.g. the 1967 No. 1 hit 'A Whiter Shade of Pale' by Procol Harum has an organ counter-melody lifted from Bach). Similarly, there was a vogue at one time for taking well-known Classical pieces and dressing them up with appropriate drum backing and increased speeds into a pseudo-pop style (e.g. Mozart's 40th Symphony).

Pop music has rarely been original in real musical terms. Since bursting out in the 1950s, it has absorbed a rich variety of styles from the classical, jazz and folk traditions, as well as from within itself. It has always been associated with young people, often making a powerful and pervasive social impact.

In 1954 a song called 'Rock around the Clock' was released on the Decca label. It was number one in the British and American charts the next year and used as the title song in a rock 'n' roll film in 1956. The singer was *Bill Haley*, with his backing group *The Comets*, and the song was to make him the first real pop star. Although we think of him (and perhaps his music) as rather old hat now, it came at a time when teenagers on both sides of the Atlantic were ready for something 'modern', and they could afford to buy records after the deprivations of World War II. New pop magazines and periodicals (*Melody Maker* and *New Musical Express*) were appearing and began to 'hype' up these new idols, and popularise them further, as did the rapid expansion of television at this time.

ROCK 'N' ROLL

Rock 'n' roll had derived from skiffle, which was a simple type of rhythmic song as sung by *Lonnie Donegan, Tommy Steele* and others. Skiffle was a British, not American, style and tended to use home-made instruments instead of normal ones – the washboard (used then for scrubbing clothes and played by scraping thimbles on it!) and tea-chest + broom-handle basses, for example. The lyrics were black-American blues style. Rock 'n' roll used the twelve-bar blues chord progression (borrowed from jazz), but it was used in a quicker and livelier fashion. It was at this time that the guitar gained enormous popularity, often using an electric pick-up to amplify the sound. *T-Bone Walker* was one of the first to use an electric guitar on record.

Elvis Presley (1935–1977) was younger, and far livelier than Bill Haley, and soon overtook him in popularity. Presley was the first white singer to sing in a 'black' style, and the effect of all this energetic and overtly sexual music and movement must not be underestimated. There were campaigns against the evils of rock 'n' roll! To some extent, there have been expressions of outrage over every new rock style ever since. Other important names then were *Buddy Holly* (1936–1959), *Jerry Lee Lewis, Little Richard* and *Gene Vincent. Chuck Berry*, a black rock and roller, tailor-made many of his lyrics to appeal to teenagers ('Roll Over Beethoven').

A 1950s TV programme called 'Oh Boy!' featured British pop music and encouraged many of our own singers and groups. *Cliff Richard* and his backing group *The Shadows* became well known in 1958 and are still performing and recording over thirty years later. The Shadows were also an instrumental group in their own right, releasing many singles and LPs of memorable numbers, some of which were vocal. The basic line-up for most groups at that time was lead guitar, rhythm guitar, bass guitar and drums, and this rarely changed – sometimes an electronic organ would be added.

In the early 1960s a Liverpool group came to the forefront of the pop business, capturing worldwide media attention as never before – the *Beatles*. The song-writing team of *John Lennon* and *Paul McCartney* produced many million-selling hits that have become pop 'classics', re-arranged for all combinations of voices and instruments, which are still often heard in their original versions. Countless other 'Mersey-sound' groups were formed in the 1960s to emulate the success of the Beatles: *Freddie and the Dreamers, Gerry and the Pacemakers, The Swingin' Blue Jeans* to name but three, but none of these were to overtake the amazing 'Beatlemania' that took hold in the middle of that decade.

By 1966 the Beatles style was becoming less stereotyped. The words became more important than in the earlier songs; listen to 'Eleanor Rigby' for instance. Their 1967 LP

'Sergeant Pepper's Lonely Hearts Club Band' is a milestone in the history of pop music, for besides a colourful and attractive cover to the album, there was a common theme of loneliness in several of the songs and several tracks merged into the next – a new departure in pop recording. The Beatles' visit to India had led to an interest in the sitar, which they used occasionally on their records.

The Rolling Stones were perhaps the main rivals to the Beatles, but were less 'polished' musically and in appearance generally. They were able to relate to rebellious teenagers (and consequently upset the parents) with the gyrating antics of the lead singer Mick Jagger and the suggestive lyrics of the songs. This aggressive style of performing had the same sort of effect on the older generation as Elvis Presley had had several years before.

At this time in pop history we can start to see a separation between the commercial 'Top Ten' type of song and the more serious, known generally as 'underground', which obviously appealed to smaller numbers of people. Frank Zappa was an inventive 'acid rock' musician who showed little interest in the three minute single, concentrating instead on making 'progressive' LP records. The Grateful Dead and Jefferson Airplane were two other notable bands who experimented with form, occasionally incorporating elements of jazz and Eastern sounds, often with long solos.

Attention switched from Britain in 1968 to the West Coast of America when the 'psychedelic' Flower Power movement briefly bloomed. The basic attitude behind this cult was a non-political pacifist stance with a flower as a symbol of love and peace (Beatles: 'All You Need is Love'), but unfortunately further brought to light the widespread use of drugs, associated for so long with the world of jazz and pop. This was the hey-day of huge pop festivals, where thousands would gather to hear a dozen groups or more. The most famous festival of all was Woodstock.

While rock and beat music was at its height, folk music was enjoying a revival, although with never quite the same frenzy that Beatlemania was able to produce. Various styles of folk music developed – 'protest' music from Bob Dylan, and later 'electric folk' from Steeleye Span who re-arranged traditional folk material into a contemporary idiom. Listen to Dylan's song 'Blowin' in the Wind' as an example of his protest against war and his interest in civil rights. Dylan is still performing and recording today; he has changed styles several times, in keeping with changing tastes, which may account for his continuing popularity. He became a Christian in 1979 and has since written some religious rock songs, a parallel to Cliff Richard in this country.

Another folk-rock musician who emulated the Dylan style was the British singer Donovan who also played a straightforward folk-guitar style in the mid-60s. (Listen to his song 'Colours'). In America, the Byrds recorded a Bob Dylan song 'Mr Tambourine Man' in folk-rock style, and two other groups worked in a similar way – Lovin' Spoonful and The Mamas and the Papas. Simon and Garfunkel were an immensely successful American duo in the mid-60s. Listen to 'Sound of Silence' (1966) and 'Bridge Over Troubled Water' (1970). Paul Simon and Art Garfunkel eventually went their separate ways as solo artists. Most people know 'Bright Eyes' which Garfunkel recorded in 1979 as a theme from the cartoon film 'Watership Down'. It was number one in the pop charts for six weeks.

The 1960s was the decade for super-groups, where the best musicians from several bands would play together. Cream, in the late 60s, included drummer Ginger Baker and the revered guitarist Eric Clapton. Although they made albums using all the latest technology, it was in stage performances that they really came alive; extended solo improvisations would be framed by references to their album songs. The Beatles eventually folded as a group, but each went his own way as a musician. Paul McCartney went on to form Wings with Linda, his wife, and John Lennon made a very successful solo career until his tragic assassination in New York in 1980. The Rolling Stones are still not officially disbanded after twenty-five years or more, and the Who reformed for a tour in 1989, even though their first hit dates from 1965 ('My Generation'). Their early concerts featured amplifier and guitar smashing, and extensive use of screeching feedback – the noise made when a microphone or guitar pick-up is too near a loudspeaker. Their theatrical rock-operas 'Tommy' and later 'Quadrophenia' were a style to be developed later by Alice Cooper and David Bowie. 'Tommy', more of a song cycle than an opera, was another attempt to make an album with a coherent theme; it was later turned into a film by Ken Russell, the controversial film director. 'Jesus Christ Superstar' and 'Hair' are other popular rock musicals from this time.

Another loud performer was the late Jimi Hendrix, regarded by many as one of the finest rock guitarists of all time. He made distorted sounds with a 'wah-wah' foot-pedal to help create his unique blues-based style.

Led Zeppelin were formed in 1968 by *Jimmy Page*, another excellent guitarist of the period. This group tended to shun publicity, preferring to release albums rather than single records. New dramatic laser stage effects combined with brilliant high-volume musical skill led to a new name for this style: 'heavy metal'. *Deep Purple* is another band you should listen to.

BLACK MUSIC

Everything mentioned so far has been British or American White Music, but nearly all pop stems in some way from the music of Black America. The Blues developed at the end of the nineteenth century, and came from the songs and chants of the negro slaves working in the cotton fields. This turned into Rhythm and Blues (R 'n' B), a very influential force on pop music. Soul Music (popular in the 1970s) came from Rhythm and Blues and Gospel Music. *Aretha Franklin* and *Otis Redding* are two early Soul singers of the 1970s. Tamla Motown is well-known in the world of Black Music. It is a very large record company in Detroit which produced records by *Diana Ross and the Supremes, Stevie Wonder* and many others. The production of all these singers became so distinctive that 'Motown' is now a word that implies a style of black pop music. One feature is the constant repetition of the 'hook-lines' (the chorus title lines) so that they really stick in the memory.

Ska, Blue Beat, Rock Steady and Reggae are all styles of Jamaican music from the 1960s onward. You can easily recognise Reggae by its emphatic off-beat rhythm and the singer's West Indian accent. *Bob Marley* (who died in 1981) is regarded as the greatest Reggae artist; he was Rastafarian and politically-minded. (Rastas believe in peace and brotherhood, and that they will eventually return to Ethiopia, their spiritual home.)

THE 1970s

The commercial pop music of the 1970s is not so memorable in many ways as that of the previous decade. It was a time of light-show spectacles and loud volume, demanding very large concert halls to stage the required effects. Ticket prices naturally reflected the cost of these extravaganzas. As before, many singers and groups were famous briefly, but soon forgotten. Some of the more successful include: *T-Rex, Slade, Rod Stewart, Wizzard, 10 CC, Abba, Status Quo, Queen, Elton John, Chicago, Leo Sayer, Kate Bush, The Bee Gees, Blondie* and *Police. Emerson, Lake and Palmer* used themes from serious composers, such as Sibelius and Copland, and re-arranged them in a heavier style, performing with real showmanship. Keith Emerson, the keyboard player, was one of the first to use a Moog synthesiser. *Pink Floyd* has created very successful stage shows (e.g. 'Dark Side of the Moon') using sophisticated electronics and a superb control of sound and textures.

You should try to hear *Mike Oldfield's* album 'Tubular Bells' of 1973 – 4 which is a blend of rock and light classical styles. Oldfield recorded nearly everything himself on this LP by multi-tracking and overdubbing. In 1992 he made a new version of this pop classic. Which of the two do you prefer, and why?

The 70s saw the arrival of Disco music. The vital ingredient here was the dance rhythm, not so much the tunes or instruments used. *Donna Summer* was the first real disco star in the mid-70s, and the film 'Saturday Night Fever' with the *Bee Gees'* music encouraged many companies to produce Disco records. All sorts of unlikely people cashed in by making disco music – even old singles and classical tunes were re-arranged for people to dance to.

Funk was first played by *James Brown* way back in the mid-60s and it developed in the 70s. It has blues, jazz and rock ingredients and tends to use distorted sounds, syncopated rhythms and a percussive bass-line (slap-bass). It is black dance music with a strong jazz feel. Try songs by *Kool and the Gang* (e.g. 'Funky Stuff').

PUNK AND THE 1980s

One new style to arrive in the late 1970s was Punk Rock – an aggressive and shocking style, often with extremely depressing lyrics. For its followers, it was more than just music; it was a whole lifestyle. Safety pins were used as jewellery (in the most unlikely places), and hair was dyed and shaped in outrageous ways. The infamous *Sex Pistols* and later *The Clash* were the epitome of this raw and extremely unsophisticated pseudo-style. The guitar sound is often distorted and simple to the point of banality, usually without solos. It had virtually disappeared in 1979, although some bands tried to keep the Punk tradition alive. Later punk music was often so fast and incoherent, that it is referred to as 'Oi music'!

New names from the 1980s include: *The Pretenders, The Jam, Roxy Music, Michael Jackson, Kraftwerk, Madness, Culture Club* (with *Boy George*), *Phil Collins, Spandau Ballet, UB40, Frankie Goes to Hollywood, Lionel Richie, Duran Duran, Wham! Eurythmics, Madonna* and *Pet Shop Boys*. This lengthy list is probably more familiar to you than the earlier names, and you will know much of the music. No-one can predict which way pop will turn next. Perhaps the wheel will turn full circle and we will revert to the simplicity of the 50s and 60s. Maybe there will be a folk revival, or something completely new. Black and white music will almost certainly continue to blend together, enhanced by new technology and changing social conditions. This is the way pop music has always evolved. Listen carefully to as much as you can, thinking as you do so about the origins of a particular style. Enjoy it!

SONGS TO LISTEN TO

Below is a complete list of the groups and singers that have been mentioned in the above section on Pop music. With so many performers in all areas of popular music, space does not allow mention of everyone. Try to get hold of albums by performers that you have not heard before, and listen to them carefully.

Are the words political? Is the song trying to make a social comment, or is it simply a fun song for dancing to? How is the song put together? Is it too repetitive, do you think? Is there a solo for any particular instrument – if so, does it fit in well with the rest of the song? Perhaps you will hear two versions of the same number, by different performers. Which do you prefer, and why?

The recordings given (with serial numbers to help you find them more easily) are only suggestions:

Bill Haley and the Comets:	*Rock Rollin' Bill Haley* BFX 15068
Lonnie Donegan:	*My Old Man's a Dustman* HMA 204 (No. 1 in 1960)
Tommy Steele:	*Singing the Blues* (No. 1 in 1957)
T Bone Walker:	*T Bone Blues* 1975 Atlantic K40131
Elvis Presley:	*Greatest Hits* 1982 RCA INT 5116
Buddy Holly:	*Greatest Hits* 1981 MCA MCL 1618
Jerry Lee Lewis:	*Great Balls of Fire* 1982 Charly CFM 516 (No. 1 in 1958)
Little Richard:	*Greatest Hits* 1984 CBS 32185
Gene Vincent:	*Singles Album* 1981 Capitol 26233
Chuck Berry:	*Rock 'n' Roll Hits* 1983 Mercury 9279 138
Cliff Richard:	*Cliff in the 60s* 1984 MFB MFP 4156561
The Shadows:	*String of Hits* 1979 EMI EMC 3310
The Beatles:	*Please Please Me* 1963 Parlophone PMC 1202
	Revolver 1966 Parlophone PCS 7009
	Sgt Pepper 1967 Parlophone PCS 7027
	Beatles 1967/70 1973 Parlophone PCSP 718
Freddie and the Dreamers:	*I'm Telling You Now* 1977 EMI 2694
Gerry and the Pacemakers:	*Best of...* 1977 EMI NUT 10
The Swinging Blue Jeans:	*Swinging Blue Jeans* 1978 EMI NUT 15
The Rolling Stones:	*Let It Bleed* 1969 Decca SKL 5025
	Rolled Gold 1975 Decca ROST 1/2
	Time Waits for No One 1979 RS COC 59107
Frank Zappa:	*Orchestral Favourites* 1979 Discreet K59212
The Grateful Dead:	*Grateful Dead Live* 1971 WB K 66009
	Dead Set Live 1981 Arista DARTY 11
Jefferson Airplane:	*Best of...* 1984 RCA Int 89186
	Nuclear Furniture 1984 Grunt FL84921
Bob Dylan:	*Times They Are A Changin'* 1964 CBS 62251
	Greatest Hits 1967 CBS 62847
	Shot of Love 1981 CBS 85178
Steeleye Span:	*Hark the Village Wait* 1970 RCS SF 8113
	Below the Salt 1972 Chrysalis CHR 1008
Donovan:	*Greatest Hits* 1969 PYE NSPL 18283
The Byrds:	*History of the Byrds* 1973 CBS 68242
Lovin' Spoonful:	*Greatest Hits* 1970 Kama Sutra 2361 002

The Mamas and the Papas:	*20 Greatest Hits* 1980 MFP 50493
Simon and Garfunkel:	*The Sound of Silence* 1966 CBS 62690
	Concert in Central Park 1981 Geffen 96008
Cream:	*Fresh Cream* 1983 RSO SPELP 42
Eric Clapton:	*Blues World of Eric Clapton* 1975 Decca SPA 387
	Steppin' Out 1982 Decca TAB 21
Wings:	*Band on the Run* 1974 Apple 10007
	Pipes of Peace 1984 Parlophone CDP 746018 2
John Lennon:	*Imagine* 1971 Apple PAS 10004
	Collection 1982 EMI EMTV 37
The Who:	*My Generation* 1980 Brunswick LAT 8616
	Tommy 1972 Track 2406 007/8
	Quadrophenia 1979 Polydor 2625 037
Alice Cooper:	*Greatest Hits* 1974 WB K 56043
David Bowie:	*Space Oddity* 1984 RCA PL 84813
	Rise and Fall of Ziggy Stardust 1984 RCA 83843
Jimi Hendrix:	*Smash Hits* Track 1613 004 (especially 'Hey Joe' and 'Purple Haze')
Led Zeppelin:	*Led Zeppelin 3* 1971 Atlantic K 50002
	Physical Graffiti 1975 Swansong K 89400
Deep Purple:	*Deepest Purple* 1980 Harvest EMITV 25
Aretha Franklin:	*Best of…* 1984 Atlantic 780 169 1
Otis Redding:	*The Best of …* 1972 Atlantic K 60016
Diana Ross and the Supremes:	*20 Golden Greats* 1977 Motown EMTV5
Stevie Wonder:	*Greatest Hits* 1972 Motown STML 11196
	Songs in the Key of Life 1976 Motown TMSP 6002
Bob Marley and the Wailers:	*The Legendary* 1984 Premier CRB 1001
T-Rex:	*Greatest Hits* 1978 Pickwick SHM 953
Slade:	*The Best of Slade* 1975 Polydor 2664 124
Rod Stewart:	*Greatest Hits* 1979 Riva RODTV 1
Wizzard:	*Wizzard's Brew* 1973 Harvest SHSP 4025
10 C.C.:	*Greatest Hits* 1979 Mercury 9102 504
Abba:	*Greatest Hits Vol 2* 1980 Epic 10017
Status Quo:	*12 Gold Bars* 1980 Vertigo QUOTV 1
Queen:	*A Night At The Opera* 1975 EMI EMTC 103
Elton John:	*Too Low for Zero* 1983 Rocket HISPD 24
Chicago:	*Greatest Hits* 1975 CBS 69222
Leo Sayer:	*The Very Best Of* 1979 Chrysalis CHR 1222
Kate Bush:	*Never for Ever* 1980 EMI EMA 794
Bee Gees:	*Saturday Night Fever* 1977 RSO 2658 123
	Staying ALive 1983 RSO RSBG 3
Blondie:	*The Best of Blondie* 1981 Chrysalis CHR 1337
Police:	*Synchronicity* 1983 A & M AMLX 63735
Emerson, Lake and Palmer:	*Tarkus* 1971 Island ILPS 9155
	Pictures at an Exhibition 1971 Island HELP 1
Pink Floyd:	*Ummagumma* 1969 Harvest SHDW 1/2
	Dark Side of the Moon 1973 Harvest SHVL 804
	The Wall 1979 Harvest SHDW 411
Mike Oldfield:	*Tubular Bells* 1973 Virgin V 2001
	Ommadawn 1975 Virgin V 2043
Donna Summer:	*On the Radio (Greatest Hits)* 1979 Casablanca 5008
James Brown:	*The Best of James Brown* 1975 Polydor 2343 036
Kool and the Gang:	*Greatest Hits* 1975 Polydor 2310 401
Sex Pistols:	*Never Mind the Bollocks* 1977 Virgin V 2086
The Clash:	*The Clash* 1982 CBS 32232
The Pretenders:	*Pretenders 2* 1981 Sire K 56924
The Jam:	*Sound Effects* 1980 Polydor 5035
Roxy Music:	*Greatest Hits* 1977 Polydor 2302 073

Michael Jackson:	*Thriller* 1982 Epic 85930
Kraftwerk:	*Autobahn* 1982 EMI EMC 3405
Madness:	*Complete Madness* 1982 Stiff HITTV 1
Culture Club (with Boy George):	*Colour by Numbers* 1983 Virgin V 2285
Phil Collins:	*No Jacket Required* 1985 Virgin V 2345
Spandau Ballet:	*Parade* 1984 Chrysalis CDL 1473
UB40:	*The Singles Album* 1982 DEP DEP 5
Frankie Goes to Hollywood:	*Welcome to the Pleasuredome* 1984 ZTT 1Q1
Lionel Richie:	*Can't Slow Down* 1983 Motown STMA 8041
Duran Duran:	*Rio* 1982 EMI EMC 3411
Wham!	*Make It Big* 1984 Epic EPC 86311
Eurythmics:	*Be Yourself Tonight* 1985 RCA PL 70711
Madonna:	*Like a Virgin* 1984 Sire 9251571
Pet Shop Boys:	*Please* 1986 EMI PCS 7303

POP AND ROCK – SOME IDEAS

You may like to follow up some of the groups or singers that have been mentioned, by considering their songs in more detail. The WJEC has included Beatles songs as set works: 'I Need You'; 'Another Girl'; 'The Night Before'; 'Ticket to Ride'; 'I've Just Seen a Face'; 'Yesterday'; 'Act Naturally'; from the *Help* cassette, side one.

If you have worked your way through the various set works in Chapter 5, you will have a good idea how to go about studying some new songs. In addition, this present section of rock and pop has given you an awareness of where the Beatles would fit in to the plethora of styles and influences which have developed over the last fifty or sixty years.

The Beatles seemed so different when they rose to fame in the early 1960s but it was their approach that was new: hairstyles, Beatle jackets, and zany personalities, not so much the music. The songs, excellent though they are, were a highly successful mixture of black and white influences: Soul, Blues, 20's Dance Band, children's songs, Motown, gospel hymns, Country and Western, Indian (the occasional use of sitar), Rock 'n' Roll – all spring to mind.

When you have listened to the songs and become familiar with both tunes and words, try to work out the influences in the above-mentioned songs and others of your choice. You should form your personal responses to each song:

a) Is it the words or tune I most like?

b) Is the song different from the ordinary? If so, is it the use of voice/voices or solos that are played that makes it sound fresh?

c) Does the song come from the early Beatles period, or the increasingly-inventive later years?

d) Which are the most successful to you – the slow ballads, or the up-tempo numbers? Why?

e) Is it acceptable that a group can 'borrow' from so many different styles? Should they stick to one style? Should they aim to be original?

f) It has been said that Ringo Starr is not a good drummer. Do you agree? Why do you think this criticism arose?

g) Do you prefer the songs where Paul McCartney is the lead singer or those which feature John Lennon? How do their styles vary?

h) Why is Liverpool so important in the history of pop? Could it be due to its position as a port on the west coast on England?

A FINAL COMMENT

"Form your own opinions."

The world of pop and rock is immense; songs that were 'outrageous' in the 1960s are classics today. Groups that were regarded as rather unwholesome by parents are now accepted, through the fullness of time, and often enjoyed. Familiarity does not always breed contempt!

Enjoy your pop music, and try to widen your listening. Young people are often wary of admitting that they like or dislike a particular sound for fear of alienating themselves from their friends. Stand your ground – and convert the others!

REVIEW SHEET

1550–1600

✎ Palestrina composed masses, _____ and _____. His music tends to be highly _____ and was constructed with the old _____, which were the forerunners of our major and minor scales. Other composers of the time were _____ and _____. In wealthy homes, _____ were sung, and instrumental pieces were played by _____ and _____, often in groups, which we call _____.

✎ When a piece in a minor key ends up with a major chord, we call it a _____. If music stops being contrapuntal for a while, and all the parts move rhythmically together, it is said to be _____.

1600–1750

✎ This period is called the _____ period. A new style of vocal music called _____ started in Florence in about 1600. To save the composer writing out every note of these lengthy pieces, the harpsichord player would read from a _____.

✎ The great violin makers of this time were _____, _____ and _____. The English composer Henry _____ wrote _____ for two violins and continuo. The continuo was made up of two instruments, the _____ and _____.

✎ The two great composers of this period were _____ and _____ who were both born in 1685 in _____. _____ composed the six Brandenburg Concertos and _____ is perhaps best known for his oratorio 'Messiah'. Domenico _____ was the composer of over 500 _____, many of which were composed in _____ Form.

1750–1830

✎ Three important composers of this so-called _____ period are _____, _____ and _____. The _____ superseded the harpsichord, and the concerto, _____ quartet and _____ were developed. Deafness was a problem for _____, who bravely overcame his handicap, and composed many pieces in total deafness such as the _____ Symphony which uses voices in the last movement.

✎ _____ composed over 600 art songs which are known as _____. One of the most well-known of these is _____ where the piano part represents the galloping horse.

1830–1900

✎ In this, the _____ period, composers really emphasised the emotional side of music. The 'Hebrides' Overture by _____ is a good example of descriptive music, cleverly evoking the _____. Some composers tried to capture the spirit of their country in their music by using folk tunes and dances. This style is known as _____, and some of the main composers are _____

_____.

✎ Wagner's cycle of four operas is called the _____ cycle. In his work Wagner employs the _____, which is a recurring theme associated with a character or event.

1900 onwards

✎ Some composers continued with the Romantic tradition: _____

_____.

✎ Others were inspired by Impressionism: _____

_____. Debussy was particularly fond of the _____ scale in his music. Forward-looking composers such as Charles Ives and Prokofiev sometimes used several keys at once in their music. This is called _____. Others, such as Stravinsky (with 'Pulcinella') looked back in time and combined their own style with an eighteenth-century flavour. This we call _____. Some avant-garde composers have written _____ music based on chance, or random sounds.

Jazz

1. Continue the 'blues' scale on the stave:

2. Write in the chords for a 12-bar blues in C:

3. Which jazz musicians played be-bop? _____

4. Which American city is associated with the birth of jazz? _____

GLOSSARY 1: COMPOSERS MENTIONED IN THIS BOOK

The following table contains brief details of composers whom you will have encountered in the book. The GCSE exam no longer places much emphasis on dates and similar factual detail, but this table is included to reinforce the information given in Chapter 15 and elsewhere. You may find some helpful notes here towards your chosen set work, but regard the Recommended Listening as the most useful column – try to hear some of these pieces, thinking as you do so about the advice given in Chapters 4–5 about **how** to listen to best advantage.

COMPOSER	DATES	COUNTRY	TYPES OF MUSIC	RECOMMENDED LISTENING
J.S. Bach	1685 – 1750	Germany	Concertos, Organ music, Cantatas etc	Brandenburg Concertos
Balakirev	1837 – 1910	Russia	2 symphonies, piano music	Tone poem: 'Tamara'
Bartok	1881 – 1945	Hungary	Piano music, concertos, operas	Concerto for Orchestra
Bax	1883 – 1953	England	7 symphonies, tone poems	Tone poem: 'Tintagel'
Beethoven	1770 – 1827	Germany	Symphonies, opera, concertos, chamber music etc	Pastoral Symphony
Bellini	1801 – 1835	Italy	Operas	Extracts; Norma
Berg	1885 – 1935	Austria	Operas, string quartet	Violin Concerto
Berio	1925 –	Italy	Electronic and avant-garde music	Sequenza III
Berlioz	1803 – 1869	France	Operas, overtures, symphonies, Requiem	'Roman Carnival'
Bizet	1838 – 1875	France	Operas, symphony in C major	'Jeux d'enfants'
Borodin	1833 – 1887	Russia	Symphonies, opera, 2 string quartets	Polovtsian Dances
Brahms	1833 – 1897	Germany	Symphonies, songs, chamber music	Academic Festival Overture
Britten	1913 – 1976	England	Choral music, operas etc	Serenade, Op.31
Bruckner	1824 – 1896	Austria	9 symphonies, masses	Symphony No.5
Bull	1562 – 1628	England	Music for viols, organ, virginals	Any piece
Byrd	1543 – 1623	England	Masses, madrigals, motets	5-part Mass
Cage	1912 – 1992	America	Avant-garde music; 'prepared piano'	'Imaginary Landscape'
Chopin	1810 – 1849	Poland	Piano music	Any piece
Copland	1900 – 1991	America	Ballet scores, orchestral, chamber	Rodeo/Billy the Kid
Corelli	1653 – 1713	Italy	Concerti grossi	'Christmas Concerto'
Debussy	1862 – 1918	France	Piano, orchestral, chamber	'La Mer'
Delius	1862 – 1934	England	Operas, orchestral, chamber	'On Hearing the First Cuckoo in Spring'
Donizetti	1797 – 1848	Italy	Operas	Excerpts: 'Lucia di Lammermoor'
Dowland	1563 – 1626	England	Lute songs, lute solos	Any piece

COMPOSER	DATES	COUNTRY	TYPES OF MUSIC	RECOMMENDED LISTENING
Dvorak	1841 – 1904	Czechoslo-vakia	Orchestral, opera, chamber, choral	'New World' Symphony
Elgar	1857 – 1934	England	Orchestral, choral, chamber	'Cockaigne' Overture
Falla	1876 – 1946	Spain	Ballet scores, orchestral	'The Three-Cornered Hat'
Gershwin	1898 – 1937	America	Songs, opera, orchestral	Rhapsody in Blue
Gibbons	1583 – 1625	England	Church music, madrigals	Madrigal: The Silver Swan
Grieg	1843 – 1907	Norway	Piano music, orchestral, songs	Piano Concerto
Handel	1685 – 1759	Germany (nat. Eng.)	Concerti grossi, choral, operas, oratorios	Excerpts: 'Messiah'
Haydn	1732 – 1809	Austria	Symphonies, string quartets, oratorios, masses	Symphony No. 104
Holst	1874 – 1934	England	Operas, orchestral, choral music	Suite: 'The Planets'
Ives	1874 – 1954	America	Symphonies, sonatas	'Three Places in New England'
Joplin	1868 – 1917	America	Piano rags	The 'Entertainer'
Kodaly	1882 – 1967	Hungary	Orchestral music, educational music	Hary Janos Suite
Lassus	1532 – 1594	Netherlands	Madrigals, masses, motets	Madrigals (any)
Liszt	1811 – 1886	Hungary	Piano, orchestral transcriptions	B minor Sonata
Lully	1632 – 1687	Italy	Operas, church music	Any opera excerpt
Lloyd Webber	1948 –	England	Musicals	Requiem
Mahler	1860 – 1911	Bohemia	Symphonies, songs	Symphony No. 4
Mendelssohn	1809 – 1847	Germany	Symphonies, piano, songs, chamber music	Violin Concerto
Menotti	1911 –	Italy	Operas, orchestral	'Amahl & the Night Visitors'
Messaien	1908 – 1992	France	Orchestral, organ, choral music, songs	'Oiseaux Exotiques'
Monteverdi	1567 – 1643	Italy	Operas, madrigals, church music	Beatus vir
Morley	1557 – 1603	England	Madrigals, church music, lute songs	'It was a lover and his lass'
Mozart	1756 – 1791	Austria	Orchestral, chamber, church music, etc	Symphony No. 40
Mussorgsky	1839 – 1881	Russia	Operas, orchestral, piano	Night on a Bare Mountain
Paganini	1782 – 1840	Italy	Violin music	La Campanella
Palestrina	1525 – 1594	Italy	Masses and other church music	Missa Brevis
Penderecki	1933 –	Poland	Orchestral, choral	Threnody for the victims of Hiroshima
Prokofiev	1891 – 1953	Russia	Symphonies, operas, chamber, piano, etc	'Romeo and Juliet'
Purcell	1659 – 1695	England	Church music, opera, harpsichord music	Excerpts: 'Dido and Aeneas'
Rachmaninov	1873 – 1943	Russia	Symphonies, operas, piano music	Piano Concerto No. 2

COMPOSER	DATES	COUNTRY	TYPES OF MUSIC	RECOMMENDED LISTENING
Ravel	1875 – 1937	France	Orchestral, chamber, piano, operas, ballets	'Bolero'
Rimsky-Korsakov	1844 – 1908	Russia	Orchestral, operas, choral, etc	'Scheherazade'
Rossini	1792 – 1868	Italy	36 operas	Any opera overture
A. Scarlatti	1660 – 1725	Italy	115 Operas, 500 Cantatas	–
D. Scarlatti	1685 – 1757	Italy	500 harpsichord sonatas	Any sonata
Schoenberg	1874 – 1951	Austria	Orchestral, choral, chamber music	'Verklarte Nacht'
Schubert	1797 – 1828	Austria	Symphonies, piano, chamber & church music, songs	'Unfinished' Symphony
Schumann	1810 – 1856	Germany	Symphonies, piano, chamber music, songs	'Carnaval' for piano
Shostakovich	1906 – 1975	Russia	Symphonies, piano, chamber music	Symphony No. 5
Sibelius	1865 – 1957	Finland	Symphonies, songs, chamber music, tone poems	'Finlandia'
Smetana	1824 – 1884	Bohemia	Tone poems, operas, chamber music, etc	'Vltava'
Sousa	1854 – 1932	America	Marches for band	'El Capitan'
Stockhausen	1928 –	Germany	Electronic and avant-garde music	'Mixtur'
J. Strauss I	1804 – 1849	Austria	Waltzes, polkas	'Radetzky March'
J. Strauss II	1825 – 1899	Austria	Waltzes, polkas, operettas	'Thunder and Lightning Polka'
R. Strauss	1864 – 1949	Germany	Tone poems, operas, songs, orchestral	'Don Juan'
Stravinsky	1882 – 1971	Russia	Orchestral, choral, operas, ballets etc	'Rite of Spring'
Tchaikovsky	1840 – 1893	Russia	Symphonies, ballets, chamber music, songs	Violin Concerto
Tippett	1905 –	England	Symphonies, operas, piano and vocal works	Concerto for Double String Orchestra
Vaughan Williams	1872 – 1958	England	Symphonies, chamber, vocal works etc	'Wasps' Overture
Verdi	1813 – 1901	Italy	Operas, Requiem	Excerpts: Requiem
Vivaldi	c1678 – 1741	Italy	Concertos, church music, operas	'Four Seasons'
Wagner	1813 – 1883	Germany	Operas (music dramas)	Excerpts: any opera
Walton	1902 – 1983	England	Symphonies, chamber, orchestral, choral	'Facade'
Weber	1786 – 1826	Germany	Operas, orchestral, piano music	'Oberon' Overture
Webern	1883 – 1945	Austria	Orchestral, chamber, vocal, serial music	Five Pieces for Orchestra
Weelkes	c1575 – 1623	England	Madrigals, church music, lute music	'Hark all ye lovely Saints'
Weill	1900 – 1950	Germany	Operas, symphonies	'The Threepenny Opera'
Williamson	1931 –	Australia	Symphonies, vocal, orchestral, songs	Any work

GLOSSARY 2 : MUSICAL WORDS

Music is one of those subjects that contains many technical terms and foreign words. You will not need to learn all of them by any means, but this glossary contains a brief explanation of words that you may come across in your GCSE course. For fuller explanations you should consult a good music dictionary, such as the *Oxford Companion to Music*. Look up the words *in italic* as cross references.

A cappella	Unaccompanied choral music.
Absolute music	Abstract instrumental music – i.e. not *programme music*.
Accelerando	(accel.) – quicken the pace.
Accent	Extra force given to a particular note, and indicated like this:
Accidental	A sharp, flat or natural which does not form part of the *key signature*.
Adagio	Slow, but faster than *largo*. A slow movement is often called an adagio.
Aleatoric music	Music where the performer is allowed to play parts of a piece based on chance – the composer allows some degree of choice.
Allegretto	Fairly quick, but not as much as *allegro*.
Allegro	Quick and lively, but not as fast as *presto*.
Allemande	A dance movement in moderate 4/4 time; part of the Baroque *Suite*.
Alto	1 The lowest female voice; 2 a clef which the *viola* uses.
Amati	Family of sixteenth & seventeenth century Italian *violin* makers, based in Cremona.
Andante	A walking speed, but not too slow.
Anthem	Protestant church equivalent of the Latin *motet*; now a term used for short religious choral pieces.
Arco	An instruction for string players to use the bow, after a passage marked *pizzicato*.
Aria	A solo vocal piece in *opera* or *oratorio*, often composed in *ternary form*.
Arietta	A short or light *aria*. Sometimes applied to an instrumental piece.
Arioso	*Aria*-like. Applied to a melodic type of *recitative*.
Art song	An artistic setting of a poem for voice and accompaniment, normally piano. This usually refers to nineteenth century *Romantic* songs (see *Lieder*).
Atonal	Music without a sense of key (*tonality*), by *Schoenberg* and others in early 1900s, which led on to *serial composition*.
Avant-garde	Very modern music – often experimental.
Bagatelle	A short instrumental composition, often for piano.
Ballad	1 From the sixteenth century, a term applied to a simple and popular song for solo voice, often describing an event of the day. 2 In the nineteenth century, either a narrative-type song, or a sentimental English drawing-room song.
Ballade	An instrumental composition (with no one particular form) by *Chopin*, *Brahms*, *Liszt* and others. They are supposed to have narrative associations.
Barcarolle	A song or instrumental piece, usually in 6/8 time, suggesting Venetian gondolas.
Baroque	A word borrowed from architecture suggesting an ornamented, detailed construction. The name is used musically for the period 1600–1750.
Bass	1 The lowest male voice; 2 The lowest note of a chord or composition; 3 The lowest member of a family of instruments, e.g. bass clarinet; 4 The lowest *clef*.

Basso continuo	Sometimes just 'continuo'. A type of *bass* line used in the *Baroque* period, with figures underneath it from which a *harpsichord* player would work out the correct harmonies. The bass line would often be doubled by a *cello*.
Be-bop	A jazz innovation of the early 1940s using *chromatic harmony* and complicated, fast-moving melodies.
Bel canto	Literally 'beautiful song'. An operatic term for a brilliance of vocal execution and beauty of tone as heard in eighteenth/nineteenth century *operas* by *Bellini* and *Donizetti* etc.
Binary form	A common musical structure, especially in the *Baroque* period. In two parts, the first changing key, the second returning to the home key before the end. Both parts are often repeated.
Blues	A style of music, associated originally with American Negro *Spirituals*. It generally has a mood of intense sadness and loneliness. Twelve-bar blues is a very common simple chord progression used in popular music. A 'blue' note is a note of the scale flattened (often the 3rd & 7th) which gives a characteristic *jazz* effect.
Bourrée	A dance movement from the *Baroque* suite, in quick 2/4 time, beginning with an upbeat.
Cadence	see page 140
Cadenza	A solo vocal or instrumental passage, usually inserted into a *concerto* for display purposes.
Calypso	A type of West Indian music; strong rhythmically and often with topical words.
Canon	A *contrapuntal* composition, or section of music where a melody given by one part is imitated exactly by one or more others, usually with overlapping.
Cantabile	In a 'singing' style; flowing and clear.
Cantata	A choral work, with or without solo voices, and usually with orchestral accompaniment. It may be sacred or secular (non-religious).
Canzona	A sixteenth/seventeenth century short instrumental work, somewhat resembling choral music, and often in several movements.
Cassation	An eighteenth century type of lighter orchestral music in several movements, often played outdoors. Sometimes called *Serenade* or *Divertimento*. This century Malcolm *Williamson* has written several Cassations for children.
Catch	A type of amusing vocal *round*, often bawdy, by *Purcell* and others up to the nineteenth century.
Chamber music	This is not a precisely defined term, but it refers to music for a small group of players who are regarded as soloists on equal terms. (See *Duet, Trio, String Quartet, Quintet, Sextet, Septet, Octet* and *Nonet.*)
Chorale	A hymn tune of the German Protestant Church. *J.S. Bach* harmonised hundreds of these tunes.
Chorale prelude	An instrumental piece (usually for organ) based on a *chorale*.
Chord	Any combination of notes played together – whether pleasant or not! (See *Triad.*)
Chorus	1 Refrain to a song, frequently recurring; 2 A group of singers singing in harmony (See *S.A.T.B.*)
Chromatic scale	A scale which goes up or down in *semitones*.
Classical	1 A style of music from 1750–1830; 2 A style of work that is standardised and 'accepted', not modern; 3 Opposite to light or popular music.
Clavier	(German = Klavier). Term meaning 'keyboard'.
Clef	Sign which fixes the location of notes onto the stave and placed at the beginning of each line of music. Treble, *alto, tenor* and *bass* clefs are used today.

Coda	A section of music to round off a *movement*.
Coloratura	A very agile style of vocal music; the very high register of the soprano voice.
Concerto	Generally a work for one or more soloists with accompanying orchestra. (See *Concerto Grosso* and *Cadenza*.)
Concerto grosso	Seventeenth/eighteenth century type of orchestral music with interplay between a larger group of players (the ripieno) and a smaller group (the concertino). Try some of *Bach*'s six Brandenburg Concertos.
Conservatoire	Special college for higher musical training.
Consort	Old English for a group of instruments.
Contrapuntal	A combination of two or more melodies which make musical sense – they are then said to be in 'counterpoint' to each other.
Counterpoint	See *Contrapuntal*.
Country & western	White American folk music, a forerunner of rock 'n' roll.
Courante	Dance movement in three time in the *Baroque* Suite. Usually in a running, rapid tempo.
Crescendo	(cresc.) Getting gradually louder.
Cyclic form	1 Work (e.g. *song cycle*) in several sections which has a unifying mood or theme; 2 Work which uses a recurring musical subject in each movement.
D.C. (Da Capo)	Go back to the beginning. A Da Capo *aria* (as used by *Handel*) returns to the opening section.
D.S. (Dal Segno)	Go back and play from the sign (𝄋) – not the beginning.
Development	A section of music (usually in *sonata form*) where themes are 'developed' – modified or expanded in some way according to the inventiveness of the composer.
Diatonic	Music that concerns itself with major/minor scales. The opposite to *chromatic*.
Diminuendo	(dim.) Becoming gradually softer.
Dissonance	A sense of 'clashing' or jarring *chords*.
Divertimento	A light-hearted work in several movements for a small instrumental group. (See *Cassations*)
Dixieland	An early jazz style for a small band, with *choruses* and improvised verses.
Dodecaphonic	*Twelve-note music*. A style of composition as devised by *Schoenberg* in the 1920s. See also *serial music*.
Dominant	The fifth note of a scale, (in C major = G); or the chord formed above this note.
Duet (duo)	A combination of two performers (sometimes with an accompaniment), or a piece for two.
Dynamics	Loud and soft expression marks.
Electronic music	Music that involves the use of synthesisers or pre-recorded tapes.
Embouchure	A term used for the application of a mouth-piece to a brass or wind player's lips.
Episode	A section of music within a *rondo* or a *fugue* intended to form a contrast.
Equal temperament	See *Temperament*.
Exposition	The opening section of *sonata form* which presents the main musical themes.
Fanfare	An introductory flourish for *trumpets* (or other instruments imitating them).
Fantasia	(or fantasy/phantasie/fancy) A vague title given by some composers when they require a 'free' rather than a set form.
Figured bass	A musical shorthand from the *Baroque* period, whereby figures were added to a bass line for the harpsichord player to embellish with appropriate *chords*. (See *Basso Continuo*.)
Fine	Literally 'finish'. Written at the end of a repeated section of music to indicate the end.

Formalism	A supposed fault in Russian composition; the Soviet authorities denounced *Shostakovich* and *Prokofiev* in the 1930s and 40s for excessive emphasis on 'form' rather than 'content'.
Forte (f)	Loud.
Fortissimo (ff)	Very loud.
Folk song	A song made up long ago and handed down aurally, the words often differing from region to region. Some composers this century (e.g. *Vaughan Williams, Holst, Bartók*) have collected folk songs and used them in arrangements of their own.
Frets	Marked divisions on the neck of a lute, viol or guitar to indicate fingering positions.
Fugue	A *contrapuntal* composition with strict rules of construction – especially in the *Baroque/Classical* times. A set number of 'parts' or 'voices' are used, with the main 'subject' being heard in each part initially. *J.S. Bach* was a great writer of fugues.
Galliard	A three-beat dance from the fifteenth/sixteenth centuries.
Gavotte	An old dance in 4/4 time which usually began on the third beat of the bar; it was used sometimes in the *Baroque suite*.
Gigue (jig)	A lively dance in 6/8 or 12/8 time; often the last movement of the eighteenth century *suite*.
Glee	A short choral piece for men's voices, very popular in England about 1750–1830.
Glissando	(or gliss.) – a slide from note to note, especially used on harp, trombone, piano and stringed instruments.
Grave	Italian word for 'slow and solemn'.
Ground bass	(see also *Passacaglia*) A piece of music built over a short recurring bass phrase. *Purcell* was a master of this form.
Harmonic progression	A series of chords.
Harmony	The art of adding appropriate chords to a melody.
Homophonic	Music where the parts or voices move together instead of showing rhythmic independence (as in counterpoint or polyphony).
Hook	In pop music, a word or short phrase that is repeated. The 'catchy' part of the song.
Idée fixe	(see also *Leitmotiv*) A recurring motto theme or figure associated with a person or action. *Berlioz* uses this idea in his 'Symphonie Fantastique'.
Imitation	A *contrapuntal* action, where one voice or part 'copies' another – strictly or freely.
Impressionism	(From painting.) A term for music (by *Debussy* and others) where the expression seems to hint at something rather than state it dramatically. Tone-colour and harmony are used to give an 'impression' – with soft, vague outlines.
Impromptu	Title for a short piece, usually for piano, giving an impression of spontaneity.
Improvisation	Music made up on the spot.
Incidental music	Music for a play; songs, dances and perhaps an overture to enhance the drama.
Intermezzo	1 Title for a short piano piece (e.g. by *Brahms*); 2 An instrumental item during an opera played while the stage is empty.
Interval	The distance measured between any two notes.
Jazz	A type of music with strong *syncopations* that came originally from Negro music in New Orleans. Although now branched out into many different styles, an important element is that of *improvisation*.
Jingle	A catchy tune – e.g. music for a TV advert.
Kappelmeister	German for 'Musical Director'; and later for 'resident conductor' of an orchestra.
Key signature	Sharps and flats at the start of a piece to indicate the key; this is then repeated at the beginning of every line.

L.H.	Left hand.
Largo	Slowly and broadly.
Leading note	The seventh note of a scale.
Legato	Play smoothly. Connect the notes.
Leitmotiv	'Leading-motive'. A recurring theme associated with a character or object in operas – especially those by *Wagner*. (See also *Idée Fixe*)
Lento	Slowly and broadly
Libretto	(Plural libretti). The text of an opera or oratorio.
Lied	(Plural Lieder). A German *art song* with piano accompaniment. *Schubert, Brahms* and *Schumann* wrote many fine Lieder.
mf	Mezzo forte = rather loud.
mp	Mezzo piano = rather soft.
Madrigal	A type of *contrapuntal* vocal composition, which flourished in the sixteenth and seventeenth centuries. *Morley, Weelkes* and *Byrd* wrote madrigals, which were often about love in some way.
Magnificat	The hymn of the Virgin Mary (My soul doth magnify the lord') which is commonly set to music.
Mass	A service of the Roman Catholic Church. A musical mass usually has five sections (Kyrie, Gloria, Credo, Sanctus with Benedictus, and Agnus Dei). Try *Haydn*'s 'Nelson' Mass.
Mazurka	Originally a Polish dance in three time. *Chopin* wrote over fifty piano mazurkas for concert use.
Mediant	The third degree of a scale.
Melodic	1 Music that emphasises the melody, rather than harmony; 2 A type of minor scale.
Minuet and Trio	Often the third movement of a *Symphony* or a *Sonata*, favoured by *Haydn* and *Mozart* and other *Classical* composers. Both Minuet and Trio are in two sections – and each is repeated before the Minuet is played once more, thus producing an overall *ternary form*.
Moderato	Use a moderate speed
Modes (modal)	A scale system in use for hundreds of years before our present major/minor system evolved. Play the white notes on a piano for an octave from any note to produce a mode (e.g. A–A = Aeolian mode, useful for a folksong-like effect).
Modulation	Changing from one key to another.
Molto	Very (e.g. Allegro molto = very fast).
Motet	A church composition for voices, usually in Latin. (See *Anthem*).
Movement	A self-contained section of a larger work, e.g. a *Symphony* normally has four movements.
Music Drama	Title given by *Wagner* to his later *operas*, which were intended by him to be a balance between music and drama.
Musical	A stage show of light entertainment (largely American-influenced). Examples include Oklahoma (1943) by Rogers and Hammerstein, and more recently, Evita, Cats, and Phantom of the Opera by *Andrew Lloyd Webber*.
Musique concrète	A term coined by a group of Paris musicians experimenting in the 1940s with the rearrangement and reproduction of existing sounds by electronic means.
Mute	A device to clip on to a stringed instrument or insert into a brass instrument to deaden the tone slightly. (See *Sordino*).
Neo-classical	Term given to a style of music by *Stravinsky* and others which deliberately avoids the expression of strong emotion. It was a reaction against the *Romantic* style of the late nineteenth century. Smaller orchestras were used (as in *Classical* days). Listen to 'Pulcinella' by Stravinsky.
Nocturne	Originally music alluding to the calmness of night-time, but now occasionally used as a title without 'nocturnal' connotations. Try *Debussy's* set of Nocturnes for orchestra.
Nonet	A group of nine players, or music for them.

Obbligato	e.g. Aria with obbligato flute – a term used where an instrument has a solo role, often in conjunction with a solo singer.
Octave	Eight notes, e.g. C - C or G - G; an *interval* of a perfect 8th.
Octet	Eight players or a piece for eight players.
Ode	A piece of music written in celebration of something, e.g. 'Ode for St Cecilia's Day' by *Purcell* or *Handel.*
Opera	A play set to music – eg 'Carmen' by *Bizet*. Sometimes the word is used to mean a company which performs opera, or the building where it is performed (e.g. the Paris Opera).
Opus	Literally a 'work'. Composers often give their compositions opus numbers, e.g. Op. 1, as a way of cataloguing them.
Oratorio	A large-scale religious work for choir, solo singers and orchestra. One of the best loved is 'Messiah' by *Handel.*
Orchestration	The art of scoring out a composition for an orchestra.
Ornaments	A general term for the decorations that are used in music (use a music dictionary to look up trill, mordent, and turn, or see Chapter 14)
Ostinato	An 'obstinately' repeated figure or phrase.
Overture	An opening piece of music to an *opera* or *oratorio* (often said to be in 'French' or 'Italian' style depending on its structure). A Concert Overture (e.g. 'Fingal's Cave' by *Mendelssohn*) stands in its own right.
p	Piano = softly
pp	Pianissimo = very softly
Partita	An alternative word for *Suite*
Partsongs	Short unaccompanied choral pieces written in several parts, often *SATB.*
Passacaglia	Another word for *ground bass.*
Passing note	A note which passes between two others
Passion	A choral work which sets the Easter story. *Bach* composed a 'St Matthew' Passion and a 'St John' Passion.
Pastorale	A term to indicate a countryside atmosphere.
Pedal	(1) Ped. is an instruction to use the sustaining pedal on the piano; (2) in harmony, a long held (or repeated) note in any part.
Pedal Board	The set of foot pedals on a church *organ.*
Piu mosso	More movement; quicker.
Pizzicato	(Pizz). An indication to pluck the strings.
Plainsong	An ancient form of church music – a single line of singing for unaccompanied voices in a free rhythm. Gregorian chant survives today.
Plectrum	A plastic 'plucker' guitarists use for strumming.
Polka	Dance in 2/4 time, originally from Bohemia.
Polonaise	Dance in 3/4 time, originally from Poland.
Polyphonic	*Contrapuntal* music – the so-called polyphonic age was the time of *Palestrina, Byrd* and *Lassus.*
Polytonality	Music composed in two or more keys at the same time. *Bartok* and *Holst* sometimes used this method of composing.
Prelude	Originally an 'opening' piece – perhaps to a *Suite*; it became a favourite pairing to a *Fugue* (e.g. *Bach's* 48 Preludes and Fugues for *clavier*). Some composers use the word instead of *overture* to open their *operas*; others use the word for any self-contained piece (e.g. *Chopin's* Preludes for piano)
Prepared piano	A way of producing new effects: the American composer John *Cage* instructs the pianist to insert screws in between certain strings!
Presto	Very fast
Prestissimo	As fast as possible
Programme music	Music that attempts to describe something – landscape, or the supernatural perhaps (e.g. the river 'Vltava' by *Smetana*).

Proms	The annual Henry Wood Promenade Concerts held mainly at the Royal Albert Hall in London, July-September. First held in 1895, some seats are removed from the arena for young people to stand with cheaper tickets. You are not allowed to walk around however!
Quarter-tone	The *semitone* is the smallest interval in Western music, but some composers have experimented with intervals half this size, making use of quarter-tone pianos, and other new finely-tuned instruments.
Quartet	A group of four players, or music for four people.
Quintet	A group of five players, or music for five people.
Raga	In Indian music (which is improvised rather than written down) a cross between a melody and a scale. There are many ragas, each made for a certain time of day or night.
Ragtime	An early piano *jazz* style with a syncopated melody played against a regularly accented beat in the left hand. Scott *Joplin* is the important composer of piano rags.
Rallentando	(Rall) Slow down.
Recapitulation	(Recap) In *sonata form*, the section which reprises the main themes after the *development* section.
Recitative	(Recit) Speech-like singing in an *opera* or an *oratorio*, often used to give information or fill in the story. The words tend not to be repeated (unlike the *aria* which it usually precedes).
Reggae	A pop style of West Indian origin, much played in the 1970s. The basic unit is a two-bar phrase, with the third beat of bar two accented.
Requiem	A *Mass* for the dead; notable examples are by *Mozart, Berlioz* and *Verdi*.
RH	Use the right hand.
Rhapsody	A title for a piece of music, suggesting a free form or *fantasia*. Try *Rachmaninov*'s Rhapsody on a theme of *Paganini*.
Riff	A short repeated musical pattern in *jazz* and pop; similar to *ostinato* in *Classical* music.
Ritardando (Rit)	Gradually slower.
Ritenuto (Riten)	Hold back, slower – immediately.
Ritornello	A passage for full orchestra which keeps 'returning' after a solo section in a *Concerto Grosso* or similar work.
Romantic	A period of musical history (c 1830–1900) when composers were keen to depict emotional feelings and their response to things outside music, such as literature or landscape. (See Chapter 15 section 4)
Rondo	A form popular in the *Classical* and later periods where the sections appear as A-B-A-C-A. Sections B and C are contrasting *episodes* to the recurring Rondo theme.
Round	A short vocal *canon* for unaccompanied singing e.g. 'London's Burning'.
Rhythm 'n' blues	A strongly rhythmic type of popular music which combines *blues* and *jazz*. The singer and guitarist Chuck Berry is a good example to listen to.
Sarabande	A slow dance in 3/2 time, originally from Spain. A regular part of the old *Suite*.
SATB	Short for: *Soprano, Alto, Tenor* and *Bass*; the regular voice parts of a choir.
Scherzo	Literally 'a joke'. From *Haydn* and *Beethoven* onwards a faster version of the *Minuet and Trio*, and usually (when used) the third movement of a *symphony* or *sonata*. It tends to be very lively – not particularly funny.
Semitone	Half a tone – the smallest distance between any two notes in Western music.
Septet	A group of seven players, or a work for seven.
Sequence	A repeated pattern at a higher or lower pitch (see pages 88–89).

Serenade	Originally a work for outdoor use (to sing outside a lover's window); in *Classical* days it was a lighter instrumental piece for a few players – often wind players. *Mozart's* 'Eine kleine Nachtmusik' is a popular string Serenade.
Serial music	Music by *Schoenberg* and others which treats all notes of the *chromatic scale* equally. It is therefore *atonal*.
Sextet	A group of six players, or a work for six.
Sforzando	(Sf) or (Sfz) – an indication to give a 'forced' emphasis to a particular note.
Sinfonia	Literally 'sounding together'. The old name for what was to become the *symphony*; it is also used for the name of an orchestra – e.g. London Sinfonia.
Singspiel	A type of *opera* with extensive chunks of spoken dialogue, popular in the eighteenth century. German is used instead of Italian.
Sonata	A four movement work for one or two instruments, depending on whether a piano accompaniment is required. Early sonatas by *Domenico Scarlatti* had just one movement.
Sonata Form	A Classically-developed structure which was frequently used for first movements in *sonatas, symphonies, concertos* and *string quartets*. It tended to follow this plan: *Exposition:* First subject in the *tonic* key. Bridge passage, or transition. Second subject in the *dominant* key. Codetta finishing off the exposition. *Development:* Some of the main themes (from the above) are developed. *Recapitulation:* Nearly the same as the exposition, but all in the same key this time. *Coda:* An ending.
Song cycle	A set of songs linked by a common theme. Try *Vaughan William's* 'Songs of Travel'.
Soprano	The highest female voice.
Sordino	(Con sord.) Use a mute on the instrument.
Spirituals	American Negro religious folk-songs.
Sprechgesang	A sort of 'speech-song', originated by *Schoenberg*, where the voice just touches the note without actually sustaining it.
Staccato	Short, crisp notes – indicated thus
Stradivarius	A name for the excellent violins made by the seventeenth–eighteenth century Antonio Stradivarius (see Chapter 15 Section 2).
String quartet	Two *violins*, a *viola* and a *cello*; or a work for this combination of instruments.
Strophic form	Term used when a song uses much the same music for each verse.
Study	(French = Etude) – a piece which originally set out to provide practice for a certain technical difficulty; now it often has artistic merit as well (eg *Chopin*'s Studies)
Subdominant	The fourth degree of a scale; or the chord above that note.
Submediant	The sixth degree of a scale; or the chord above it.
Suite	A collection of short movements – in the *Baroque* Suite they were mainly dances: eg *Allemande, Courante, Sarabande* and *Gigue*. Later on, it came to be the name for the instrumental extracts from an *opera* or ballet.
Supertonic	The second degree of a scale; or the chord above it.
Swing	The 'Swing' Band era was during the 1920s and 30s; Benny Goodman was one of the first band leaders to produce a swinging *jazz* style.

Symphony	1 A four-movement work (rather like a *sonata*) for orchestra which developed around the time of *Haydn*. At least one of the movements will be in *sonata form*. 2 A short way of referring to a symphony orchestra – an orchestra large enough to play symphonies.
Symphonic poem	Or Tone Poem. A one-movement work for orchestra based on a story or sequence of events, e.g. 'Vltava' by *Smetana* which describes the course of a river.
Syncopation	A rhythmic effect made when a weak beat is accented.
Tango	A favourite ballroom dance in the early part of this century. Originally from Argentina, its characteristic rhythm is

♩. ♪♩ ♩

Temperament	A word used in connection with tuning of instruments. Modern keyboard instruments use equal temperament where each semitone is made to be an equal interval. Thus G flat and F sharp are made to be the same sound. With this system it is possible to change key without any 'sour' notes sounding.
Tenor	A high male voice; a clef sometimes used by cello and bassoon.
Ternary form	A three-part structure (designed as A B A), where the second A section is a repeat of the first.
Theme and variations	A popular form. A melody (either borrowed or original) is chosen by the composer, and any number of variations are created around it. Sometimes the theme may be simply decorated, or missing in a variation altogether. Listen to *Brahms'* 'Variations on the St Anthony Chorale'.
Timbre	The 'colour' or sound quality of a particular instrument.
Toccata	A keyboard piece with difficult finger-work.
Tonality	A sense of key – where a piece is composed around a certain scale. (See also *Polytonality* and *Atonality*.)
Tone poem	See *Symphonic poem*.
Tonic	The 1st degree of a scale; or the chord above it.
Transcription	A work rearranged for another instrument; *Liszt* transcribed hundreds of orchestral pieces into piano pieces.
Transposition	Moving a piece higher or lower to another key.
Transposing instrument	One that produces notes either higher or lower than actually written. A Horn in F will be written a perfect fifth higher than it sounds. Other examples: Trumpet in B flat, Clarinet in B flat – here written C sounds B flat.
Tremolando	(Tremolo) A rapid bowing on a stringed instrument – for dramatic effect.
Triad	A three-note chord, e.g. C-E-G.
Trio	A group of three players or a work written for three.
Tutti	Literally: 'everyone' – an indication in a piece that all should play.
Twelve-note music	See *Serial music*.
Valves	The mechanism on a brass instrument for producing different notes.
Variations	See *Theme and variations*
Vibrato	The slight 'wobble' that a singer or player produces to improve tone quality.
Virtuoso	A top-class performer.
Vivace	Lively.
Voluntary	A composition for church organ.
Walking bass	Term for a bass part in a composition which is continually moving along.
Waltz	(French = Valse) A dance in 3/4 time; very popular in nineteenth century Vienna. The *Strauss* family were famous composers of waltzes.
Whole-tone scale	A scale consisting entirely of tones – e.g. C–D–E–F sharp –G sharp – A sharp – C. *Debussy* frequently used it.

GLOSSARY 3:
MUSICAL INSTRUMENTS

GCSE requires a general knowledge that covers music from all ages, and many cultures. This glossary does not pretend to describe all the musical instruments that the world has seen. It covers, however, all the well-known Western European ones and introduces you to some instruments of the past, some of which are being heard again as musicians continue to explore the beauties of pre-classical music with reproduction instruments. Some mention, too, is made of the more common non-European instruments. This section should help you with the general musical knowledge required for the Musical Perception, Literacy and Set Works sections of the examination. It may even give you some ideas towards your composition!

Factual information of this sort is of little use unless you hear the sound of these instruments. There is every opportunity for this by choosing suitable pieces or programmes from radio and television; you could join a record library, and go to all sorts of concerts.

Accordion	A box-shaped reed organ that has metal reeds which vibrate with air from bellows which are pushed and pulled by the player. The right hand plays the melody keyboard while the left hand operates the harmony buttons. It is frequently associated with French café music.
Bagpipes	These have existed for over 3000 years and are played all over the world – not just Scotland. It is a reed-pipe wind instrument with air stored in a bag which serves as a reservoir, to be slowly squeezed out by the player's elbow, so that the flow of sound is unbroken when the player has to breathe. Try to hear the difference in sound between the Scottish bagpipes and the gentler Northumbrian pipes. Which do you prefer?
Balalaika	A triangular, three-stringed Russian guitar in various sizes. Played on its own, and in bands.
Banjo	A fretted, long-necked lute with a parchment-skin belly and usually four or five strings. It was popular with 'Negro Minstrels' and jazz bands in America as it is quite loud and could be heard where the guitar would be overpowered.
Baritone horn	The baritone horn in B flat is one of the various saxhorns used in brass bands. Music for it tends to use the treble clef.
Bass	A general word – it can mean an electric bass guitar in pop music, or double bass in jazz; we tend to say double bass when referring to the orchestral instrument.
Bass clarinet	A larger version of the standard B flat clarinet and pitched an octave lower.

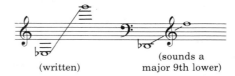

(written)   (sounds a
                   major 9th lower)

Bass drum	A huge orchestral drum of indefinite pitch, and played with a soft headed stick (Try the 'Dies Irae' section from Verdi's Requiem for its powerful effect! In a drum kit the stick is attached to a foot pedal.
Bass guitar	A four-stringed electric guitar used for the bass part in pop music. It was developed in the 1950s, and soon overtook the double bass in popularity because of its convenience.
Basset horn	A single-reed instrument of the clarinet family pitched in F. It has been rarely used since Mozart's day.

Bassoon A bass woodwind instrument found in the orchestra and military band. It is sometimes found as a soloist and in chamber music. It uses a double reed. (Try Mozart's Bassoon Concerto, K.191)

Bongos Small Cuban drums (usually a pair joined together) played with thumb and fingers.

Brass A term which covers wind instruments made of (any) metal and using a mouthpiece: trumpet, French horn, trombone and tuba comprise the orchestral brass family, while the brass band includes the cornet, tenor horn, baritone horn and euphonium.

Bugle A brass instrument without valves, so it produces only a few notes (usually in B flat). Used by armies as a band instrument, and for signalling movements.

Castanets A Spanish percussion instrument. Two small hollow pieces of wood for clicking together, or (in the orchestra) attached to the end of a stick which is shaken.

Celesta A percussion instrument which looks like a small upright piano, and sounds like a glockenspiel. Listen to Tchaikovsky's 'Dance of the Sugar-Plum Fairy' from the Nutcracker ballet.

'Cello Full name violoncello. Four-stringed bowed member of the string family, and used as the lowest instrument of the string quartet, as well as a solo and orchestral instrument.

Cimbalom A Hungarian folk instrument having horizontal strings struck with hammers. Kodaly uses it in his opera 'Hary Janos'.

Clarinet A single-reed woodwind instrument used in the orchestra, military band and in jazz. The standard instrument is pitched in B flat, but one in A is sometimes used. See basset horn and bass clarinet.

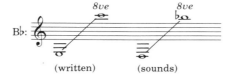
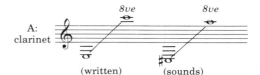

Clavichord A small, soft-toned keyboard instrument popular in the sixteenth–eighteenth centuries. The strings are hit by metal tangents, and a vibrato effect is possible by shaking the individual keys. It was used in the home as it was too quiet for concert use.

Cor anglais A woodwind instrument of the oboe type, but pitched a fifth lower. The nineteenth century Romantic composers were the first to use it regularly in the orchestra. Its name 'English horn' has never really been accounted for.

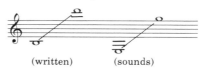

Cornet B flat brass instrument resembling a small trumpet. Much used in brass bands, and occasionally in the orchestra.

Cornett An obsolete wooden wind instrument having a small mouthpiece (like brass instruments) but finger-holes, not valves. Originally played in groups with sackbuts.

Crumhorn	An obsolete, curved double-reeded wind instrument, with the reeds covered by a windcap. It appeared in many sizes as its range was limited. It produced a quiet buzzing tone.
Curtal	Used throughout the sixteenth and seventeenth centuries as a bass instrument, this was the forerunner of the bassoon.
Cymbals	A percussion instrument. A plate of metal which can either be clashed against another, or struck with a drumstick. No definite pitch but modern composers often require several, in varying sizes. Drum kits include hi-hat cymbals.
Double bass	(See also *Bass*). The largest of the modern string family; its flat back is for strength. Rarely used in chamber music. It can be bowed or plucked.

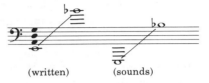

(written)   (sounds)

Double bassoon	The lowest woodwind instrument. Similar to, but larger than the ordinary bassoon.

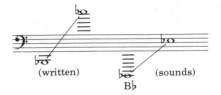

(written)   (sounds)
B♭

Euphonium	A tenor tuba, mainly used in military and brass bands. It is pitched in B flat.

Flugelhorn	A valved brass instrument made in various sizes and used mainly in brass bands for lyrical melodies.

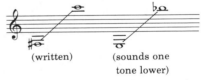

(written)   (sounds one tone lower)

Flute	A horizontally-held woodwind instrument. It has no reed and the higher notes are produced by blowing rather harder (over-blowing).

French horn	A coiled brass instrument. Originally played until about 1850 without valves. Horn notes are written a fifth higher than they sound.

(written)   (sounds 5th lower)

Glockenspiel	A pitched percussion instrument which uses beaters to strike tuned metal bars.
Gong	Sometimes called tam-tam. A bronze percussion instrument in various sizes, struck with a large soft beater.
Guiro	Latin-American 'scraper' percussion instrument.
Guitar	Popular stringed instrument. The Spanish guitar has six strings and is played unamplified, unlike the electric guitar. The

Hawaiian guitar uses a sliding metal bar (a 'steel') across all the strings to produce its characteristic sound. (see also *Bass guitar*)

Harmonica   Also called the 'Mouth Organ'. A small wind instrument in different sizes, using metal reeds. The better models are chromatic. The sound is continuously maintained by alternately blowing and sucking.

Harmonium   A small reed organ operated by foot pedals which, when pushed alternately, pump the air.

Harp   A plucked stringed instrument with a range of nearly seven octaves. Each of the seven foot pedals can lower or raise each note by a semitone.

Harpsichord   A plucked-string keyboard instrument with one or two manuals. Although used frequently today, it was prominently used between about 1550–1750. Stops and couplers are used to change the tone-quality.

Heckelphone   A rarely used type of bass oboe.

Hurdy-gurdy   A portable, mechanical instrument. One hand turns a handle which activates a wheel-type bow; the other stops the strings inside by means of a tiny keyboard.

Kettledrum   See *Timpani*

Koto   A Japanese zither. Thirteen strings are stretched over movable bridges that are moved with one hand; the other plucks the strings with plectra that are attached to the fingers. Six feet long.

Lute   A fretted stringed instrument with a pear-shaped body; plucked by the fingers. Used as a solo instrument, or as an accompaniment to songs from about 1400–1700. The sizes and tunings of lutes varied.

Mandolin   A plucked stringed instrument. Originally Italian. Eight strings tuned in pairs (GDAE) and played using a plectrum.

Maracas   Latin-American shaker percussion instrument. A pair of dried gourds with seeds inside.

Marimba   A deep-sounding xylophone with metal resonators under the keys.

Oboe   A double-reeded woodwind instrument used in the orchestra and military band, in chamber and solo music. (Listen to Britten's 'Ovid Metamorphoses'

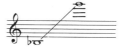

Organ   A church organ is a keyboard instrument (with one to four manuals), through which air is blown by bellows. Combinations of stops are used to vary the tone, and bass notes are produced by foot pedals; the electronic (or Hammond) organ has no bellows – sound is produced electronically.

Percussion   A general term for any instrument that is struck or shaken in some way.

Piano   Invented around 1700, the piano differs from the harpsichord because the strings are struck by hammers. Either upright (vertical strings) or grand – that is, horizontal strings.

Piccolo   A high-pitched flute used in the orchestra and military band.

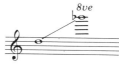

Psaltery   An ancient and now obsolete plucked stringed instrument. A simple kind of zither.

Racket   An obsolete bassoon-sounding instrument of amazingly short dimensions for its low pitch.

Rebec	An obsolete forerunner of the violin with three or four strings.
Recorder	A family of flute-type instruments in various sizes, ranging from sopranino down to the bass.
Regal	An obsolete portable organ (fifteenth–seventeenth century.)
Sackbut	An early trombone; virtually unchanged.
Saxophone	An instrument which gets its name from its maker, Sax, who produced several sizes of saxophones in the 1840s. It is a single-reed woodwind although made of brass; popular in jazz and the military band. Not so common in the orchestra.
Serpent	An obsolete curved woodwind instrument played with a brass-type mouthpiece.
Shawm	An old, loud-sounding woodwind instrument with a double reed. Superseded by the modern oboe.
Side drum	(Snare drum). A small drum, played to the side when used by marching bands, also used in jazz, rock, and the orchestra. There are two skins on the drum, the lower one in contact with wires (or snares) which give it its distinctive rattling sound.
Sitar	An Indian stringed instrument. Rather like a long-necked lute, but with seven strings and about twenty movable frets which arch over a wide neck. These frets enable the player to 'bend' the notes slightly.
Sousaphone	A type of tuba which actually fits over the player's body with a big forward-facing bell. Associated originally with the American band led by J.P. Sousa.
Spinet	A small harpsichord, but wing-shaped not rectangular. A popular domestic keyboard from the sixteenth–eighteenth centuries.
Synthesiser	Popular modern electronic instrument which constructs sounds when given precise instructions by the player.
Tabla	A set of two Indian hand drums capable of producing a range of different tone colours.
Tambourine	A small circular drum with metal jingles around the edge.
Tam-tam	Another name for a *Gong*.
Tenor horn	Really a tenor saxhorn – a brass band instrument pitched in E flat.
Theorbo	A large lute, popular in the seventeenth–eighteenth centuries.
Timpani	Italian for kettledrums. Tuned drums played with softsticks. Pedal 'timps' enable quick tuning, and make possible the use of a glissando.

Triangle	An un-tuned metallic percussion instrument, struck with a metal beater.
Trombone	A brass instrument which produces notes by means of a slide, rather than valves. Used in jazz, the orchestra and military bands.

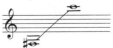

Trumpet	A three-valved brass instrument; extremely popular in jazz, and indeed all types of ensemble. Pitched in B flat (although 'Bach' trumpets in D are used for Baroque high trumpet parts.

Tuba	The lowest brass instrument, dating from about 1835. It is only rarely used as a soloist, but Vaughan Williams wrote a concerto for tuba.

Tubular bells   A set of suspended bells (tuned metal tubes) which are struck with mallets to give a sound rather like church bells.

Ukelele   A very small four-stringed guitar-like instrument. Popular earlier this century with singers like George Formby.

Vibraphone   Or Vibes for short. A tuned percussion with flat metal bars like a glockenspiel. Beneath the bars is an electrically powered motor which gives a vibrato effect to the tone.

Viol   A family (or 'consort') of bowed stringed instruments which came before the violin family. There are three principal sizes, the lowest being the viola da gamba. They have frets (unlike the violin) and use a different type of bow. Even the smallest size was played vertically like a cello, and had six strings.

Viola   A bowed stringed instrument, larger and therefore lower and mellower in tone than the violin. Its strings are tuned to C-G-D-A.

Viola da gamba   A sixteenth century bass viol, played when resting it vertically on the knees. It had six strings.

Violin   The smallest of the violin family; tuned to G-D-A-E. See *Stradivarius* in Glossary 2.

Virginals   A simple domestic keyboard instrument without legs, similar to the harpsichord, and popular in the days of Elizabeth I. Basically a rectangular box (and often highly decorated) with a short keyboard.

Woodblock   A simple non-pitched percussion instrument. A piece of hardwood with a cavity for resonance, hit with a wooden beater.

Woodwind   Collective term for piccolo, flute, clarinets, oboe, cor anglais, saxophones and bassoons.

Xylophone   A wooden tuned percussion instrument. Different sized rosewood bars are struck with beaters.

Zither   A central European folk stringed instrument plucked when resting on the knees or a table. Some of the strings can be 'stopped' like the violin – others are fixed in pitch.

GLOSSARY 4: WELL-KNOWN PERFORMERS PAST AND PRESENT

You should be aware of the top performers of different instruments, as sometimes you are asked to name who might have recorded (or conducted) a particular extract. The list is kept deliberately brief; you should try to remember who was playing, singing and conducting when you listen to any music.

○ deceased   △ jazz player

FLUTE
James Galway
Jean-Pierre Rampal
Susan Milan

BASSOON
Archie Camden○
Roger Birnstingl

VIOLA
Lionel Tertis○
Peter Schidlof○

SOPRANO
Elizabeth Soderstrom
Emma Kirkby
Frederica Von Stade
Elly Ameling
Heather Harper

HARP
Marisa Robles

TENOR
Peter Schreier
Peter Pears○
Robert Tear

TROMBONE
Jack Teagarden○△
Tommy Dorsey○△

DRUMS
Buddy Rich○△

COUNTER TENOR
Alfred Deller○
James Bowman

PIANO
John Ogdon○
Earl Wild
Alfred Brendel
Jorge Bolet○
Oscar Peterson△
Fats Waller○△

OBOE
Heinz Holliger
Evelyn Rothwell
Nicholas Daniel

SAXOPHONE
alto: Charlie Parker○△
tenor: Stan Getz△○

CELLO
Jacqueline du Pré○
Rostropovich
Paul Tortelier○

TRUMPET
Don Smithers
Bram Wiggins
Miles Davis△○
Dizzy Gillespie△○

TUBA
Paul Lawrence

GUITAR
Julian Bream
John Williams
Django Reinhardt○△

CONTRALTO
Kathleen Ferrier○
Janet Baker

BARITONE
John Shirley-Quirk
Brian Rayner Cook
Dietrich Fischer-Dieskau
Geraint Evans○

HARPSICHORD
Trevor Pinnock

CLARINET
Jack Brymer
Benny Goodman○△
Woody Herman○△
Thea King

VIOLIN
Yehudi Menuhin
Itzhak Perlman
Stephane Grappelli△

DOUBLE BASS
Rodney Slatford
Charles Mingus○△

FRENCH HORN
Dennis Brain○
Barry Tuckwell
Alan Civil○
Ifor James

PERCUSSION
James Blades
Tristan Fry

ROCK GUITAR
Jimi Hendrix○
Eric Clapton

MEZZO SOPRANO
Felicity Palmer
Sarah Walker

BASS
Stephen Varcoe

ORGAN
Peter Hurford
Simon Preston
Marie-Claire Alain

SYNTHESIZER
Jean-Michel Jarre
Rick Wakeman
Keith Emerson

CONDUCTORS
André Previn
Herbert Von Karajan○
Leonard Bernstein○
Bernard Haitink
Georg Solti

BRASS BANDS
William Fairey Engineering
   Band
Brighouse and Rastrick
   Band
Black Dyke Mills Band
Grimethorpe Colliery Band

STRING QUARTETS
Allegri
Amadeus
Borodin
Endellion
Lindsey

ORCHESTRAS
London Symphony
Berlin Philharmonic
Chicago Symphony
Cleveland
New York Philharmonic
Vienna Philharmonic

OPERA COMPANIES
Royal Opera House (Covent Garden)
English National Opera (Coliseum)
La Scala, Milan
New York Metropolitan (The Met)

RECOMMENDED FURTHER READING

These books may help you to follow up topics that interest you, in further detail.

INSTRUMENTS AROUND THE WORLD by Andy Jackson, Longman (1988)
A very useful book for those interested in instruments from other cultures; each of the eleven sections deals with one instrument and the culture from which it comes. There are also comprehensive notes on how to construct and play each of the instruments.

MUSICAL INSTRUMENTS by Paul Sturman, Longman (1989)
A very comprehensive book on a wide range of instruments with excellent illustrations and examples for following-up.

OFF BEAT – A PRACTICAL GUIDE TO POP AND JAZZ FOR GCSE by Richard Crozier, Bell and Hyman (1987)
A book to encourage composition and performance in a variety of popular and jazz styles – from blues to writing a pop song. The development of 20th century popular music is covered, from early gramophone records to the compact disc.

JAZZ by Michael Burnett, Oxford Topics in Music, OUP (1985)
Interested in jazz? This is the book for you – a book to just browse through, or a concise reference source for exam projects. From the roots in slavery to free-form jazz today, a well-illustrated and informative book.

RAGTIME AND BLUES by Paul Farmer, Longman Music Topics (1979)
Short of ideas for your ensemble piece? Try the Maple Leaf Rag or The Entertainer by Scott Joplin, or perhaps the simple twelve-bar blues from this short book. A valuable background to two popular jazz styles.

STEELBANDS AND REGGAE by Paul Farmer, Longman Music Topics (1981)
A good guide to Reggae music and its players, with some ensemble Reggae tunes for you to try out. There are notes on steelbands and how the pans are made.

JAMAICAN MUSIC by Michael Burnett, OUP (1982)
Although part of a series designed for 11–14 year olds, this is the perfect introduction to the instruments and general background to Jamaica and its music. Mention is made of Rastafarians, religious music, and ska/ rock steady/ reggae.

MUSIC IN SHOWBUSINESS by Paul Farmer and Frances Reilly, Longman Music Topics (1986)
Some useful assignments here that might give you some ideas for composition. A brief guide to theme tunes and music for advertisements, radio and film, and backgrounds to the Musical, Opera, Ballet and Modern Dance.

AN ILLUSTRATED GUIDE TO CLASSICAL MUSIC ed. Peter Gammond, Salamander Books (1980)
An excellent reference book to the major classical composers from the 15th to the 20th centuries. 124 biographies, arranged alphabetically and well illustrated, including references to all their major works.

DISCOVERING MUSIC (Books 1 and 2) by Roy Bennett, Longman (1983)
Learning about music in the traditional style – historical notes on composers and pieces with appropriate pictures and quotations. Some of the extracts discussed are included on a cassette which accompanies each book.

LISTENER'S GUIDE TO CLASSICAL MUSIC by Kenneth and Valerie McLeish, Longman (1986)
A good, comprehensive reference book. Over 1000 individual works are covered in this selection of over hundred composers; helpful follow-up suggestions and recommendations are made.

ENJOYING MODERN MUSIC by Roy Bennett, Longman (1983)
A helpful introductory guide to 20th century music. The 27 chapters each present an important work by 25 composers in a concise and interesting way.

CREATING MUSIC by Paul Sturman, Longman (1982)
Although designed for people younger than GCSE level, there is much to be gained from reading through this book. The nine topic sections could well stimulate ideas for composition or improvisation.

COMPOSING IN THE CLASSROOM (OPUS 2) by David Bramhall, Boosey & Hawkes (1989)
Really intended for 12 – 13 year olds, but if you are rather weak on the composition side you will probably benefit from going right back to these early stages of melodic and chordal work.

GCSE MUSIC SKILLS: COMPOSING by Martin Hinckley, Longman (1989)
Ten assignments, including TV title music, Making Arrangements, Song-writing and Music for a Play. Many useful ideas for imaginative composition work here.

IMPROVISE MICROJAZZ by Christopher Norton, Boosey & Hawkes (1988)
This book is designed to get the improviser started by highlighting the basic elements of improvisation. The author's aim is to provide material that will stimulate original ideas and encourage freedom in playing. A book to either dip into or work through in sequence.

STARTING TO IMPROVISE JAZZ PIANO by Lewis Riley, Boosey & Hawkes (1988)
This book contains ten units, each highlighting a different rhythm style found in jazz today (Latin American, Jazz Rock, etc). To be used with a teacher where possible, a useful preparation for jazzy improvisation (or composition)

ROCK MUSIC (Music Matters Series) by Clive D.Griffin, Dryad Press (1987)
A book for those who require more than mere biographical detail about rock stars. It discusses the growth of teenage cults and changing social conditions, and shows how rock music reflected all of this, from the early days of rock n'roll up to synthesiser rock. Highly recommended.

ROCKSCHOOL (Guitar * Bass * Drums) by D. Cartwright, G. Nicholls, H. Thomas, BBC (1984)
The book from the BBC TV 'Rockschool' series (1983–4) which looks in great detail at the technology, techniques and musical vocabulary for playing in a band, in many different styles. For the serious practical rock musician.

GENERAL MUSICIANSHIP by Roy Bennett, CUP (1984)
Intended as a 4th and 5th year textbook, but you will find this very helpful for all aspects of 'serious' music.

INTO THE MODERN CLASSICS by Paul Farmer, Longman (1981)
A short revision booklet on 5 major 20th century composers: Stravinsky, Bartok, Schoenberg, Shostakovich and Britten.

INDEX